UNIPOLARITY
AND THE
MIDDLE EAST

D1479377

UNIPOLARITY
AND THE
MIDDLE EAST

Birthe Hansen

St. Martin's Press
New York

Unipolarity and the Middle East

St. Martin's Press Scholarly and Reference Division, 175 Fifth Avenue, New York, N.Y. 10010

First published in the United States of America in 2001

Printed in Great Britain

ISBN 0-312-21521-5

Library of Congress Cataloguing-in-Publication Data

Hansen, Birthe.
  Unipolarity and the Middle East / Birthe Hansen.
    p. cm.
  Includes bibliographical references and index.
  ISBN 0-312-21521-5
    1. Middle East–Politics and government–1979– 2. United States–Foreign relations–Middle East. 3. Middle East–Foreign relations–United States. 4. World politics–1989– I. Title.

DS63.1 .H365 2000
327'.0956–dc21   00-059178

To Edith

Contents

Preface   x

1   Introduction   1

2   Neorealist Analysis   7
    The problem and the argument   11
        The transformation   14
        The change of polarity   15
        The specific change of great powers   15
    The end of the Cold War   16
    Unipolar dynamics   17
    From US-Soviet rivalry to US unipolarity: the Middle East   22
    The method   25
        The analytical procedure   29

3   Bipolarity and the Middle East   32
    Subsystemic alignments   42
    The loosening and end of the rivalry   46

4   A Model for Unipolarity   49
    Neorealism and unipolarity   51
        Anarchy and the balance of power   53
        Security   55
        The unipole: strength and strategies   56
    Unipolarity and the international system   57
        Stability   60
        Peace and war   61
        Nuclearity   62
        The unipole and the other states   63
            The single option   64
            Flocking   65
            Hard work   67

Systemic transformation 68
Systemic change leads to realignment 69
The end of the Cold War 73
The number of poles 79
Summary: the model and the change 80

5 The US World Order 82
The US international policy in general 83
US and the Middle East 89
The American way 92

6 The Unification of Yemen 93
The Yemens and the US-Soviet rivalry 95
The Soviet retreat and the choice of the Yemens 98
The 1994 civil war 100
Uniting the republic 104

7 Iraq's Invasion of Kuwait 106
Iraq and the subsystemic balance of power 108
The Iraqi response 112
The calculations 120
Iraq and the emergence of unipolarity 121

8 The Formation of the International Coalition 124
The participation 126
Unipolar management 135
Massive support 137

9 End of the Lebanese Civil War 139
From the National Pact to the Ta'if Accords 139
Syria and the end of the civil war 145
The Lebanese challenge 147

10 Operation Desert Storm 149
US objectives and agenda 151
The leadership and the coalition 153
The Kurdish safe haven 155
The US-Iraqi stand-off 157
The Gulf War 160

11 The Western Saharan Cease-fire 162

12 The Gaza-Jericho Accords   165
   The Declaration of Principles   168
   Israel, the PLO and the US   171
   Palestinian autonomy   176

13 The Arab-Israeli Peace Process   179
   End of the Cold War and the Arab-Israeli relationships   181
   Israel and Jordan   185
   Israel, Syria and Lebanon   188
   A complex process   190

14 Survey: The Middle East 1989–1998   191
   State strategies   192
      Turkey   192
      Iran   194
      Libya   196
      Algeria   197
   Subsystemic alignments   198
   Geographical and political cooperation   200

15 The Transformation of the Middle East – Conclusion   202
   The model for unipolarity   212
   Future research   214

16 Security Challenges in the Middle East   216
   The Arab-Israeli-Palestinian peace process   217
   Succession and democratisation   220
   The major powers in the subsystem   222
   Nationalism and failed states   223
   US dominance   224
   Future patterns   225

Notes   226

References   232

Index   239

Preface

During the 1990s the Middle East underwent a profound political transformation, a process which has not yet come to an end: there has been war, the signing of peace accords, and realignment of states in the region. The aim of this book is to offer a way of understanding and explaining the process of change in theoretical terms and, through the development of a model for unipolarity, to demonstrate a connection between the large international change of power which followed the end of the Cold War and the Middle Eastern transformation. Obviously, the framework does not pretend to tell the whole truth about all the individual events in the transformation, not to say about Middle Eastern politics. I turned my blind eye to several important dimensions, but I did it in order to isolate and highlight others: the post Cold War transformation and the following general trends of Middle Eastern international politics.

The book is the result of a three year research project. My research grant was financed by the Danish Social Science Research Council, and major travel expenses were provided by the Research Council, the Danish Institute of International Affairs, and the Institute of Political Science at the University of Copenhagen.

I owe very special thanks to dr. Carsten Jensen for discussions, ideas and support. For their useful contributions during the research process I want to thank Professor Bertel Heurlin and dr. Lars Erslev Andersen. I also want to thank Morten Poulsen-Hansen and Sami Mølbak for excellent assistance, and many thanks to historian dr. Lars Bœrentzen who read and commented the whole manuscript. In 1993, I studied in the Department of War Studies at King's College, London. I had inspiration from many, in particular from dr. Efraim Karsh. Finally, I want to thank my colleagues and students at the Institute of Political Science, University of Copenhagen, and the staff at the Danish Institute of International Affairs.

Chapter 1

Introduction

The aim of this book is to present a theoretical model for unipolarity and to explain the development in Middle Eastern international politics from the end of the Cold War in 1989 to 1998 by means of the model. That is, to demonstrate how the end of the Cold War affected the Middle East by connecting the developments in the area to theoretical statements derived from the model; and to make a contribution, with this study of one particular area, to more general research on the effects of the 1989 changes. The main argument is that 1989 brought about security conditions different from those of the Cold War and that this had an impact on patterns of conflict and cooperation in the Middle East.

The model for unipolarity is based on the neorealistist theory (Waltz 1979), which provides a general, structural framework for dealing with international politics. Yet a neorealist model for unipolarity has so far been lacking. The end of the Cold War in 1989 highlighted the need for such a model, as the post-Cold War world order apparently emerged as unipolar; i.e., characterised by the presence of only one superpower – the US. If world politics, as it is argued in the neorealist theory, is deeply influenced by the number of superpowers, the 1989-change should be expected to have profound effects worldwide. Accordingly, the analysis of international politics – including Middle Eastern politics – after 1989 might benefit from the inclusion of this variable of change.

When the Second World War ended it was evident that a new era was beginning. The former European great powers were replaced by the United States and the Soviet Union. The colonies began to win their independence, norms were changing and the division of the world into two new camps was beginning. Two generations later the Cold War ended, but not nearly as spectacularly as had both the two previous World Wars. In many ways, however, the end of the Cold

War was similar to and as significant as the end of the great power 'hot' wars, and the effects were no less profound: as the conclusion of the Cold War is now at some distance, it has become clear that it was followed by remarkable events which turned many aspects of international political life upside down. In the Middle East the Yemens unified, Iraq invaded Kuwait, the Israeli-Arab peace process commenced, and a series of other events took place during the 1990's.

While the many sudden events in the Middle East were not foreseen in the traditional scenarios, they are arguably explicable and comprehensible. Neorealist theory (Waltz 1979) provides a structural approach to analyse international systems, which is applied below in order to explain the Middle Eastern development. The theory points to similarities as well as variations of international politics, connecting them to the different numbers of great powers[1] in existence. Analytically, the prevailing number of great powers corresponds to a specific structure, which induces specific dynamics and patterns of alignment. When one structure is replaced by another, a systemic change takes place and as a result a series of outcomes comprising patterns of conflict and cooperation are to be expected. The structural approach is general and, in principle, it should comprise all variations of the anarchical international system, whatever the context of their emergence. It follows, therefore, that the end of the Cold War is encompassed by this theory, as it represents a transition from one structure to another and thereby a systemic change. This structural approach provides the point of departure for dealing with the basic question: how did the 1989–systemic change affect the international politics of the Middle East?

The Middle East is characterised by a combination of many specific attributes. Religion plays a major role, there are unresolved border issues, ethnic conflicts recur, the states still struggle with their colonial past; and wars have frequently been fought. At least as far as the discipline of International Politics is concerned, the politics of the Middle East are often dealt with in terms of these attributes. In many works the developments in the area have been treated as unpredictable, divergent and deeply influenced by many unique attributes. The area's attributes notwithstanding, neorealism approaches from a different position: from a neorealist perspective, all states have to secure themselves because of the anarchical self-help condition, which is, itself, subject to structural variations. Here it is taken for granted that such a structural variation took place in 1989 when the Cold War ended, thereby halving the number of great powers. In neorealist terms, a systemic change took place and bipolarity was substituted for unipolarity. This also entailed the Middle Eastern states having to care for themselves in conditions different from that of the bipolar period. A combination of neorealist statements about systemic change and the theory's general validity suggest a problem and an argument.

The problem can be stated as the following question: in which ways has the systemic change penetrated Middle Eastern politics, in spite of the area's apparent and immanent potential to resist systemic change?

The argument is as follows: the international politics of the Middle East were deeply affected by the systemic change, because systemic change in general brings about asymmetrical realignment and different self-help conditions, in this case a shift from a bipolar self-help condition to a unipolar one. As a consequence, the Middle East was transformed: the political issues linked to the bipolar arrangement were set free and placed in another context. The new context favours different patterns of cooperation and issues of conflict, as the states, it is assumed, attempt to help and secure themselves within the given international condition, which is now different. The analysis deals with what arguably resulted in the transformation of the Middle East: Using neorealist structural theory, a ten year period of Middle Eastern politics from 1989 to 1998 is analysed in order to demonstrate and explain the impact of the systemic change. This has required a demonstration of how:

- Bipolar patterns and issues of conflict and cooperation have been challenged and possibly vanished.
- New patterns and issues of conflict and cooperation have emerged.
- The new patterns and issues are compatible with what must be the expectations of the new unipolar condition (in its specific US version).

Indeed, the period in question was a turbulent one for the area. The list of major international political events of conflict and cooperation is long. Once deadlocked positions gained momentum or were turned around during a process which started with the unification of the Yemens. In chronological order, the other events were: the Iraqi invasion of Kuwait, the formation of the international coalition, the end of the Lebanese civil war, Operation Desert Storm, the Kurdish upheaval and Operation Provide Comfort, the beginning of the peace process between Israel and its neighbours, the accords on Palestinian autonomy, the peace treaty between Israel and Jordan, the Yemeni civil war, and the Iraqi-UN crises of 1997. These events took place against traditional expectations, and they also revealed complexity and indicated that the majority of Middle Eastern relations appear to be fragile and subject to further development. However, whatever the future development, the outcome of the events between 1989 and 1998 seriously affected the Middle East, and each of them have, more or less, changed the political relations. The outcomes as well as their impact are thus interesting objects for analysis.

The empirical material is analysed using theoretical statements derived from the neorealist, structural approach. The approach consists of two closely linked elements: Waltz' neorealism and Hansen's model for unipolarity (which is presented in Chapter 4). All the basic assumptions are derived from neorealist theory (Waltz 1979), according to which the decisive principle in understanding the overall conditions of interstate politics is the number of great powers. The theory provides specific models for the cases of bi- and multipolarity, but so far it does not include any specific analytical model for the case of unipolarity – nor for systemic transition itself. It follows from the assumption of a unipolar distribution of relative strength resulting from the end of the Cold War, that a unipolar model is essential to deal with post-1989 international politics, including the Middle East. Because such a model was lacking, part of this research has been to construct one. A way to deal with systemic change is added as well.

The interaction between the Middle Eastern states is approached in light of the structural conditions, which are considered to *select* the strategies of the units (the states) as well as the outcomes of these strategies. Each unit always has two options: it may adapt or oppose, but in the long run the selection will favour adaptation. The interaction process consists of 'myriads' of minor unit level decisions (Waltz 1979), all taken within the structural constraints and opportunities. Although each decision may be taken with a unique motive, and many will contradict each other, the trend may nevertheless be clear (Waltz 1979). Thus the starting point is the series of major international political events which took place in the period in question. A deductive method has been applied in order to provide the explanation. Events were analysed using abstract theoretical statements in order to demonstrate the connection between the statements and the empirical findings. When the question *why* arises, reference is made to the statement(s). Furthermore, comparison was carried out to demonstrate how the (US-specific) unipolar dynamics affected Middle Eastern conflict and cooperation patterns in a way which was different from the impact of the bipolar dynamics.

A systemic change is a relatively rare phenomenon compared to most other international events. So far the intervals between such changes are, roughly, between one and two generations. Such a low frequency may point to the limitations of the systemic-structural approach, most international politics being carried out beyond the effects of a systemic change. However, all international politics take place either within the context of systemic change or, in relatively stable periods, within the context of the given structure and its effects. In between the systemic changes, it is necessary to look for more subtle yet decisive structural selection of outcomes, most notably the local balancing of power. In addition it is important to distinguish between the effects of the transformation itself and the unipolar effects in order not to exaggerate the unipolar impact – and to be aware that the first five years after a systemic change are probably the most turbulent years. A period of five years is often used as an operational measure of the likely timespan from a cause to the emergence of an effect (Singer and Small 1968).

While the structural change is considered to be the most important and decisive variable, the analysis, of course, does not pretend to be recording everything about the Middle East during the period in question, and a lot of interesting details and dimensions are neglected. Instead, the theory's minimalist selection of variables hopefully makes it possible to point to trends and connections which might otherwise disappear out of a concern to show the multiplicity of important variables. The demonstration of the impact of the systemic change of 1989 aims at providing understanding and explanation of the functioning of Middle Eastern politics with regard to these states' care for their position and their mutual relations, as well as providing an identification of major trends. Last, but not least, by dealing with the effects of 1989 in one particular area, a contribution may be made to the research concerning the end of the Cold War and what followed. To sum up, the research process produced the following results:

- The creation of a theoretical model for unipolar international political systems with an emphasis on security conditions.
- An analysis of how Middle Eastern international politics were penetrated by the 1989 systemic change to unipolarity.

- A demonstration of the differences between the bipolar and unipolar impact on conflict and cooperation issues.
- An explanation of the transformation of the Middle East which serves as an example of the effects of the 1989 systemic change.

The book consists of this introduction and the following chapters: the theoretical and empirical prerequisites for the analysis are dealt with in the specification of the argument (Chapter 2), the analysis of the impact of the Cold War on the Middle East (Chapter 3), the presentation of the model for unipolarity (Chapter 4), and the specific US unipolar approach to the area (Chapter 5). The empirical analysis comprises all the events (Chapters 6–13) and the general tendencies (Chapter 14). Conclusions are drawn regarding the patterns and issues of conflict and cooperation (Chapter 15); and finally the new conditions of conflict and cooperation in the Middle East are discussed as well as the security challenges for the years to come (Chapter 16).

Chapter 2

Neorealist Analysis

The neorealist theory was presented in Kenneth Waltz' *Theory of International Politics*. The book was published in 1979, and since then the core concepts and statements of neorealism have come to a widespread use as well as the theory triggered intense debate. Kenneth Waltz put forth the point that structural analysis is essential to the analysis of international politics, which was analysed as a system comprising the units (the states) and the structure. His additive concept of structure entails the comparatively stable features of anarchy (i.e., the lack of an authority with a monopoly of power); functional similarity (i.e., any unit has to care for its position); and the less stable feature of the number of great powers in existence. The units are analysed as trying to care for their security.

Security is understood as a state's position relative to other states' positions, and as being a function of the state's aggregate capabilities[1] vis-à-vis others'. Increase in a state's relative capabilities implies that its position improves with more security being the bi-product, and vice versa. Their ability to care for their positions are closely linked to the self-help condition of the system in question. If the number of great powers is subject to change, the self-help condition should be analysed by means of a structural concept encompassing the different numbers. Across structural variations (as long as the anarchical organization prevails) balances of power tend to occur, and the units tend to adapt to the particular self-help condition. Some units may not, but in the long run a significant tendency is expected, as those which do not adapt will suffer, and units as such tend to imitate the more successful ones. Neorealism thus points to a likely range of outcomes which is selected by and depending on the specific distribution of capabilities across the units. Accordingly, the range of outcomes is expected to be subject to change as an effect of systemic change. These concepts and statements are essential to the elaboration of the model for unipolarity and the analysis below.

Since the publishing of *Theory of International Politics*, neorealism has been tested, applied and criticised. The criticism has often focused on the theory's few variables and the structural emphasis, and as a result interesting debates, clarifications and elaboration of neorealism have taken place. The model for unipolarity aims at contributing to this process of further development of the theory, and it aims at providing a theoretical response to the end of the Cold War, which posed an additional series of theoretical challenges.

Neorealism should be elaborated accordingly, and apparently it holds the potentials. Like most theories on international politics, neorealism emerged during bipolarity, and 1989 was therefore the 'big test' regarding its capacity to survive its own original context. Neorealism included three notions on the fate of the Cold War: Firstly, it would come to an end, because the mutual overlapping interests of two great powers could not be reconciled in the long term. While it has been argued that bipolarity is a comparatively stable arrangement (compared to tri- and multipolarity), neorealism never assumed bipolarity to be eternal. Secondly, the Cold War would probably end in a peaceful way due to the war-restraining role of nuclear weapons. Thirdly, the post-Cold War world would not necessarily turn into a peaceful one, because the problem of the Cold War was arguably not the character and attributes of the Soviet Union but the tension between two great powers. In the light of the actual development these core neorealist notions appear reasonable and valid. The next question is if the theory also has the potential to deal with the post-Cold War order.

It might be argued that the world is rather multipolar, characterised by hegemony, or is no longer a 'great power world'. However, international politics are still organised in an anarchical fashion (there is still no international monopoly of power), and the units still have to care for their own security. Thus the two comparatively stable features of the neorealist concept of structure are still considered analytically adequate (the anarchy and the functional similarity), and there is no reason *a priori* to exclude neorealism from the range of viable post-Cold War theories. Additionally, the advantages of neorealism may well be useful for future analysis: to analyse a realm of such complexity as international politics regarding essential questions, to point at general tendencies of international outcomes and state behaviour, and to be applicable while still providing general explanations.

However, one problem remains to be solved: Neorealism does not comprise a specific theoretical statement on the case of unipolarity as it does on the cases of bi- and multipolarity. To qualify as a general theory with an emphasis on the importance of the distribution of strength, it should also include theoretical statements on unipolarity. In principle, unipolarity cannot be ruled out as a variation, nor is it uncontested whether or not historical precedents are available (as possibly the Roman Empire). Finally, but not least, international politics after 1989 appear to qualify in terms of unipolarity if the neorealist criteria for identification of polarity are applied (cf. Chapter 3). As international politics has hardly become less complicated, the model may contribute to understand and explain the 'new'. For these three reasons, a model for unipolarity appears to be an important addition to the neorealist theory.

That international politics remain a complicated realm is illustrated by the 1990's development in the Middle East, where political processes apparently lead in contrasting directions. The Middle East still poses a lot of questions with respect to the international development, and in case of the post-Cold War period it is a challenge to investigate whether or not the neorealist model for unipolarity encompasses the capacity to explain the development. The neorealist focus on the importance of great powers does not exclude the analysis of the socalled other states: they are affected by the international system's dynamics and the security conditions, and they interact with the great power(s). In this context the other states relate to each other in terms of the self help condition and balancing of power. Being less capable to project power compared to the great powers, most of the time the other states primarily focus on the other states in their proximity.

The Middle East is analysed as an international subsystem. 'Subsystem' merely conceptualises a part of the international system which is selected for research purposes. Yet the concept implies that the subsystem is a part of the totality and subject to the structural dynamics. When dealing with the Middle East as a part of a totality rather than with a totality including the Middle East, more attention is paid to the symmetrical relations (the relations between the selected group of other states), though the asymmetrical relations are still vital (the relations between the other states and the great power(s)) – especially in case of security concerns (for the distinction, see Morrow 1991). In Chapter 3 the interaction between the relations are specified. Specifically the part of the totality is defined in accordance with the broad and conventional Middle East, "extending from Morocco to the Arabian Peninsula and Iran" (Encyclopædia Britannica 1993, Vol. 8:108).

Chronologically the analysed development is very close to the end of the Cold War. Most importantly the first period after a systemic transformation does highlight the changes, because strength is redistributed and the units cannot stand back and wait for other or better times to respond. On the other hand, all being so close to the transformation the events might only represent the immediate repercussions of that very change and therefore exaggerate the effects of the new. The strategy for overcoming this problem has been to state and distinguish between what are arguably the effects of the transformation and the unipolar impact. Besides, even though a systemic change naturally induces most turbulence in its very aftermath, this is how it manifests itself and makes the new conditions clear. After the clearance, the units tend to adapt (or may be forced to) and the states' mutual relations are taking place in the realm of the given new international arrangement. To avoid the risk of over-explanation, a comparison is carried out in order to identify continuity and change across the end of the Cold War.

The neorealist emphasis on strength and power balancing implies that the analysis and the explanatory process proceed chronologically, as the units are considered to relate to each other and are continuously responding to even minor developments as well as putting their mutual relations of strength on trial: after each outcome, the situation is different, and the other units respond to that. Politics under unipolarity are therefore not a static state of affairs; unipolarity conditions a range of dynamic political processes.

It is important to further emphasise the lack of concrete predictions of the model. Neorealism and the model for unipolarity claim predicatory power in the sense of predicting a range of probable international political outcomes in the course of time. And there is no guarantee that all states will adapt successfully to a given international structure. The general prediction, however, is, that most states will adapt in the long run as they will face very strong obstacles and weakening – even death – if not (Waltz 1979). In addition, structural pressure is not expected to produce identical outcomes. What specifically results from the pressure is uncertain and depends on unit level attributes. However, some common features are expected to be part of the majority of outcomes; in this analysis the common features reflect the content of the theoretical statements regarding unipolarity.

THE PROBLEM AND THE ARGUMENT

The complexity and the particularities of the Middle East are often stressed both empirically and theoretically. As mentioned above, there is a strong tendency to deal with the area's political life in terms of its many specific attributes (and consequentially to assume different state behaviour compared to states in other areas, like the European states), and consequently internal factors are often seen as constituting an obstacle to impact from the outside and thus preventing major developments. It has been argued that the lack of cohesion between the elites of these states and their societies makes them less adaptive to external inputs than to internal threats. When the elites' struggle to survive in power is considered to exceed these units' concern for their positions, systemic effects become secondary. Similarly, when it comes to analyses of the great powers and the area, two notions have prevailed: one pointing to the internal roots of the conflicts outdoing the great powers' attempts to manipulate the region, thereby stressing the importance of the local level. The consequence of such an approach is that the disappearance of either of the bipolar great powers would not substantially affect the conflict patterns. The other perceives US-Soviet rivalry as a unique and artificial overlay. The consequence of this approach is that the disappearance of the rivalry would bring back some kind of natural functioning in the area.

The area has specific attributes and many internal variables are undoubtedly at play. Any great power may face insurmountable obstacles when trying to pursue its interests and to influence a local actor. The theoretical debate, as well as the political context, thus raise the question of whether Middle Eastern attributes and dynamics were strong enough to obstruct the expected impact of the 1989 systemic change, and of what exactly happened when the US-Soviet rivalry came to an end. The theoretical approach and the argument here are general in their nature and do not regard the Middle East as neither a comparatively complex object, nor a comparatively specific one. This leads to different expectations from those summarised above, and frames the problem concerning how the end of the Cold War affected the Middle East:

Firstly, 1989 not only affected Middle Eastern international politics, but it did so to a substantial degree because the internal variables are held to be subject to the structural impact. Moreover, this particular area was bound to be transformed, because it occupied a high position on the great power agenda during bipolarity, increasing its sensitivity to a change. *Secondly*, the end of the rivalry is not to be regarded as an end to the area's sensitivity to structural impact; the area has rather become subject to another kind of structural impact. This is not to say that US unipolarity will affect international relations in the area in the same way and to the same extent as did the 1945–1989 bipolarity; but all Middle Eastern states face the unipolar self help-condition and need to relate to the US approach.

The argument is based on the fundamental assumption that systemic change implies altered relations of strength symmetrically as well as asymmetrically, and leads to asymmetrical de- and realignment,[2] and thereby to a different range of outcomes and patterns regarding conflict and cooperation among the units. This is depicted in Figure 1, where the arrows indicate processes of selection, and where 'range' indicates the likely space for the majority of outcomes making up trends:

A systemic change paves the way for resolving conflicts and undermines settlements which were linked to the previous relations of strength (structure). The reason for this is broken down into a *chain of effects*: The systemic change is based on a redistribution of aggregate strength which leads to realignment. As a consequence, international politics are affected, because strength and added strength are at the core of the ability of each state to secure its international position. The impact spreads: not only are the other states exposed to new conditions, but their mutual relationships are also bound to change. The different conditions entail different asymmetrical alignments and support, thereby altering the relative positions of the smaller states and leading to symmetrical realignment as well. It is an essential part of their self help condition that their positions are affected by systemic change, and it is that change which arguably brings about different issues and results in different patterns of conflict and cooperation.

When examining this chain of effects, it is important to pay attention to the steps in the process of the systemic transformation in

Structure 1	$\rightarrow$	Range of outcomes and patterns 1
Δ Structure	$\rightarrow$	Δ Range of outcomes
Structure 2	$\rightarrow$	Range of outcomes and patterns 2

Figure 1

question: after a period in which the old system begins to dissolve, the transition takes place, and the first step is the disappearance of the old. The next step is that the new structure manifests itself. The transformation itself is a high-risk period: "Force is least visible where power is most fully and most adequately present", as Waltz has stated (1979:185). After a systemic break-down, force becomes particularly visible because power vacuums arise and are filled, and because it is easy to miscalculate in such a confusing context. After a systemic change brought about in an extremely peaceful and quiet way, as was the case in 1989, the risks are not necessarily reduced: it was less clear immediately after 1989 that the US was a winner than it was after World War II – or that the Soviet Union was a real loser, at least until later when the empire collapsed. The third step concerns the process after the new system has become manifest and the new dynamics are taking over. Within the framework of structural analysis, however, it is a question of either/or: the relative distribution of strength makes up one structure or another, and, accordingly, the response to the events of the high risk period should be dealt with in terms of the succeeding structure and its effects. However, the process of politics at a unipolar condition should not be confused with the state of unipolarity: during the process 'ups and downs' may take place and political decisions and events each leading in a different direction will occur. The prevailing tendency, however, arguably reflects the unipolar conditions, and presumably it is possible to detect a unipolar content in the individual events.

Moreover, the effects of the systemic change depend on the specific qualities of the change. Basically this is a triple question. The first question concerns which of the structural elements is subject to the change. In principle, any of the elements in the additive neorealist concept of structure could be changed. The two elements of organisation and function are so far more robust, however, than the third one of polarity. Thus, the primary focus – which is also the relevant one in the 1989 case – is the structural element concerning polarity. A change of polarity implies the chain of effects described above. The second question concerns what kind of polarity (with specific dynamics) was replaced and by what kind. In this case the shift was from bi- to unipolarity. The third question is about the change of the great powers involved. Great powers have different interests and different clashes, so the way which other states are affected by a given structure depends on both the general dynamics and on the specific great power agenda. In 1989 the rival Soviet-US great powers were replaced by the US in an exclusive position. The impact, thus, consists of the effects of both unipolarity and the specific US approach. These considerations are relevant to the specification of the scope and range of the expected impact on the post-1989 self-help condition of the states. The next task is therefore to consider the three dimensions of the 1989 systemic change in order to specify them and make it possible to separate them in the analysis.

The transformation

The systemic change itself is one dimension of the resetting of international relations according to the new relations of strength. When one or more great powers withdraw, power vacuums emerge, and the states which were formerly supported by the retreating great power(s) are weakened, at least in the first place. Formerly supported other states, nations and groups, are subject to weakening because distributions of strength and power change with the great powers' change; they are affected by the asymmetrical dealignment from the retreating power(s). Other states are subject to asymmetrical as well as symmetrical changes of strength, and the changes may lead to even armed trials of relative positions in cases where the new is unclear or a state perceives alternatives to be lacking. States may take high risks out of fear or because they perceive a window of opportunity to obtain long wished for gains while everything is in a mess or because they want to prevent others from doing the same. Additionally, a general confusion and an increased risk of miscalculations follow the very transformation of the system and its spread horizontally and vertically. This increases the risk of warfare while new alliances and relations of strength emerge and are tried and revealed. Outbreaks of war due to the increased risks of miscalculation, the temporary rise of power vacuums and following trials of positions related to the re-/ dealignment as well as to areas and issues liberated from the previous relations of strength are, thus, among the expected impact of any systemic change, including that of 1989. On the other hand, the change paves the way for peace settlements which were not within reach in the framework of the former great power relationship. In some cases the change of one international arrangement into another one even affects the internal political organisation of states which are vulnerable to the loss or gain of a specific international constellation of strength; states primarily based on the disappearing great power arrangement are prone to collapse into civil war, which may be followed by external intervention and/or disintegration – possibly fission. The range of potential effects thus comprises the rise of new states, the disappearance of others, and fission/fusion. The period after a systemic change is a high risk period. The emerging structure affects the substance of the potential results, which include: the rise of new conflicts and the settlements of previous ones, new alignments (symmetrical as well as asymmetrical), birth and death of states, a new agenda, and a different selection of the states' strategies.

Together this leads to a resetting of interstate relations, which is intense during the immediate aftermath of the systemic change. The loosening of what was linked to the previous arrangement, however, is met by the new structure and its specific dynamics. While the period immediately after the change contains high risks, some effects of the change may occur in the course of a longer process (as the decolonisation process following the 1945 systemic change).

The change of polarity

Polarity affects the self-help condition of the other states through the nature of the game among the great powers, the other states' options for obtaining support with respect to the amount of external security guarantees available, and the lines of conflict and alliance-making. It also affects their mutual symmetrical relationships, which are created in light of the self-help condition. These core conditions are all related to the number of poles. In 1989 unipolar dynamics replaced the bipolar dynamics: the zero sum game and the double option of external security guarantees available to the other states disappeared with bipolarity. Instead, unipolarity provides only one option, no dominant great power balancing, or no great power alliances as in the case of multipolarity, and the unipole is in a comparatively privileged position to pursue its interests and set the agenda. The change of structure also implies a resetting of the subsystemic relations of strength: the dealignment and the weakening of the dealigned is followed by realignment and a reassessment of allies. The new arrangement thus provides all states with new opportunities and restraints regarding their security concerns.

The specific change of great powers

Any unipole arguably has strong incentives to preserve its position (cf. Chapter 3). To many political processes it is, of course, of the utmost importance which state emerges as a unipole. The result is a different arrangement of specific great power interests, commitments and agenda-setting. The 1989 change included the end of US-Soviet rivalry and the rise of the US as the exclusive great power. The US policy immediately after the end of the Cold War was defined as a general concern for what was called the 'New World Order', including the non-proliferation of nuclear weapons. With respect to the Middle East, there was also a primary concern about the supply of oil and, later, a commitment to the Israeli-Arab peace process. During the period in question, the policy was changed slightly, and it is bound to change during the political process of unipolarity. The unipole's specific policy, however, needs to be taken into consideration: Does it commit itself, on which 'conditions', and how does it define the agenda? Here the combination of unipolarity and the US being the unipole and pursuing concrete policies, particularly the spread of free market capitalism and liberal democracy, is referred to as the US World Order for analytical purposes. This should not to be confused with the American political notion of the New World Order.

* * *

The major international political events in the Middle East from 1989 to 1998 are consequently dealt with in terms of a common reference to the transformation of the international system in 1989 rather than as individual, coinciding events. This transformation arguably comprised the end of US-Soviet bipolarity, the high risks of the systemic change itself, and the emergence of unipolarity in its specific US version. All states, including those in the Middle East, were affected because they, and their mutual relations of strength, were all exposed to a new structural variation of the self-help condition. Consequently, their mutual relations were reset, and the patterns of cooperation and conflict were challenged.

THE END OF THE COLD WAR

It is obvious that the Cold War was not a static period. The United States and the Soviet Union were confronting each other, but they also had their moments of cooperation, and as time proceeded nuclearity provided them with a common incentive to avoid a major war. Within their rivalry the Middle East was not in the center: The center, of course, was their bilateral relationship within which the focus increasingly was directed towards their nuclear weapons. Outside the center Europe was the strategic political 'theatre'. As the Cold War spread and intensified, the Middle East grew more and more important and is usually considered second to Europe in the rivalry (Zakaria 1990). In the first place the Middle East was a possible military theater but in the course of nuclearisation the superpowers became more careful and tended to replace their own, direct commitment to 'proxies' in the area. In the middle of the 1980's the Soviet Union began a major reorientation of its foreign policy during the Gorbachev leadership, and the confrontation in the Middle East was eased. The end of the Cold War thus was a process of Soviet retreat during which the Middle Eastern states were fearing abandonment as well as superpower imposed solutions resulting from their improved bilateral relationship (Taylor 1991). In addition, the Gorbachev leadership began to reduce Soviet commitments in the 'periphery' prior to the Cold War termination. This had consequences for Middle Eastern politics, where some states and groups began to act, and where some developments took place, but the major impact did not occur until the Cold War had finally come to an end.

To define the date of the very end of a major war is always a more or less arbitrary task. A common way to define the end, however, is to focus at one party's surrender. In case of the Cold War the 21 September 1989 is interpreted to be the date of the Soviet Union's actual surrender (Hansen 1991). The structural transformation is consequently dated to September of 1989, and from then bipolarity is considered history as well as the high risk period of transformation is considered operative while the new international arrangement emerges – and is revealed and manifested. This, of course, does not exclude the fact that systemic change, including that of 1989, is a process emerging over several years, or that some units may react to or anticipate the development according to their particular perception of the time and the consequences of the change.

UNIPOLAR DYNAMICS

Above it was argued that the conditions of the other states will change in the case of a structural change. But what will they be like in the specific case of unipolarity? Below four statements of the essential qualities of unipolarity are forwarded. These statements are derived from the model of unipolarity (fully presented in Chapter 3), and the analysis aims to demonstrate the unipolar character of the transformation of the Middle East by means of these statements. As mentioned above, it should be emphasised that neorealism makes only one stratification of states: into great powers and other states. The category of other states comprises all states except for the unipole. The first three statements below concern the essential self-help conditions of the other states, including the Middle Eastern states, and the fourth concerns the unipole itself. The statements do not tell everything about unipolarity, and they should always be dealt with in the framework of neorealism as such, as many international dynamics are at play, and the specific unipolar dynamics are unfoldning in the context of more general dynamics like the balancing of power, the tendency to avoid great power dominance from the other states' point of view, and the tendency to avoid 'unnecessary' conflicts. The purpose, however, is to point out some specific and crucial unipolar dynamics.

Flocking: Firstly, the other states will tend to flock around the unipole. In a conflict, a state can hardly afford to go against the other ones plus the unipole. Other states may prefer not to align or, if possible, to keep the unipole at a distance, but in moments of truth, i.e., when security is at stake, they will tend not to go against their small adversaries and the unipole. On the contrary, they are inclined to take part in the polarisation process, as the unipole is the only one capable of providing other states with adequate security, and as international tension tends to force the parties to choose side. In the cases of diminishing threats, flocking becomes a less likely behaviour although some states may maintain this policy for other, indirect reasons. This is not to say that all the states will always flock or that the relationship between the other states and the unipole will be exclusively positive. In many cases the other states may fear domination and entrapment or their interests will be in conflict with the unipole's interests. If the other states are able to keep a distance they may likely prefer to do so, and they will also face a series of strong conflicts of interests with the unipole. However, when security is at stake, the unipole becomes the center, and when the unipole sets the agenda, other states have to address the agenda. Therefore, although the relationship between the unipole and the other states is characterised by conflicts of interests, fear of domination and many problems, unipolarisation is highly probable in the case of serious security concerns. The possession of weapons of mass destruction (WMD), primarily nuclear weapons, may temper the incentive to flock: the possession provides a state with a strong deterrent and reduces its need for obtaining security guarantees in relation to matters of survival. It also makes it less vulnerable to pressure from the unipole which otherwise has a superior amount of instruments suited for pursuing its political objectives.

The single option: Secondly, the other states have no alternative to the unipole if they need great power guarantee. Such guarantees are often preferred to those from neighbours: an external great power is able to supply the small state with a large amount of additional security (Morrow, 1991:913) and the primary adversaries are usually found within the neighbourhood (Walt, 1987:23). When turning to the great power option in case of unipolarity, other states have only one choice. Similarly their bargaining position *vis-à-vis* the unipole is weaker relative to a case of more great powers. Their great power ally does not need to fear that the other states may turn to another great power and thereby inflicting losses to the great power's spheres of influence, i.e., the great power's international position. This counts even though the losses may seem marginal, for the rationale of the unipole to ally with other states, adding nil or only little to its defence, is the extension of autonomy and broadening of spheres of influence (Morrow, 1991). By comparison to bipolar dynamics, the former Soviet allies were provided with a new option after 1989 in terms of alignment. The option was a US relationship while previous US allies might have to share their former guarantee with those who were formerly their adversaries. On the other hand, the unipole will tend to restrain itself from getting involved if its own interests are not at stake or if managerial tasks are not urgent.

Hard work: Thirdly, unipolarity demands hard work. Depending on the absolute strength of the only great power, the other states need to make greater efforts themselves to secure their positions. By comparison to the bipolar rivalry, unipolarity provides reduced opportunities to shelter behind the only pole as its need for smaller allies has decreased with the vanishing of the zero-sum game. If the great power has comparatively few incentives to entering broad-scale non-strategic commitments, the other states consequently face the challenge of sorting out more problems about their positions by their own means – either by forming comparatively more symmetrical alliances or by cooperating in other ways. All in all, they have to work hard to secure themselves, and have to relate to their geopolitical context in a closer way, which comparatively increases regional activity whether this is characterised by cooperation or conflict.

The unipole's agenda: Fourthly, the unipole will affect the international agenda most strongly. It has the best position to do so;

and it will do it according to its own strategic interests and in order to carry out managerial tasks and maintain the system, and indeed its own precious position. Moreover, it will set a balance between its internal and external resources. It has incentives to economise with its resources but gives priority to halting potential challengers; to attempt to halt 'free-riding'; to attempt to contain most conflicts or to keep them at a low level in order to avoid its exhaustion; and to promote its own interests. However, it is comparatively free to define its interests and objectives. Compared with the bipolar epoch, the US does not have the same incentives to select allies among the other states, as they are no longer potential instruments against the adversary, nor are they gains or losses in the game. This does not imply that it has lost incentives to commitment, but the causes and the effects of commitment will differ. The strategy for containing the Soviet Union belonged to the bipolar Cold War, and after 1989 the US was expected to reassess each of the Middle Eastern states as well as its overall regional commitment in the light of the new American position. Now the other states have become pieces of a puzzle which could be labelled 'assembling the US world order'. This should not be confused with the assumption of a 'US grand strategy' or 'master plan'; the metaphor aims at highlighting the result of many American actions regardless of the intentions or strategies. In many cases the unipole will face serious troubles when pursuing its policy, it is always facing the trap of exhaustion as well as the dilemma between internal and external use of its resources, and the managerial tasks will constantly provoke dissatisfaction and related conflicts. A unipole is not omnipotent, yet it has the best possible relative position in the international system measured in terms of aggregate capabilities. According to Kenneth Waltz (1979), all great powers have an incentive to undertake managerial tasks in the international system as this serves to maintain their own positions. The unipole has this incentive, too, and this incentive may be even stronger than any other as its position is so precious. Likewise, the managerial task is huge as the unipole is the only great power in existence and therefore the only 'real' manager.

'The US world order' was understood as the sum of the US' position as a unipole and its specific agenda and policy at a given time. Unipolarity implies that the US world order will spread. The spread has more consequences. It will facilitate further US improvement of its position on the one hand, on the other hand it will increase US obligations and problems. Among the problems will be the resistance which the spread of the US world order cannot help but trigger. Some states and groups will be offended as they are not suited for adaptation or because they have fundamentally different interests. As they cannot obtain alternative support from another great power or its compering system, they have to unite their efforts with smaller parties and direct their resistance directly against the US and US allies. Liberal democracy and free market capitalism are centrepieces of the current US world order, and they are not welcome everywhere. Currently another important part of the US policy is the non-proliferation of nuclear weapons. This part especially challenges states not ready to embrace other parts of the US world order. Nuclear weapons provide a state with an ultimate deterrent capability, and obstacles to obtain such a deterrent in times of other challenges risk creating conflict. However, no states are able to ignore the world order, and, expectedly, most states will adapt in some way and to some degree. The US world order is bound to change over time according to changes in the US policy and agenda.

* * *

In summary, the core statements regarding other states and their interaction in the case of unipolarity are: they will tend to flock around the unipole in case of security problems, they have only choice in terms of asymmetric alignment; and they have to work hard for their security and need to cooperate/ally symmetrically as well as to deal with conflicts, i.e., regional activity will tend to be high. On the other hand, the unipole will concentrate on avoiding potential challengers and check them when rising, economise with its resources, and be free to choose its objectives (symmetrically) unchecked; it will, however, still be available as the (only) ultimate external backing and as its strategic interests, and it has to face the task of management in the context of conflicting interests. These characteristics are expected to be part of the majority of international outcomes in the long term. In addition, at the specific level, it also makes a difference with regard to the other states which great powers have left and which survived or replaced the old ones, because the relationship between great powers and the other states is marked by great power pursuit of their interests. In order to identify the new, the old needs to be stated. The next task is, therefore, to describe the issues and the patterns of the US-Soviet bipolarity, and then to focus at the specific post-1989 international arrangement.

FROM US-SOVIET RIVALRY TO US UNIPOLARITY: THE MIDDLE EAST

The systemic change of 1989 was not unique in the sense that systemic changes recur. The emergence of bipolarity in 1945 had also extensive effects on the Middle East. The systemic change into bipolarity ended the pre-1945 multipolar condition in which the European great powers had imposed their specific mandatory rule on the area.

The two post-1945 superpowers both aimed at reducing the European dominance in the area and substituted the principle of mandates by that of dividing the territory into sovereign states, as illustrated in the case of the UN partition plan of 1947. The redivision included the formation of the Israeli state. This was the most controversial part of the bipolar transformation, because it was a decision which most Arab entities opposed. They had two reasons to oppose the plan and its implementation: the Israeli state comprised territory of interest to some of them; and they might fear that the Israeli state would become a medium for renewed extra-regional influence. Shortly after the United States and the Soviet Union had, by their similar efforts, reduced the influence of the old great powers and changed their rules, they began their own rivalry which lasted until 1989. From the Suez crisis in 1956, the Middle East seriously became part of the rivalry and was polarised in a way one would expect from the bipolar condition and dynamics, mainly the 'zero-sum game' and the 'double option'; i.e., the option of two superpower guarantees.

The Cold War affected the area in three main ways regarding patterns of conflict and cooperation. Firstly, the Middle East was divided into pro-US states and pro-Soviet states. Secondly, the Middle East was divided into moderate and radical states within the subsystem. And thirdly, a number of issues became connected to the bipolar rivalry: the main issue was the Israeli-Arab conflict over Palestine which during the Cold War became a point of confrontation, a primary political battlefield between the superpowers. Other issues were: the proxy battle inside Lebanon; to a lesser extent the relationship between the two Yemeni states; and the question of Western Sahara. The superpower game came to involve these conflicts and in the course of the Cold War the conflicts and the positions of the parties involved 'froze'. Over time the nuclearisation of the superpowers' rivalry also had effects in the Middle East: the superpowers began to pursue their objectives in more cautious ways so as to prevent escalation. The emergence of nuclear technology in the

22

Middle East further encouraged the superpowers to be cautious, and this became obvious after the 1973 war. During bipolarity the nuclear-related cautiousness led the superpowers to an indirect pursuit of their policies and to a reliance on proxy struggle.

The Middle East was the secondary external battlefield of the Cold War rivalry, second to Europe. The United States approached the area with two main objectives: to contain the Soviet Union and to secure oil supplies. The Soviet Union, on the other hand, tried to avoid encirclement, to expand its influence and to secure its access to the area's waterways. The objectives of both led them to search for influence and to align Middle Eastern states in opposition to the other's allies. During the Cold War the bipolar 'double option' was beneficial to most Middle Eastern states. Iraq and Egypt changed their superpower affiliations, and the Yemens also benefited from the double option. Bipolarization and the bipolar patterns, however, were strengthened as the Cold War intensified, but when it was over, they were arguably all up for change. The bipolar game and its rules were no longer present to condition Middle Eastern politics. A new game and a new set of rules, however, was soon presented to the regional actors, just as it had been in the aftermath of the Second World War.

In order to provide the background for the empirical analysis, including the possibility of identifying the break with the bipolar impact, bipolar issues and patterns of conflict and cooperation in the Middle East are summarised as follows. The bipolarised issues were the Palestine question, the control of Lebanon, the Yemeni relation-ship, and the Western Sahara quest for independence. In these cases the US and the Soviet Union took up diverging positions in the course of the Cold War (expressed, *inter alia*, in the United Nations), and they supported the parties politically, economically and sometimes militarily. The issues were not zero-summed to the same extent: the Lebanese and the Western Sahara conflicts took place mainly in a very indirect way by the proxies' proxies. The issues had both conflictive and cooperative dimensions: the US and the Soviet Union confronted each other, and so did those Middle Eastern states which were involved. On the other hand, symmetrical as well as asymmetrical cooperation was part of each issue. The Palestine question involved primarily Israel (supported by the US), Syria (supported by the Soviet Union), Jordan (supported by the US), and the PLO (supported by the Soviet Union). The struggle for rule of Lebanon involved primarily Israel and Syria, supported by the US and the Soviet Union, respectively. In addition, the proxies had their own proxies in

Lebanon. As for the Yemeni division, the People's Democratic Republic of Yemen (PDRY – South Yemen) was linked to the Soviet Union and the Arab Republic (YAR – North Yemen) primarily to the US. The struggle for independence of the Western Sahara Polisario Front movement involved support from the Soviet camp to the Polisario Front, while its adversary, Morocco, was supported by the US. The various dimensions of the bipolar effect were closely linked: the local parties involved in the issues were each supported by one of the superpowers, which gradually zero-summed the conflicts. As a rule, the weaker part, which opposed the *status quo*, was supported by the Soviet Union. These states were looking for a great power ally to help against their adversary which was supported by the US. The area as such became bipolarised. When the Cold War was at its peak in 1985, the area was divided into the US camp (Egypt, Israel, Jordan, Morocco, Oman, Saudi Arabia, Tunisia and United Arab Emirates were full members, while Kuwait and North Yemen were affiliated to a lesser extent) and the Soviet camp (Algeria, Iraq, Libya, South Yemen and Syria, with the PLO and the Polisario Front being given political support). Only Iran, from 1979, was outside these camps. It should be added that Iraq was supported against Iran by the US, and that the Iraqi-American relationship gradually improved during the late 1980's.

The area divided into two bipolar camps, though not to the same extent as in Europe, where the superpowers had explicit spheres of influence and where any shift between the camps was almost unthinkable. Nevertheless, while the Cold War was at its height, the Middle East had divided in a comprehensive and stable way, which included nearly all the states with the major exception of Iran after 1979.

The analytical depiction of the subsystemic, symmetrical, division is more difficult than the bipolar systemic division because of the subsystem's 'multipolar' character. By its nature this makes divisions less clear and allows for a greater degree of shifting alignments. However, the Middle East also divided symmetrically. The symmetrical division had two dimensions: the Arab states boycotted Israel except for Egypt after the Camp David Accords, and the Arab world was split internally. During the bipolar period, Arab states gradually adjusted their mutual relationships by forming a huge number of alignments (for a survey, see Taylor, 1982). One tendency prevails, however: the main division which developed was between a group of radical states and a group of moderate states. Although shifts took place between the groups over time, the stable radical states were Algeria, Iraq, Libya, South Yemen and Syria, and the PLO was also linked to this group, while the moderate block came to include stable members such as the oil states at the Arab Peninsula, Egypt and Morocco. Since March 1979 and the signing of the Camp David Accords, the pattern became stable. From 1980 the Cold War in general intensified and developed into its last phase.

The bipolar issues and the patterns of conflict and cooperation were arguably challenged by the 1989 systemic change: the US was still present after the Soviet defeat and it had to reassess both its objectives and its relations to other states. The general expectation of a unipole is that it cares for its position and this includes a restraint from commitment to non-strategic conflicts in order to be capable of facing stronger challenges. The US policy is thus considered to be an important factor, and in reality the US policy is a fact that the Middle Eastern states may oppose but are hardly able to ignore. Specific US objectives in the Middle East for the period in question became clarified between 1990 and 1992: a solution to the conflicts between Israel, the Palestinians and the Arabs; the dual containment of Iraq and Iran as long as they were regarded to be socalled 'rogue' states, that is hostile states with a WMD-capacity; and the maintenance of the free flow of oil at reasonable prices.

THE METHOD

The purpose of the analysis below is to investigate the effects of the end of bipolarity on the Middle East, to identify the possible unipolar impact, and to explain the post-Cold War Middle Eastern development by means of the model for unipolarity. 'Explaining' here is understood as the connection of theoretical statements to the empirical material. As the statements are derived from a coherent, neorealist approach, and if the criteria are satisfactorily met, the connection exceeds a mere demonstration of co-existence, at least if the following three-step procedure is adhered to: the theoretical statements are derived from their coherent context, the empirical development is described, and then the analysis is carried out by means of deduction, interpretation and comparison in order to provide the ground for the conclusions.

It is evident that interpretation has been an important part of the empirical analysis. Interpretation characterizes many analyses of international politics and it has become a part of the application of theory for the purpose of understanding and explaining. However, interpretation needs to be carried out by means of explicit assumptions and statements, and it has to be carried out in a systematic way. The unit level interaction is analysed in the light of the theoretical statements (deduction). This is done with a focus on the major international political events, which are considered and interpreted in such a way as to demonstrate the new. In addition, the issues and the patterns of conflict and cooperation are related to the bipolar state of affairs as well as to the new unipolar state of affairs in order to highlight the changes (comparison). Comparison highlights the differences in the conflict and cooperation issues across the point of the systemic transformation in order to establish whether unipolarity had a distinct impact. Eventually the outcomes are compiled in order to assess the scope and range of the penetration.

The unipolar model is systemic by nature, and a systemic explanation may be applicable to any of the cases without being mutual exclusive to other explanations. The systemic idea, on the contrary, aims to establish notions across individual cases, thus counting for more than each case. However, the status of the explanation is non-exclusive: to any of the events other explanations may apply as well, not least in the attempt to achieve a fuller understanding of the individual event.

The empirical material consists of international political developments in the Middle East from the end of the Cold War in September 1989 and through the following almost ten years to the end of 1998; these have been summed up into a series of major international events. The list thus includes all the events, disseminated in time, space, and character, during the first ten years after the systemic change in order to assess the extent of the systemic impact on the area: the greater the number of events that are referred to the theoretical statements of the change, the greater the impact; and the greater the difference between the events, the wider the range of the impact. The events result from interaction among the parties involved. Their positions and strategies are, therefore, also subject to analysis: how did they change? When the units adapt to a new condition of self-help, they change their positions and strategies, and when more units do the same and meet, the events are completed. The focus is the outcomes, but the units' interaction and behaviour are means to carry out the analysis.

To ensure that the analysis of developments in the Middle East is a balanced one, attention is also devoted to continuity across the systemic change and whether major, residual bipolar patterns survived

1989. The general tendencies, ongoing issues and patterns of conflict and cooperation are also dealt with using the same framework as for the events. The purpose is to ensure that the impact of the systemic change is not exaggerated. A bias might occur if bipolar patterns and issues not subject to change were left out. On the other hand, it would not be a proper method only to deal with the bipolar departure point and investigate its fate: this would exclude the second half of the assumed systemic change and that which was brought about by the emergence of unipolarity.

Selection entails exclusion and limitation. As mentioned above, the most general limitation in this case is that the application of the systemic-structural model implies that many aspects of the Middle East's development and many interesting details are left out in the analysis. This is a cost, when the aim is to identify and explain generalities and broad tendencies as opposed to searching for the unique. To get a full understanding of all the factors involved in each event and of the specific motives of the actors, supplementary and detailed studies of each are required.

The scope of the theoretical model applied is limited to the unipolar arrangement, and so are the unipolar dynamics. Just like previous international systems, the US unipolarity is expected to come to an end. When the international distribution of strength is altered again, or if another element of the additive structure were to change, the Middle East would be subject to another resetting of issues and patterns. How a future systemic transformation will affect the area depends on the same qualifications introduced above about the specific change of polarity and the specific great power interests in question. Until these identities are known, it is not possible to forecast exactly what will occur beyond US unipolarity using the structural approach. It is possible, though, to foresee another turbulent era when the unipolar system is transformed. Even during the present era of unipolarity, the US unipole may redefine its policy and priorities. Because of the unipole's unique position, a unipole is comparatively free to pursue its interests and define its policy. The unipole may be restricted, however, by the rise of potential challengers. Also, because of its exclusive position, it has to watch and manage the whole world, and this may be felt by the less strategically vital areas. Issues, policies as well as the degree of commitment, may be redefined in order to free resources for something more urgent somewhere else. Issues of conflict and cooperation may also rise locally or regionally, not least in the case of unipolarity, where hard work matters. It is therefore impossible to give a full picture of the post-1989 Middle East only by means of the structural approach. On the other hand, the model of unipolarity provides a number of guidelines for the general trends. For instance, the conditions for which local or regional issues likely remain unaltered depend primarily on the unipole's incentives to manage and interfere. Issues which are strategic for the unipole are likely to be subject to response. In addition, the unipole's balancing of its internal and external use of resources will make a difference. These considerations are important, because the empirical analysis only comprises the development in the Middle East during the first phase of unipolarity, and even though the unipolar dynamics continues to be operative, neither polarity arrangement so far has been a static arrangement regarding the multitude of unit level processes and interactions.

The analysis was derived from a mixture of sources. The sources were selected to provide a comprehensive and representative description of each event, including the development of the issues and of interstate cooperation and conflict, as well as the development of the units' positions, capabilities, alignments and actions during the period in question. The first substantial criterion for selecting sources was the principle of representation. The second criterion was that sources also had to provide information about what was not changed or done, so as to isolate the changes. As for positions, sources had primarily to inform about official international signals. The weight given to official statements, contrary to e.g. secret negotiations, is based on the fact that these are the signals which commit the states externally and internally – and by which the states commit themselves. As the official statements only provide one indication, sometimes a seriously misleadig one, it is also necessary to refer to the actions of the units, in this case particularly their military deployments and other security related activities. Consideration of the actions of the units is based mainly on the annual version of *The Military Balance* (IISS), the comprehensive surveys of facts by Anthony H. Cordesman, and other sources. In addition, the study relies on a series of comprehensive works and results regarding the development of the neorealist theory in addition to *Theory of International Politics* (Waltz 1979), most notably on *The Origin of Alliances* (Walt 1990). Other important results regarding neorealism and/or alliance theory were provided by G. Snyder 1984, Christensen and J. Snyder 1990, David 1991, Morrow 1991, and Garnham 1991. Concerning the analysis of Middle Eastern politics the study has benefited from the works of especially Taylor 1982, Walt 1990, L. Freedman and Karsh 1993, volumes edited by Robert O. Freedman, and current sources provided by civil servants, fact-finders, and journalists.

The analytical procedure

The analysis is undertaken in a chronological order, and the procedure consists of description, comparison and deduction. Each event is subject to the following procedure.

First, what took place is described in order to put forward the selected empirical facts. The descriptions of the events put a special emphasis on capabilities and strength, alignments, strategies and positions.

Second, the events are analysed in the light of change: what was changed compared to the bipolar patterns and what was not. Even though the expectations and the findings coexist, the findings may be related to something other than the systemic change, and as a consequence the analysis must proceed.

Third, the changes are interpreted and the impact of the systemic change to unipolarity is demonstrated by means of deduction. The empirical findings are connected to the statements on self-help and security conditions, i.e., whether they reflect flocking (unipolarisation), the single option, hard work and the US unipolar approach, thereby analysing and demonstrating the unipolar impact of the events.

Then post-1989 the issues and patterns of conflict and cooperation are compared to those of bipolarity in order to sum up the impacts of the change, and to define the specificity of the unipolar issues and patterns of conflict and cooperation. Each event is subject to the same questions to secure a similar treatment across the seemingly divergent character of the events. The procedure is to ask three questions of each event (later the answers are compiled). After considering these questions and the answers of the analysis, general conclusions are drawn about how the 1989 systemic change penetrated the Middle East: what was affected and in what direction? The questions which serves as criteria for positive explanation of the Middle Eastern transformation are:

- Which bipolar issues and patterns of cooperation and conflict were still in operation, and which were not? This question implies that the findings are related to the bipolar set-up.

- Did any new ones emerge? This question is close to being answered by the very occurrence of the events. It is not, however, necessarily the case that all the events represent a break with the bipolar set-up, or that there is a break with the bipolar set-up as a whole. The question also includes the status of the events position regarding the expected outcomes of the systemic transformation. The question concerns the potential scope and range of the transformation.
- Is the new distinct in a unipolar way? This question is about stating the connections between the findings of the deduction procedure and that identified as new, to ensure that the new is, specifically, a unipolar impact.

The general comparison across the systemic change reveals the degree to which and the range in which the change has had effects. The conclusion is based on partial conclusions about individual events – made by cross-examination for residual bipolar patterns.

Finally, considerations will be given to the usability and explanatory power of the model for unipolarity regarding its ability to explain the Middle Eastern development between 1989 and 1997. Within the neorealist tradition a strong criterion for assessing a theory is whether or not it seems useful and brings about results. This criterion can also be met by the model's very use. Empirical results are, therefore, the measure for a potential assessment of this model.

When approaching the three questions to each event, the points of departure are the bipolar issues, those issues which were drawn into the zero-sum game: the conflict between Israel and the Palestinians, between Israel and its Arab neighbours, the internal Lebanese struggle (where proxies fought each other), the Yemeni relationship, and the question of the Western Sahara. The patterns of conflict and cooperation are divided into two camps of asymmetrical alignments as well as into a subsystemic division into moderates and radicals. These patterns are a part of the interaction process, but they also contribute to the set-up of strength and thereby frame the issues.

In order to complete the analysis, it is necessary to ask all the three questions. If the bipolar patterns alone had disappeared, one could not be sure that this was an effect of a systemic change: it might equally be referred to as one of the above mentioned alternative arguments in the research on the Middle East. For example, it could be referred to the argument that the area was subject to US-Soviet neo-colonialism or overlay, which, if it vanished, would allow the region to function 'naturally'. The second question of whether new issues and patterns emerged is essential to demonstrate the impact of the changing conditions on all states. The third question, which concerns the distinct unipolar features of the new issues and patterns, is posed to isolate the impact of unipolarity and separate it from, for example, a so-called natural regional functioning or from a case of hegemonic influence. The way to measure the unipolar impact is to add the results of all the events and compare across 1989. In practice, the answer to the third question regarding the distinct unipolar impact depends on the double presence of the stated unipolar effects (established by means of the deduction) and the findings of the comparative differences with the bipolar state of affairs.

*   *   *

According to the initial argument, the Middle East was penetrated by the effects of the end of the Cold War. The analysis, however, only covers the first phase of unipolarity from 1989 to 1997, and therefore some perspectives concerning current and future Middle Eastern politics are added after the analysis, as the Middle East is still a volatile, vivid area in political development – and as unipolarity is also a condition open to comprise dynamic development.

Chapter 3

Bipolarity and the Middle East

The Napoleonic invasion of Egypt in 1798 was a manifestation of the attention of and the pursuit of interest in the Middle East by external great powers. The area has been attractive to the great powers for varying reasons and to various degrees; and it has been a battlefield for them. Up to World War I the Ottoman Empire, which had a dominant position in the Middle East as well as being a pole in the then multipolar international system, and the European poles strived for influence and pursued strategies of colonization. The European great powers did it in different ways: while the Ottomans were comparatively less inclined to reform their seizures, France pursued its *mission civilisatrice*, and the other major European power in the area, Great Britain, carried out a less centralised rule relying on local administrations. For both the Ottomans and the Europeans the Middle East was a natural centre for expanding their markets and extracting resources. For the Europeans the region held additional assets: the control of the Suez Channel and the surrounding territory was vital in order to secure the seaway to India, China and other colonial areas. The importance of the Middle East thus made it a battlefield when World War I broke out between the colonial powers. When the Ottoman Empire, which had chosen the defeated side, was dissolved after its defeat in World War I, the victorious European great powers took over what they did not already hold. They divided the region and reorganised the vital parts into mandate territories and protectorates inspired by the Sykes-Picot agreement of 1916. The results provided for suzerainty under British and French protection.

The European great powers, however, had serious problems with their gains in the Middle East during the inter-war period. Strikes, rebellions and growing nationalism were on the Middle Eastern agenda. The European great powers, however, had worse problems with each other. The Second World War broke out and was, in the beginning, fought mainly between the European great powers. For them, it was the beginning of the end of their dominance in the Middle East (and other areas); but two new great powers were ready to take over.

The first actions of the US and the Soviet Union regarding the Middle East were taken in the spirit of similar interests.[1] Their agreeable decisions implied that the old great powers should leave, that the area should be liberated from their rule, colonialism, and that it should be transformed into a group of modern sovereign states. This was the concept and its implementation was begun immediately. France and Great Britain began a process of withdrawing except from some selected positions. They had privileged positions within the Western alliance and served to fill potential vacuums of power in the process of US enlargement of its positions. France maintained its rule of Algeria and some other strongholds in North Africa, while Great Britain was influential, in cooperation with the US, in the Israeli-Arab parties (Gold 1988:115), as well as in the Southern Gulf States, which were, however, to be subject to a slow but steady process of obtaining independence.

The implementation was the result of the post-Second World War negotiations and the reorganisation was confirmed by the United Nations, the new global institution, with support from both the US and the Soviet Union. The reorganisation included the establishment in the area of a new, Jewish state – Israel. The Soviet Union and the US agreed both on the question of formal sovereignty and that of substantial reorganisation; this was reflected in the UN votes on the Partition Resolution. The agreement included the addition of Israel to the Middle Eastern map next to a Palestinian state and otherwise in general the maintenance of the post-World War I Arab borders. This act challenged all the adjacent Arab nations whose ambitions of independence and strength had been nurtured during the European decline. Earlier in history they had been centres of power themselves and had spread across the region. For example, Syria once covered the territory of Lebanon and parts of the modern Iraq, and, even though this was a short period, the concept of Greater Syria was maintained and promoted when opportunities to do so were present. Nationalist movements had built up scenarios of restoring the historical extent of their nations and ridding the regions of external influence. The formation of the Israeli state reduced the potential territorial gain for each of the surrounding Arab states, and it was furthermore seen as an imperialist bastion in their midst. For all of them the establishment of the new state was an obstacle to their ambitions in the region and seen as a threat.

At the end of the Second World War the Middle East was of secondary interest to the emerging new great powers. While the Middle East later became part of the zero sum game, the initial attraction was related to specific interests. The US primarily aimed at securing oil supplies. Since the 1930's, American firms had sought to gain access to the region's specific resource asset – its oil wells – and they had succeeded. Moscow had strived to secure its borders and its traditional interests; the Soviet Union gave priority to Iran in order to secure the Southern Soviet border and Turkey in order to secure the access to the Dardanelles and Bosporus Straits. Besides, the Soviet Union brought these two aims into the post-war negotiations in order to obtain acceptance of a Soviet sphere of interest (Golan 1990). For the US the region held no traditional attraction based on geopolitical conditions, unlike its adversary. It declared, however, a commitment to the security of oil production in the Arab Peninsula. The US was also promoting the formation of pacts in order to prevent Soviet influence and was improving the prospects for establishing military bases. In the initial phase of the Cold War the Middle East was, therefore, conceived as being inside the rivalry but also, less important than Europe. The US Joint Chief of Staff chairman General Bradley put is it this way: "We just feel we cannot defend Europe and the Middle East at the same time – we would still win a war despite the loss of the Middle East, which would not be true of Europe" (Gold 1988:115).

The two specific historical interests of the Moscow empire have been to secure access through the Turkish straits of the Dardanelles and the Bosporus to compensate for the lack of warm water ports outside the Black Sea as well as to secure against enemy access to the Black Sea, and to have good relations to the (various) adjacent states at its long borderline. Historically, these interests have been at the centre of Moscow's policy towards the south. Russia and later the Soviet Union had long border lines in the area, especially with Iran. The specific interests in the Southern area, however, became second to the core strategic interests of securing western frontiers with Europe, and in the east with Asia (Golan 1990); and this was still the case right after the end of the Second World War. In addition, the emergence of the Cold War put an emphasis on the Soviet Union's need for a buffer zone in light of the US strategy of Containment.

After the Second World War, the Middle East became subject to a process of general reduction of European influence. Immediately after the war the superpowers gave priority to their aims elsewhere, in Europe and East Asia. The specific strategic importance of the area was subordinated to the major task of reorganising the post-war political landscape in Europe and to the emergence of the nuclear weapons. The phase of similar goals among the new great powers was a short one, however; a new rivalry soon emerged.

In March of 1947 the American President Truman declared his doctrine against the spread of Communism. The doctrine was triggered by American fear of potential Soviet interference in the Greek Civil War in the Southeastern corner of Europe. The European theatre was crucial to the two large powers: if either of the two could gain control of major parts of the theatre this would decisively affect the global balance in favour of the one in control. The Truman Doctrine may well be interpreted as the start of the Cold War, and it became the actual launching point of the American strategy of Containment, aimed at containing the Soviet Union in all fields. The Soviet Union responded by developing a counter strategy labelled the Two Camp Strategy which was based on full-fledged (political/ economical/ideological) competition. The Soviet strategy was initially characterised by confrontation and led to the first serious trial of strength: the Berlin blockade. From then on competition began in two areas, perceived by both to be the strategic ones: the European theatre and the nuclear weapons race. The process of bipolarisation accelerated; they built up their abilities of power projection. But meanwhile they still cooperated in some other areas.

During the 1950's, the superpower rivalry expanded horizontally. Initially, the West, most energetically Great Britain but also the US, had tried to establish a comprehensive Middle Eastern organisation against the Soviet Union. The Middle East Defence Organisation did not succeed, primarily because of the Egyptian refusal to join, but efforts were continued and led to the establishment of the Baghdad Pact (Walt 1990:58). In 1955, Turkey and Iraq signed the treaty, and shortly afterwards Iran, Pakistan and Great Britain joined the Pact, in which the US became an observer in 1957. The US then became a member of the Military Committee in the Pact, which it had encouraged as part of a process of creating pacts around the Soviet Union. The Middle East was now becoming seriously involved in the struggle for influence; the Suez conflict in 1956 had made it clear that the European great powers had been replaced by two new powers. The conflict demonstrated that even though Great Britain and France still had interests in the Suez area, they no longer possessed accepted spheres of interests. This, however, led to a power vacuum which the Soviet Union tried to fill and which made the Middle East part of the Cold War. The US position was given by the Eisenhower Doctrine of 1957, in which President Eisenhower said that "the existing vacuum in the Middle East must be filled by the US before it is filled by Russia" (quoted in Walt 1990:67), and later the Congress authorised the use of "armed force to assist any nation or group of such nations requesting assistance ... against any nation controlled by international communism" (Ibid.). Subsequently, the US provided extensive economic and military aid to its allies. In summary, the Suez conflict finally ended the European epoch, clarified the American position and seriously brought the Soviet Union into the region.

The Eisenhower Doctrine had encouraged US protection of Saudi Arabia, Jordan and Lebanon 1957–58 (Walt 1990:71), but the Soviet appearance as a superpower had provided the Middle Eastern states with another option: Iraq left the Baghdad Pact, which was then renamed the Central Treaty Organisation (CENTO), and Pakistan improved its relations with the Soviet Union. Thereafter, CENTO began to fall apart and the defence dimension was given up in favour of economic cooperation. While Iraq left the Pact, its local rival Iran remained aligned to the US.

Iran's early affiliation to the US had been seriously challenged by an internal crisis at the beginning of the 1950's. The crisis concerned Iran's share of the oil revenues which had been limited by the British government. The Iranian opposition leader (the National Front), Muhammad Mossadeq, was promoting extensive Iranian demands. The US interfered, fearing Soviet influence, in order to reinstore and maintain the Shah's pro-US rule, and provided aid to Iran on a grand scale. The Mossadeq crisis and later the Suez Conflict fuelled the polarisation process, and Middle Eastern states began gravitating to the superpowers. In Iraq a crisis erupted, too. In 1958, General Abd al-Karim Qassem toppled the Hashemite monarchy. Iraq broke with the Baghdad Pact and approached the Soviet Union, although the alignment was short-lived.

Afghanistan, on the periphery of the area, had good relations with the Soviet Union which contributed to keeping it out of the pro-Western pact; and from 1953 it had begun to receive Soviet aid (Calvocoressi 1992:423). It remained pro-Soviet, but in the late 1970's internal unrest followed a coup. In 1979 the Soviet Union invaded fearing the loss of an ally and stayed there until 1989. However, Afghanistan being a client state of the Soviet Union, it was never really included in the political Middle East although the Soviet Union tried to enlarge the perception of the region in its attempts to gain influence through the Middle Eastern periphery. Towards the end of the 1950's, Iran, Jordan, Lebanon, and Saudi Arabia had affiliated with the US, while Egypt and Syria like Afghanistan had aligned with the Soviet Union. Iraq ended its US orientation and was turning towards the Soviet Union. The Soviet camp was growing.

Egypt was centrally situated and a leading power within the subsystem. This made it of great interest to both the superpowers. The Soviet Union had won the first round by offering considerable support to the construction of the Aswan Dam in the aftermath of the Suez crisis. The US, however, still aware of Egypt's importance in the struggle for regional influence, continued to support the country financially in spite of its Soviet orientation. Enjoying this beneficial position, Egypt, although adhering to its non-aligned status, maintained its close cooperation with the Soviet Union for more than ten years. Egypt was a declining power in the subsystem, however, and after the 1973 War, it changed its direction. Its economy was deteriorating; its population was growing rapidly; and, above all, it had suffered a regional setback because of its only modest oil reserves. Soviet advisers were sent home during the short superpower détente and Egypt turned to the American alternative. The US was able and willing to guarantee the Israeli front *and* contribute to the restoration of the Egyptian economy (Barnett and Levy 1991).

The growing power after the rise of the oil issue was Saudi Arabia. It had aligned with the US in 1957, and the alignment was upheld throughout the bipolar epoch although it was done discreetly. Saudi Arabia was very dependent on external guarantees because of its vast territory, many fronts, lack of military might and other resources – except for oil and its related revenues. The Iraqi record was similar, although the opposite of the Egyptian. Iraq initially affiliated with the Western camp, aligning to the US and Great Britain in the 1950's in the Baghdad Pact. The Baghdad Pact did not contribute to Iraqi ambitions in its rivalry with Egypt. Iraq could not attract other Arab states and became regionally isolated (Karsh and Rautsi 1991:12); it benefited, therefore, from the double option: Iraq broke with the Pact and, after a short period of declared non-alignment, establishing a relatively close alignment to the Soviet Union. Another state closely aligned to the Soviet Union was Syria, which turned towards the Soviet camp early in order to obtain assistance against its main enemies within the subsystem, Israel, Iraq, and Turkey. The People's

Republic of Yemen (PDRY) had also become aligned to the Soviet Union from 1968, which also tried to be on good terms with the Yemen Arab Republic.

The war in June 1967 between Israel and the Arab states of Egypt, Iraq, Jordan, and Syria changed the balance in the Middle East. In fear of war preparations in Egypt and Syria, Israel launched a preemptive strike and seized the Golan Heights from Syria, the West Bank from Jordan, and the Gaza strip from Egypt. Consequently, the Western camp expanded, and to the front line states the threat from Israel increased: Israel had demonstrated its military and political strength, it had gained territorial room for manoeuvre, and it had deprived the front line states of territory as well as of strategic assets.

As the Cold War intensified, the superpowers increased their commitments and rivalry. Their influence grew, but it was in the light of the bipolar condition that the Middle Eastern states always had another option. At the same time these states had a common interest. They wanted to avoid the external powers acquiring too much influence. Their room for manoeuvre was reduced, however, by the growing intensity of the Cold War. During the 1960's the region became even more polarised, with Iran, Saudi Arabia, Jordan and Israel aligned to the US, and Egypt, Syria, Iraq and PDRY to the Soviet Union. Only Egypt's shift during the end of the superpower détente in the middle of the 1970's, and the Iranian revolutionary disentanglement from the bipolar camps changed this picture. From the hardening of the US positions in the Cold War in the beginning of the 1980's, no further changes took place.

After 1973, even proxy war was no longer a possible way of changing the balance. The war in October 1973 was a turning point in the area's status as a 'proxy theatre'. The US ended the war by issuing a nuclear alert. Firstly, it had been revealed that Israel was close to become a nuclear power. Third party possession of nuclear weapons was a complication which might prevent the superpowers from managing their mutual deterrence at a proper level. Secondly, and most importantly, at that time both superpowers had developed a convincing second strike capability and an ability to cope with all steps of the escalation ladder, and therefore the nuclearised rivalry had become even more dangerous: the superpowers risked that a conflict in the Third World might escalate to a level in which their own mutually devastating nuclear arsenals might be involved. The 1973 War had been stopped by a cease-fire brought about by diplomatic efforts. But the cease-fire did not last and the Soviet Union began to alert its military forces. The US responded by issuing a 'Defense Condition III Alert' (Garthoff 1985:379) which involved strategic nuclear forces. This alert was the most serious superpower confrontation since the Cuban crisis, and it clearly signalled to the Soviet Union that the Middle East was not only subject to the horizontal spread of the Cold War, but had also become part of the vertical intensification of it, and that the US set the limits. It also signalled to the Middle Eastern parties that they could not exploit the rivalry beyond the limits demarcated by the US.

The conflicts in the Middle East became a problem to both the US and the Soviet Union, as the struggle for influence and the divisions in the area was subordinated to the danger of escalation. Neither superpower dared to risk a Middle Eastern conflict running out of control and escalating to the level of nuclear weapons. This was one of the two important events which marked the self-imposed restrictions which characterised the rivalry from the 1970's and onwards. The other one was the superpowers' shared notion of non-interference directly in the Iran-Iraq war, which had become the militarily strongest powers among the Middle Eastern states. Although both the Soviet Union and the US had strategic interests in the Gulf area, they were careful not to interfere and tilt the balance as this could have led to a worst-case situation between themselves (Heller 1988).

The centre of the general rivalry had become the conflict over Palestine. From the early 1960's the US took a definitive position in the conflict in favour of Israel; and the Soviet responded by supporting the demands of the nationalist Palestinian movement and the radical Arab side, the weaker parts, most eager to obtain a change in the regional order. This was primarily American in the beginning and, therefore, the natural objects of Soviet attention. Outside the centre both superpowers were on the lookout for strongholds, the US in support of containment and the Soviet Union to avoid encirclement. This led to a Soviet counter strategy in the Red Sea Area, where the PDRY became a useful ally. Similarly, the Soviet Union tried to expand in North Africa, offering support to Algeria after French withdrawal and the African periphery of the Middle East. On the other hand, the Middle Eastern states benefited from the double option and had relatively large room for manoeuvre inside the camps until the Reagan Administrations began to forcing the Soviet Union back.

The nuclearisation of the relationship between the superpowers made them both aware of the danger of escalation. Their rivalry in this volatile region carried a risk of involvement in an escalating, direct conflict. A consequence of this was self-imposed restraint, a conviction that wars should be limited and kept at a low level. The Nixon Doctrine of July 1969 stated that the US "must avoid the kind of policy that will make countries in Asia so dependent on US that we are dragged into conflicts such as the one that we have in Vietnam". The implication was that the US would primarily rely on war by proxy and be reluctant to enter formal alliances in the area. The Doctrine pointed to the maintenance of the Middle East as part of the Cold War, while delinking it from direct action which was the opposite of the link expressed in the Eisenhower Doctrine.

The 1973 War had revealed the dangers of Middle Eastern conflicts, and both of the superpowers had become even more careful. When the Reagan Administration hardened the US position in the Cold War the proxy-concept was completely challenged, which is illustrated by the fate of the proposed US-Israeli strategic alliance. The Reagan Administration proposed the formation of a strategic alliance with Israel against Moscow as part of hardening the positions and halting Soviet influence in the so-called Third World, and in November 1981 an agreement was reached on the intentions. The proceedings with the formation of the alliance, however, were suspended only a month later because the US disapproved of the extension of Israeli law by Israel to the Golan Heights (Quandt 1993:339). The alliance never materialised largely because of US concern that Israel wished to interpret the scope of the alliance to include its regional adversaries as well. This was certainly not the American intention, because it could have endangered the superpower relationship in an uncontrollable way, and the dilemma between the hardening of positions in the proxy-sphere and the problem of controlling the related dangers was accentuated.

During the terminal phase of the Cold War in the late 1980's the Soviet foreign policy became subject to rethinking and change under Mikhail Gorbachev's leadership, and the changed foreign policy was presented as the socalled the 'New Thinking'. The New Thinking policy represented a Soviet retreat at the outer circles of the Cold War: confrontation should be turned into cooperation on the less vital Cold War issues and areas. This included the Middle East where the Soviet Union signalled a new attitude. The first and very important element was a readiness to withdraw from Afghanistan where the Soviet intervention in 1979 had been of great concern to the US, which considered the invasion of Afghanistan a qualitative upgrading of the

Soviet Third World engagement. The invasion gave rise to the Carter Doctrine and later contributed to what is interpreted as the eventual Cold War offensive implemented by the Reagan Administration in the beginning of the 1980's. A second element was a conciliatory approach to the peace process; and a third a decrease in support to states and movements within the Soviet alignment network.

The superpower strategies for peace and their plans had developed over time and had resulted in different antagonistic positions just like the superpowers' position within their own arms control negotiations. With respect to the Arab-Israeli peace process both the superpowers adhered to the need for peace, but each party promoted its own version of how to achieve peace. As prerequisites for peace in the Arab-Israeli conflict, the US had emphasised the security of Israel, while the Soviet Union had emphasised the need to take into consideration the rights of the Palestinians. Similarly, the Soviet Union promoted its standard policy: an international conference on peace in the area – like the then CSCE in Europe. The Soviet Union was prone to try to internationalise conflicts, for example, its efforts in the United Nations, in order to make up for its weaker position in the Middle East compared to the US and to halt further progress of US influence. Numerous proposals and votes in the UN Security Council reflected the different superpower approaches. Resolution 242, which was adopted after the June War in 1967, was the most striking illustration of the superpower struggle, the positions of each party, and the extent as well as the limitations of the Soviet Union's success in securing influence.

Other issues were brought into the rivalry to a lesser extent. The Soviet attempt to gain influence in the area around the Red Sea area and the Horn of Africa resulted in the special status of the Yemens. They were rivals, they could not unite, but each benefited from the rivalry. In Western Sahara and Lebanon the conflicts were fought by proxies of the proxies. In Western Sahara decisive Moroccan control would strengthen the American camp and its allies, while a solution in favour of the Polisario might have become part of the zero-sum game to the advantage of the Soviet camps and its allies. This would have altered the indirect superpower balance in North Africa. Similarly, total Syrian or Israeli control in Lebanon as an end to the 1975 civil war would have changed the balance in the Arab-Israeli conflict.

As for the Lebanese civil war, the US did not just fear a total Syrian takeover; it was even more concerned that a strengthening of the then Syrian-Palestinian side might lead to Palestinian attacks on Israel, which might subsequently be dragged into the war, along, eventually, with Syria and Egypt as well (Quandt 1993:247). In such a case, the US and the Soviet Union would risk direct confrontation with each other, and the danger of escalation. On the other hand, during the Cold War offensive of the Reagan-administrations' years, the US again began to resort to the use of military force in the Third World (Garthoff 1985:1020). The US bombardment from the battleship USS New Jersey of positions in Lebanon sent a strong signal to the Soviet Union and its proxies about the limits of their potential gains. The US did not convert the intervention into any decisive action (which is why it was seen as a failure by many observers), but it did convey a strong signal, one which was apparently received. After that, all the parties, except the Lebanese factions, became more cautious. In the late 1980's, the Soviet Union began to temper the ambitions of its proxies and to signal a more cooperative approach towards US positions.

The Cold War even produced an enlargement of the concept of the Middle East. The Soviet Union attempted to increase its influence via the area's periphery, which was still open to influence: the Horn of Africa, the Red Sea area, North Africa and Afghanistan. The Soviet policy thus attempted to enlarge 'the Middle East', and consequently, these areas were considered more and more to be Middle Eastern by the US, whose aim was to contain the Soviet Union. Similarly, the strong demarcation of Europe forced the North African states to orientate towards the Middle East. The republics in Southern Caucasus and Central Asia had become part of the Soviet Union in the 1920's, and they consequently remained outside the 'Middle East' during the Cold War. On the other other hand, this squeezed out any space between the Soviet Union and the Middle East. Since 1989 even the concept of the Middle East, including the bipolar enlargement, was also open to change. Figure 2 shows some important developments in the Cold War and the superpowers' engagement in the Middle East.

SUBSYSTEMIC ALIGNMENTS

During the Cold War, the units in the Middle East not only aligned with the superpowers, they also aligned with each other. In the period between 1945 and 1989 there was a high number of symmetrical alignments in the Middle East, and the alignments encompassed various degrees of intensity as well as laterality. That is, the alignments comprised different members some of whom were

1945	End of the Second World War
Late 1940's	Similar US and Soviet efforts to end previous European colonial and mandatory rule in the Middle East
1947	US declares the Cold War
1950'	The US and the Soviet Union are aligning with Middle Eastern states; momentum after the Suez-crisis
1960's	Secondary bipolar competition in the Middle East
1970's	The Soviet Union gains influence in the so-called Third World, including the Middle East
1973	The superpowers become more cautious in the Middle East because of the level of their own nuclear rivalry and of the perception of Israel as a nuclear threshold state
1980's:	The US launches its Cold War offensive and bipolarisation increases and freezes
1987	Loosening of the bipolar rivalry and signs of Soviet retreat in some areas, including the Middle East
1989	End of the Cold War
1991	Manifestation of unipolarity

Figure 2 Important Cold War Fluctuations and the Middle East: Timetable

formerly allied against each other. The primary characteristics of the majority of the alignments were that they were rather soft and *entente*-like, of short durability with the exception is the Gulf Cooperation Council (GCC) , and that they tended to be lateral.

Not until the middle of the 1960's did any firm asymmetrical pattern amongst the Arab states appear which corresponded to the patterns of asymmetrical alignment. Then the Arab states had divided into groups of moderate and radical states, the moderate group corresponding to the symmetrical group of pro-US states, while the radical group corresponded to the pro-Soviet states, roughly speaking. This pattern coexisted with the Arab front against Israel, being a firm pattern as well. The Arab-Israeli pattern did not correspond to the asymmetrical patterns; the one side included only Israel, while the other comprised all Arab states, though their positions diverged within a range of rejectionist degrees and they belonged to either of the asymmetrical camps.

The many and lateral alignments reflected the 'multipolar' distribution of strength in the subsystem. During bipolarity, the

Middle East was characterised by more regional powers as well as by changes in the ranking among the regional powers. When several powers are competing and trying to check each other, many and changing alignments expectedly occur. Viewed as a multipolar subsystem, the Middle East has been characterised by the functioning of a balance of power between several subsystemic powers: Iran (balanced primarily by Iraq until the revolution and thereafter still balanced by Iraq but also by the major Arab states, including Syria and Saudi Arabia), Israel (balanced by the major Arab states, most notably Egypt; from 1979 most notably by Syria and the radical Arab states), Egypt (balanced by Iraq and Israel; from 1979 by the radical Arab states), Iraq (balanced by Iran, and then Saudi Arabia with the GCC states), Syria (balanced by Egypt, Iraq and Israel) and Saudi Arabia (balanced by Iraq, Egypt and Iran). These tendencies could not help but to offset each other now and then because balancing one state meant cooperation with others, and the fact that each major regional power faced more threats and rivalries prevented the emergence of subsystemically stable fronts.

In general it appears reasonable to connect the origins of the main divisions in the area from 1945 to 1989 to the post-Second World War reorganisation: Iraq, Syria, PDRY and Libya, and also the organisations the PLO and the Polisario, were the parties wanting to change the resultant reorganisation; while the Southern Gulf States, Israel and Morocco were relatively privileged and wanted to maintain it. Egypt was a radical state until the Camp David Accords and strove for leadership of the Arab states, as well as being deeply involved in the Arab-Israeli conflict. Weakened by the wars against Israel and its modest oil reserves compared to the Southern as well as the Northern Gulf States (which was highlighted in the oil crisis which followed the 1973 War when the quadrupling of oil prices raised the income and position of the oil rich states), Egypt became a moderate state.

Except for the Egyptian change of asymmetrical alignment, that is the shift from Soviet to US alignment in 1975, the relationship of radical versus moderate states in the subsystem was characterised from 1973 by a stalemate. Although Iran played an important role in the Middle East, it was outside the Arab rivalry and alignments. Neither of the Arab states were able to overlook the strong but peripheral Iranian position when aligning each other. Iran was able to stay clear of the complex Arab aligning owing to its privileged position in the US camp. However, Iran abolished asymmetrical alignment after the revolution and thus contributed to a redistribution of strength within the subsystem. West of Iran only the Camp David Accords between Israel and Egypt changed the balance. It did so in favour of the moderates: the formerly monolithic alliance between the radical, so-called Arab front line states had been broken by what was perceived as an Egyptian defection. In return, the Iranian revolution brought about an end to the close relationship between Iran and the US in the South Eastern part of the area. Iran clearly disentangled itself from both superpowers and this helped it stay out of any zero-summing game but exposed Iran to subsystemic problems. Apparently, the Iranian government perceived Iran to be strong enough to cope with its subsystemic counterparts without superpower backing. However, the disentangled Iran was not able to deter Iraq from invading in 1980 shortly after the revolution. After all, Iran was the stronger part relative to Iraq, at the longer term. Iran succeeded in preventing Iraq from obtaining any substantial gains. Iraq had probably lost the war if Iraq had not obtained support from the West. To both Iraq and Iran the war, which ended by the 1988 cease-fire, became a very costly affair.

The subsystemic and the systemic dynamics interact, and in the Middle East the dynamics obviously interacted during bipolarity. The neorealist theory set forth the expectation that the systemic dynamics will become superior to the subsystemic dynamics in case of systemic tensions, and this seems to have been the result in case of the bipolar Middle East. The stabilization of the moderate and the radical camps materialised in accordance with the rising tensions among the superpowers at a time, when the Middle East had become seriously involved in the bipolar rivalry – though the protagonist had become more careful with respect to their pursuit of interests because of the nuclearisation of their own rivalry – and later of the introduction of nuclear weapons into the region (van Crefeld 1993:119; Ch. 4).

During bipolarity the Middle Eastern subsystem was characterised by a multipolar distribution of strength with various regional powers, allowing for shifting alignments and rivalries. In addition, the Middle Eastern powers had to come to terms with the political facts with an origin from the 1945 systemic change: the creation of Israel and the Middle Eastern borders in general. These factors, however, were subordinate to the fluctuating bipolar rivalry, and when the Cold War entered its concluding phase from the early 1980's, the subsystemic alignments came to be subordinate to the asymmetrical alignments and were frozen accordingly, and so were the subsystemic issues as the

Palestinian problem, the Lebanese civil war, and the Yemeni relationship.

This interpretation of bipolar Middle Eastern international politics leaves out important developments because of its narrow focus: during bipolarity the Middle East had developed into a modern state system after being subject to the systemic change from multipolarity to bipolarity in 1945. Consequently, the period from 1945 to 1989 contained the efforts of the new or reorganised Middle Eastern units to survive and to co-exist, and the socialisation of the units' domestic governance to the bipolar models for free market capitalism and liberal democracy respectively plan economy and socialism/one party systems – naturally in the context of the units' own characteristics. However, the Middle Eastern states generally were consolidated as modern states. They succeeded in achieving the foremost goal of any state: survival, but they went through state building processes in spite of long odds as boundaries arbitrarily drawn. The processes included internal unrest, coup d'états, authoritarian rule and problems of succession. The end of the Cold War thus left the comparatively new modern states with the challenges of adapting internally to the spread of the currently dominant model of liberal democracy and free market capitalism in addition to the new external challenges. Furthermore, the internal adaptation has to take place alongside the efforts to overcome the problems of succession. Many of these problems are inclined to revive during unipolarity in addition to nationalism, unresolved border issues and the dilemma between adaptation to the US world order and local resistance from primarily Islamic fundamentalist opposition.

THE LOOSENING AND END OF THE RIVALRY

The Middle East was one of the first areas to be subjected to a Cold War retreat by the Soviet Union, and the process began when the Soviet Union agreed to withdraw from Afghanistan within the context of improved superpower relations after the agreement on the INF Treaty in 1987. The Soviet withdrawal was directly followed by the outbreak of an intense Afghan civil war, and presented the Middle East with some softening of the Soviet positions regarding the Israeli-Arab conflict. Furthermore, the US-PLO relationship was improved in the end of 1988, and the formation or revitalisation of regional organisations began to take place. The loosening of the superpower rivalry triggered a process of subsystemic activity which exploited the increased room of manoeuvre as well as decreased superpower attention. The activity, however, also took place in light of fear of abandonment. The states feared they might become victims of superpower reconciliation and therefore receive less support in order to manage their problems in the subsystem, against each other (Taylor 1991). However, in the aftermath of the Soviet withdrawal from Afghanistan, no definite asymmetrical changes took place because the rivalry had not ended. It was as if the subsystemic units were not in a position to burn their bridges. The loosening might be turn out to be a temporary fluctuation in the Cold War, there had been others, but they began to resettle their mutual relationships in the light of the loosening.

At the beginning of 1989 two cooperative blocs were formed in the Middle East: the Union of Arab Maghreb (UMA), and the Arab Cooperation Council (ACC). They completed the organisational division of the inner Middle East, and left out only Syria and Israel. The blocs primarily addressed economical and developmental cooperation, although they soon turned to focus on political matters. Algeria, Libya, Mauritania (later), Morocco and Tunisia formed the UMA. UMA aimed initially at establishing a single market on the North African coast. This is still a far away aim, but in the beginning of the 1990's, UMA succeeded in planning, approving or implementing a number of joint projects as a free trade zone, free movement of citizens and a joint airline (Nonneman 1992). The other cooperation bloc was formed in February 1989. Initially, the ACC also addressed the free movement of citizens, joint projects in transportation and communication, and planned to integrate trade and monetary policies, but it also turned into a political alignment. However, shortly afterwards the ACC broke down, as Iraq invaded Kuwait and the members of the ACC which were Iraq, Jordan, Egypt and North Yemen (later RoY) were split on the Iraqi invasion. This cautious subsystemic regrouping mirrored the loosening of rivalry in the Cold War. There were no shifts between the polar camps because the rivalry still being in existence despite the area's now lower priority. The subsystemic dynamics became more active, but they did so in the context of the loosening but still bipolar condition. Figure 3 shows the bipolar patterns of conflict and cooperation, and the particularly bipolarised political issues.

In summary, the bipolar arrangement of the Middle East was characterised, by and large, by the development of a correspondence between the symmetrical and asymmetrical patterns in accordance

Asymmetrical patterns	Symmetrical patterns	Issues
• US camp vs. Soviet camp	• Moderate vs. radical Arab states • Arab states vs. Israel	• The Palestine Question • The status of Western Sahara • The Yemeni division

Figure 3 Bipolar patterns of conflict and cooperation in the Middle East

with the development of and fluctuations in the Cold War: a pro-Soviet camp with radical states versus a pro-US camp with moderate states, Israel being isolated in the subsystem, and Iran outside the camps since 1979. The predominant issues on the bipolar agenda were the Israeli-Arab conflict in the centre, the Lebanese civil war, and, in the periphery, the Yemeni question and the conflict about Western Sahara. The United States and the Soviet Union had adopted proxi-approaches, and after the 1973 Arab-Israeli war they became even more cautious. After the loosening of the rivalry from 1987, both the superpowers and the Middle Eastern states began to act more freely. However, not until 1989 dramatic events begun to take place. From 1989 the bipolar patterns of conflict and cooperation as well as the issues were at stake, as the conditions on which the patterns and issues had evolved were dramatically changed.

Chapter 4

A Model for Unipolarity

Much has happened on the international political stage since the end of the 1980's, and not only in the Middle East dramatic and bloody events as well as peaceful settlements have taken place. Even though there is no theoretical agreement within the discipline of International Politics on how to assess the changes or how to address the 'new', a major theoretical debate has taken place and many interesting proposals have been put forth. One proposal, however, is still lacking: a model for unipolarity. The purpose of this chapter is to suggest how to construct such a specific, theoretical model for unipolarity in international politics from the point of departure of the classic neorealist theory developed by Kenneth Waltz (1979), and to present a discussion of the effects on stability and security within that model's framework. A "model" is understood as a complex of coherent theoretical statements within a broader theory, which covers a specific object or problem. In this case, the general theory is neorealism, which points to specific cases of structural variations and aims at answering the ever present questions of when, how and why sovereign states form alliances, wage war or make peace. The questions have been elaborated and tested within the neorealist framework as well, as they are already the subject of specific statements regarding their characteristics and dynamics[1] with respect to the two prevailing types of international systems discussed by Waltz: multipolar and bipolar systems; the model below provides a similar complex of statements for the case of unipolarity.

The addition of the model is important to the neorealist theory for at least three reasons:

- A theory which claims to be general and comprehensive needs to incorporate unipolar systems, too, because these cannot be excluded a priori as a variation of the international system.

- Previous unipolar arrangements may have occurred, the Roman Empire possibly an example.[2]
- As it is argued here, current world affairs ought to be analysed in terms of unipolarity.

The specific assessment of the current distribution of power is an empirical question, however, as discussed below: even if the concept of polarity is accepted for analysis, it is not generally agreed that unipolarity is the present state or that it will endure.

In *Theory of International Politics*, Kenneth Waltz just mentions the problems of a world government and, because it is non-anarchical by nature, it appears as if it is implicitly equated to any case of unipolarity – which is in contrast to his fundamental theoretical arguments on the 'virtues of anarchy'. Later, Kenneth Waltz has pointed to the emergence of multipolarity (1995), and does not pay much attention to unipolarity, as he has stated that multipolarity is already emerging and that unipolarity, as such, is only a transition period. According to Waltz, unipolarity is the least durable power arrangement in international politics because all the other states have incentives to balance the only superpower. In the first place, the argument here is that if this is so, the potential rise of multipolarity or something else does not exclude the necessity of a model for unipolarity, because a general theory has to cover all possible arrangement within its own scope. In the second place, unipolarity might not *necessarily* be so undurable as Waltz has argued. At least, the current unipolar arrangement has lasted for over a decade. The ultimate length of the era notwithstanding, a period of minimum ten years in international politics should not be left unattended, and the first ten years in question were clearly not ten quiet years.

When constructing the model, the obvious questions are: what does a unipolar distribution of power imply for systemic stability, the dynamics within the system, and the self-help condition? The robustness and durability of a unipolar system (its stability) need to be considered. A given system can be characterised in terms of relative stability; this is of interest to all its units, because the basic self-help condition depends on the specific structure of the international system. Unipolar stability is therefore a core matter. Additionally, the intra-systemic dynamics of stability and security are essential issues. All realist and neorealist thinking emphasises the unstable conditions of international affairs. Thus, war and peace within the system are primary elements to be included in the model. In the midst of war and peace, states tend to align. This is a way of achieving a balance in international politics, but in unit level strategies it is also a primary option to enhance security. Theoretical statements on alignment in a unipolar international system must therefore be presented in order to characterise the nature of such a structural variation. Before these questions are considered, however, the difference between a unipolar international, but anarchical, system and its hierarchical counterpart is discussed. The difference is important in order to distinguish between the effects of unipolarity and those of, e.g., a world government.

The lack of previous cases of unipolarity implies that there is also a lack of evidence, which can be used to identify empirical patterns in support of constructing the model. Consequently, it has been necessary to rely on the theoretical logic, and it appears obvious that the model will have to be elaborated and revised in the light of further empirical evidence.

What can be achieved by a model for unipolarity, and how can it be applied? A model for unipolarity points to a range of probable outcomes, selected by the structural impact. When applied in order to explain, 1) such outcomes should be found; 2) the outcomes should encompass a major trend; and 3) the outcomes should be expected to have a 'unipolar' content that reflects the structural selection.

The model is presented in the following order. Firstly, it is related to the basic neorealist concepts, and the compatibility of unipolarity with the balancing of power is discussed. Secondly, the unipolar model is constructed with special attention paid to the international system, the unipole, and the other states. Thirdly, the problem of unipolarity and the contemporary world is discussed, including the systemic transformation of 1989, the end of the Cold War, and the post-1989 distribution of strength.

NEOREALISM AND UNIPOLARITY

When Kenneth Waltz presented the neorealist theory in *Theory of International Politics* (1979), it provided a new combination of a systemic-structural approach and the realist tradition. Waltz' choice of a systemic approach required the construction of a system consisting of the units of international politics and a structure which describes the principle by which the units are arranged. In addition, it is an analytical necessity to treat these elements as analytically distinct in order to be able to explain and predict (Waltz 1979). The structure and the unit level developments interact, but the basic guiding analytical principle is that the structure selects from among the strategical options within the unit-level and the structure thereby holds the decisive explanatory power (Hansen 1995a). Waltz' three part concept of the international political structure is characterised by being distinct from the national structure. It comprises (Waltz 1979):

- Anarchy: the anarchical condition which does not necessarily imply chaos, but does imply the lack of an authority holding a legitimate monopoly of violence
- Functional similarity: the units being functionally alike as they all have secure their position at the self help condition in contrast, the units in a hierarchical arrangement are functionally specialized
- Polarity: the relative distribution of capabilities across units conditions the functioning of the system and the constraints and opportunities of the unit-level interaction

The relative distribution of capabilities, polarity, is the one most frequently subject to change among the three structural tenets, and the balancing of power and the impact on world politics vary according to the number of poles. A *pole* is defined as a great power which possesses a superior quantity of capabilities relative to other states. Because it has a privileged position in the system, it has a specific incentive to manage world affairs and with specific qualities compared to other states, such as abilities to threat and dominate as well as to secure and attract others. Poles make up nodal points in the system. Their primary concern is other poles, and consequently, the game between poles becomes a profound international dynamic.

The main characteristics of multipolarity and bipolarity are, according to Waltz, as follows: in a bipolar world the lines of conflict will be few and so will the number of alliances being formed (Waltz 1979).[3] The system tends to be comparatively durable and robust. In a multipolar world there will be many political units acting in any conflict and there will be several potential alliances. This is shown by the formula $((n-1)/2)$; where n is the number of poles (Waltz 1979:135). As a consequence, the system will be neither robust nor durable. In sum, these characteristics lead to the expectation that bipolarity will be a more stable condition than multipolarity. The other states enjoy the benefits of having two large partners available to protect them and their surroundings are relatively stable. The zero-sum game tends to subordinate the alignment of other states if this is in conflict with vital great power interests. It follows that other states lack the incentive to enter into full and demanding symmetrical alliances.

The multipolar impact on other states is different. Other states have more partners available to protect them, but they cannot rely on these partners to act according to the rules of the bipolar zero-sum game. A great power might abandon a smaller ally used against one adversary in order to face another. The other states' external environment also tends to be relatively unstable. It follows that compared with the bipolar system, other states have a major incentive to enter into small-symmetrical alliances with all the potential costs.[4] Multipolar systems generate multilateral games where each move counts, not only in relation to a primary adversary, but also to the others.

Anarchy and the balance of power

Two important, and narrowly related, neorealist concepts may appear to contradict the notion of unipolarity and thus have to be addressed and qualified in order to sustain the unipolar approach: the anarchical condition, and the balance of power. Concerning the anarchical condition, the question is whether a unipolar case is still to be described in terms of anarchy, or if the strong state is rather to be seen as an authority? This is related to the questions of the balance of power and how the power balancing works in a unipolar system.

In the neorealist theory, the concept of anarchy describes an organising principle by which the units are arranged without any authority. A single great power may be so much stronger vis-à-vis the other states that it will be able to interfere in their internal affairs and to obtain an international monopoly of violence. In this case, the great power should be treated as an authority in a hierarchical system. The arrangement of the units is, therefore, different from the description of the anarchy, and the structure will change: the neorealist concept of anarchical structure then ceases to be the proper analytical instrument. However, there is no reason to assume *a priori* that the unipole shares the features of an authority. The single great power may be characterized as only the strongest in relative terms and thus the system still qualifies as being anachically organised. The single great power will share some features of the position of an authority and thereby encourage some consequential and similar dynamics. As a result, the functioning of a unipolar anarchical arrangement of the units resembles a hierarchy in more ways, even though a hierarchy describes the internal organisation of the states (units) from which it differs substantially. In hierarchical systems, the acting units are not functionally alike, but they are vertically and horizontally specialised with an authority on top, which is exclusively able to intervene in and among the other units.

A unipolar distribution of power, led by an authority, may have no historical precedents and may even theoretically be regarded as a less probable case. It cannot be ruled out, however, that a single great power qualifies as an authority – and it may very well aspire to such a position. In some cases, the great power should be treated as an authority, in other cases it should not.

Consequently, it is necessary to distinguish between different sorts of systems with the same distribution of relative power. On the one hand, there are state systems dominated by the basic anarchical conditions. They can be treated using Waltz' additive concept of structure. On the other hand, there are hierarchically organised systems which cannot be properly analysed within the anarchial neorealist framework. The distinction is important to determine the relevance of neorealism in cases of a specific power distribution. If the anarchical condition is fading, the importance of a theory, which is based on the anarchical effects on state behaviour, will be quite modest. But if the anarchical condition is still present, a theoretical elaboration is needed to overcome the lack of a unipolar model.

These considerations are also important with respect to the question of the balancing of power, occuring in the context of an anarchical condition. Some might reject the notion that balances of power will occur with only one great power. Waltz has argued that a balance of a power among only two poles is stable, because in a bipolar world the two great powers can divert resources from internal to external use and vice versa. In this way, they can balance each other without allies. Two great powers are the minimum requirement for the balancing of power in an anarchical type of system (1979:118). Later, Waltz argued that balancing takes place even in the absence of two great powers, as "states are frightened by a concentration of power in one state and will seek to balance against it" (Waltz 1995:16). However, other states' balancing of a great power will differ from symmetrical great power balancing. The other states will be inclined to perform power balancing in an 'ad-hoc' manner, as they primarily care for their own interests, disregarding systemic manage-ment and general approaches. Yet it is a strong point that in anarchical systems, there is no obvious reason to confine the ability to perform balancing by one's own means to the condition of having one or more adversaries. One great power can divert and redivert its resources between internal and external purposes as can two great powers. But what is balanced will differ because of a lack of equally strong adversaries: it is the unipole's commitment to the world affairs that is balanced. Thus, the symmetrical great power balancing cannot function because there is no one to balance. Instead the external commitment is balanced and a balancing of different capabilities by different other states may take place. Though this will resemble functional specialisation in its effects, it is not external (symmetrical) balancing. It is a result of the unipole's balancing of its resources. No competing great power is present to challenge the position of the great power or balance it, but different states may balance it on different issues and areas, and in the long term other states grow into challengers and counter-align. A web is spun out of specific and strategic interests, and in time the web's extent will increase. With respect to this web other states will, one after another or together, balance the great power in different realms and *vice versa*. The effects of these dynamics will resemble those of multipolarity, and a hierarchical-type effects will also be present, as the political agenda predominantly is set in one centre.

Security

Another important concept is state security. This concept is highly controversial and contested and therefore needs a few comments. 'Security' is here understood as one state's position vis-à-vis others'. An increase in a state's relative capabilities implies that its position improves with an increased level of security as being the bi-product and vice versa). Capabilities comprise the classic neorealist range of size of territory and population, economic and military capacity, ressource endowment, and political competence and stability (Waltz 1979). This concept of security is useful in different situations ranging from times of a so-called 'soft' security agenda, which also appeared temporarily after e.g. the end of World War II when issues as de-colonization, population growth and develoment were on the political agenda; to times of a 'hard' agenda. Another advantage is that it is possible to identify what the agenda will be, and when, applying the neorealist notion on when security turns hard, i.e., in the event of changes in the relative distribution of strength or in the event of unclear relations of strength (*Op. cit.*). Likewise, this concept of security makes it possible to explain why states cannot relax in peaceful times but instead must increase other capabilities in the absence of military threats – which are the worst kind of threats as the use of force may destroy the whole range of capabilities and end the life of a unit. Yet the states cannot afford not to progress in economic capacity, e.g., if other states do; partly because military capacity demands an economic basis, partly beacuse a deficiency in one capability is reflected in the aggregate capabilities. Competition comprise them all, the level of threat defines which ones are given priority.

The ability to improve security depends partly on the state's relative progress in any capability, partly on the self-help condition in question, including the options of alignment, and the power balancing.

The unipole: strength and strategies

When considering the abovementioned single great power which is an authority and a unipole, which just takes up a comparatively large amount of space within the system, it is evident that some kind of power gap exists between the two variations: at the very least, a unipole is part of an interacting group of units in an anarchical arrangement. The upper extent is when the unipole turns into an authority. The question is what possibilities, the unipole has. When there is only one power which is stronger relative to other states, this power and its capabilities become increasingly significant. To what extent will it be able to influence world politics, what will world politics be like, and what will be the consequences for the security (self help) conditions of other states? When dealing with these questions, it is useful to apply the concepts of specific and strategic interests worked out by Glenn Snyder. In his consideration of alliance formation in multipolar systems, Snyder makes a distinction between the strategic interests of states concerning matters of security and general position, and their specific interests, including economic, ethnic, ideological and other such interests and values (Snyder 1984: 464). This distinction can be applied to the relationship between a unipole and its surroundings and be linked to measures of capability – to the size of the 'power edge', i.e., the size (being 'weak' or 'strong') of the relative, aggregate advantage of the unipole. If the power edge is significant, the unipole will easily be able to take care of its specific as well as its strategic interests. If it is weaker, having a smaller power-edge, it will tend to care for its strategic interests and draw back from pursuing specific interests when these interests lead to confrontation with others.

It is not easy to put such a distinction into operation and it poses conceptual problems as well. The great power defines, to a large extent, whether or not an interest is strategic or specific. Besides, to maintain its position as the only great power, more interests may be converted into strategic ones in order to keep up the edge and demonstrate its presence, should there be any doubts about it. If the size of the power edge is so important a dilemma arises. Should a secondary stratifying principle be added in order to distinguish between a strong and a weak unipole? Or should attention be directed to the strategic level, specifying the range of strategic options available to a unipolar distribution of power? A useful approach may be to distinguish between two main unipolar strategical options, the minimalist one corresponding to the expected behaviour of a 'weak' unipole, and the maximalist one corresponding to the expected behaviour of a 'strong' unipole. These two ideal types correspond to the diversion of a unipole's resources as above. That would allow the attempt highlight unit level strategies, themselves still analysed as being selected by the unipolar structure within the framework of a systemic theory. The unipole may shift between the two different strategies in response to external developments and as a result of its own resource balancing. The unipole may pursue a predominantly minimalist or a maximalist strategy or balance its commitments by means of changing the minimalist and the maximalist strategical elements.

In summary, the concept of unipolarity is reserved to cases in which the single great power qualifies as a unipole rather than an authority, and anarchy thus still describes the international system. In cases of unipolarity, it appears reasonable to qualify the notion of power balancing in the following ways: The symmetrical balance of power does not work between the unipole and other great powers. It will still work in three other respects: firstly, symmetrically among the other states, secondly, when the other states balance dimensions of the unipole's policy in an ad-hoc way, and thirdly, when the unipole's balances between its internal and external resources.

UNIPOLARITY AND THE INTERNATIONAL SYSTEM

The first question to ask of unipolar international system regards the stability of the system. The question may be broken down into two sub-questions reflecting different dimensions of the system's ability to remain stable: the system's robustness which is about the pressure on unipolarity, and durability which is about how long unipolarity is expected to last. One logic which concerns the element of robustness seems to confirm its stable quality and is based on the lack of equal adversaries. Another logic which concerns the element of durability points to instability: the relationship between the great power and the other states tends to undermine the position of the former in the long run.

If the great power pursues a predominantly minimalist strategy, it does not enforce its will on other states with respect to its specific interests. Thus, the other states are not seriously offended by the efforts of the great power to pursue its own specific interests or its attempts to define the interests of the system. Instead, they have incentives to test the unipole on a series of issues, and they have to solve mutual problems by themselves. this includes the risk of conflict. Nor will the great power obtain major benefits, and it may leave influence to others and thereby reduce its own room for manoeuvre.

If the great power also pursues specific interests, it is prone to offend the interests of other states, and force the system in a direction favouring itself and its own values and interests to an extent, which is incompatible with the interests of the other states. The number of small conflict lines between the great power and the other states on the other hand will increase, and this will draw the unipole into many costly confrontations of interests, which in the long run will provide the other states with a strong incentive to resign from previous mutual cooperation or even enter into one or more strategic alliances against it as the relations of strength change. In the long run, therefore, challengers will rise: their rise is nurtured by the free-riding option which may eventually change the relative distribution of power. The process is fuelled because the unipole cannot help offending the interests of others, even though this is not its intention.

The dynamics and the struggle over management issues is illustrated by the striking example of the US-European rift on intervention in Bosnia and Hercegovina in 1993. The EU itself and major individual European states wanted intervention, but were reluctant or unable to intervene. The US urged the EU to intervene and argued that the Europeans had to take responsibility for their own backyard. After many months of arguing about the ifs, whoms, and hows of intervention, a US-led NATO force intervened with the resulting peace in Dayton, Ohio. According to the model, such struggles are normal rather than special in the case of unipolarity. On the other hand, when the unipole manages world affairs it cannot help offending the interests even of its good friends in order to pursue its own interests or to solve collective problems. There are many examples of this (see Waltz 1995). Over time, they will aggregate to provide the small powers, which meanwhile may have benefited from the free-riding, with the incentive to balance the unipole in many dimensions or possibly to emerge as new poles.

In the long run, unipolarity is also challenged by the potential 'free riding'. The free riding option for systemic tasks and management is strong in the case of unipolarity, although the other states also face the incentive to work harder to secure their position (see below), while the unipole manages the totality. The other states will be able to free ride while being sheltered behind the great power regarding the management of world affairs. From the unipole's point of view, this is most serious if the free riders are the strongest among the other states. The free riders thereby slowly become stronger, richer and more complacent, and they keep open options for future alignments. The states are able to devote their efforts to securing their own, narrower interests while benefiting from the unipole's management of the system and even relying on the unipole for additional security. They can, therefore, occupy themselves with building up their own capabilities, which will lead to an extension of their external interests. This will lead to an increased risk of conflicts with the great power in the long run or to the unipole's risk to struggle to exhaustion to meet challenges and fulfil its obligations as a dominant centre of power.

All great powers tend to manage the system (Waltz 1979), although in different ways and to different extents. The unipole also faces and undertakes managerial tasks. Doing so helps it to preserve its most important interest: to preserve or even improve its position as number one, the best a state can strive for in the international system. These managerial efforts will also facilitate the pursuit of specific interests. The unipole is expected to carry out its managerial efforts in light of the pressure dynamics on the unipolar structure. This leads to attempts to avoid free riding, to keep down challengers, and to counteract the formation of counter-alliances. A minimalist strategy the response only to incidents and developments which affect a major part of the international community or when the unipole's strategic interests are at stake. Both cases would endanger its very position as the principal power. A maximalist strategy may trigger resistance even when specific interests are at stake as the unipole pursues its aims and interests to an extent which could, in principle, be unlimited, although a successful pursuit of these may eventually change the system into a hierarchical organisation.

Stability

No power arrangements are expected to last forever, and certain kinds of pressure are present and particularly strong in the case of unipolarity. The criterion of assessesing systemic stability includes the dimensions of robustness and durability. In the case of unipolarity these two tenets seem to contradict each other. The unipolar arrangement precludes challengers or serious challenges. By definition, equal adversaries are absent, and the number of symmetrical lines of conflict or counter-alliances is, therefore, zero. This indicates a high degree of robustness. On the other hand, the intra-systemic dynamics indicate several challenges, which indicates a low durability. These considerations lead to the expectation that unipolarity is a comparatively less durable condition, and considerations are thus given to the pressure against the structure. If the unipole balances inwards or pursues a minimalist strategy, power vacuums may arise. The power vacuums will trigger responses by others states, which may lead to the strengthening of these. Alternatively, if the unipole does respond, it risks exhaustion and internal decay. Finally, the continuous occurrence of confrontations of specific interests between the unipole and individual other states may bring about a counter-coalition among the latter, in the long term probably around a potentially power pole. These intra-unipolar dynamics all result in pressure on the structure and thus challenge its durability.

A concrete factor, however, may help the US remain a unipole for a prolonged period: order. The unipole is in a unique position to forward its policy and aims, and globalization as well as the high level of international interactions accelerates the spread. The actions will tend to be loaded with impact from the unipole, and the current world order is shaped according to US interests with the spread of liberal democracy and free market capitalism (Jensen 1998). States well suited for competing within this context have a comparative advantage in capitalizing from their capabilities in general. It is interesting to see whether or not this dimension adds to the robustness and durability of the US unipolarity, and how it will try to avoid the inherent traps of a unipolar power arrangement. After all, the ability of other states to progress in aggregate capabilities, relative to the US, depends not only on the unipolar dynamics but also on a series of unit level developments.

Peace and war

So far the main focus has been one half of the Waltzian concept of security and stability: the system as such. The second half comprises the security and the stability within the system: how secure is it to be a state within a given international system, in this case a unipolar one; and what is the frequency and magnitude of wars? The answer for the unipole is easily defined, as there are no equal challengers present, although they may be in the making.

For the other states the answer can be illustrated by an analogy to hard work: they have to care for more by their own means. Compared with bipolarity, it is expected that more alignments will be formed and that more minor conflicts will break out as more cooperation will take place. Compared to the cases of multipolarity and, especially, bipolarity, conflicts among other states tend to be less dangerous for the great power because there is no risk of conflict intervention by the equal great power rivals (the filling of power vacuums) or bipolar zero-summing.

The other states have two ways of succeeding in sharing their conflict with the great power, and thus obtain additional security against their adversaries: one is to get involved in the great power's care for its own interests or protection of the world order, its management; the other is to combine great power attention with a strategy of rapprochement (a less reliable way of obtaining additional security). The only moderation to this expectation derives from the unipole's fear of exhaustion. Exhaustion may occur if there are too many small conflicts. Such conflicts may offend the outstretched interests of the unipole, and the dilemma is ever present: should the unipole respond and risk resistance and exhaustion, or should the unipole leave its interests and let others gain influence? However, the hard work dynamic keeps the other states active by leading to a high degree of regional activity.

In sum, unipolarity is logically free of great power wars, leads to comparatively more wars among small units, and specific require-ments for unipolar intervention in wars of the small units. What is equally more important for peace and war, though, is nuclearity, which has partly changed the form of armed conflict.

Nuclearity

An important challenge to the neorealist emphasis on structural analysis concerns the status and the effects of nuclearity, which is especially important concerning the question of the frequency of wars. How should post-conventional systems, international systems after the introduction of nuclear weapons (*cf.* Wagner 1993), be further labelled and analysed? Is the shift from bipolarity to unipolarity less important than the 1945 shift to nuclearity? The end of the bipolar period, which had begun simultaneously with the introduction of nuclear weapons, was also the start of a period of analytical approach, which separated the two phenomena. But there are no empirical answers to the question of whether it was the bipolar condition or nuclear weapons which determined the long peace after the Second World War. It will not be possible to find convincing answers until there are a minimum of two cases available both including nuclearity, but with different distributions of strength; at least not if the answers are to be based on empirical evidence and cross-examination. Until then, it is necessary to rely on theoretical arguments, and to be aware of nuclearity as a major attribute of international politics but to continue analysing in terms of polarity. Thus, the way to deal with the international dynamics will be by reference to the structure, and with the conflicts among nuclear powers by reference to the hot war-negating effects of nuclearity. This is especially important when considering the fate of unipolarity, which might be challenged from a range of growing powers within a foreseeable time. Apparently, there is no reason not to rely on the so far undisputed and empirically supported fact that nuclearity induces cautiousness and its introduction of a shift in the nature of conflict between nuclear powers from hot to cold wars. There is also empirical evidence, e.g. in case of the 1973 October War in the Middle East (see Chapter 3), and after that the bipolar powers tended to rely on proxy struggle rather than direct confrontation. Thus, in the case of a systemic change away from unipolarity in the nuclear age, the expectation is that the protagonists will not resort to hot war – as long as nuclear weapons have not been neutralised by something else. These reflections on nuclearity are of relevance to systemic change as well as to the relationship between nuclear powers.

In 1988, Kennth Waltz stated that traditional war had become a privilege of states in the periphery of the international system (Waltz 1988) as a result of nuclearity. The states without nuclear weapons, or other weapons of mass destruction (WMD), are able to engage in wars, so are WMD-states against non-WMD-states, while it is unlikely that WMD-states will wage war against each other at this technological stage of nuclearity. The development of first strike capabilities or of effective defence systems may change that.

In terms of management, WMD-capacity poses a major problem to the unipole. It cannot threaten or put pressure on WMD-states in the same way as on non-WMD-states. This is one thing, another is that the unipole gets a strong incentive to prevent states from achieving a WMD-capacity. Among the WMD-states, those who defy the US world order pose the major managerial problems. Of course, states may change from being categorized as WMD-states to non-WMD-states and they may change their approach to the world order from defiance to acceptance or support. Figure 4 illustrates the relationship between managerial problems and the WMD-capacity/world order approach of the other states.

WMD-capacity/ World Order approach	World order accept	World order defiance
WMD-states	Low degree	Very high degree
Non-WMD-states	Very low degree	High degree

Figure 4 Degree of managerial problems posed to the unipole

The unipole and the other states

Another dimension of unipolarity regards the other states' relationship to the unipole, and how unipolarity thus affects these asymmetrical relations. First of all, there is no other source of power that other states can rely on, if they wish to align with a great power in order to substantially enhance their security. Nor is there any other great power to rally around if they want to align against the great power. Furthermore, there is no other great power around, which is generally able to affect the behaviour of the other states as in bipolar and multipolar systems, or which can offer challenging alternatives. These basic conditions lead to some specific features of unipolarity which are:

- The single option (only one great power to align).
- Hard work (the need for other states to secure themselves by a greater degree of own means)
- flocking (uni-polarization in the case of security problems).

The single option

Not only in the most extreme cases of threat and danger is this a weakening of the other states in the asymmetrical relationship, but also in the daily politics. The other states are deprived of a bargaining asset compared to the cases of bi- and multipolarity: they cannot threaten to change their great power alignment, nor can they exploit the fear of the great power in question that internal developments may lead to another alignment. Such threats may cause concern in the centre, but no panic, since there are no competing poles. Local symmetrical alignment between other states, though, may be seen as a large advantage from the unipole's point of view, as long as the symmetrical alignment does not hinder the unipole's interests and as long as the alignment contributes to the minimising of costly involvement or free riding. In general, this condition may be labelled the single option.

Compared to two or more poles, a unipole lacks the incentives to be strongly engaged internationally on behalf of certain partial interests against others, unless the other's interests coincides with the unipole's strategic interests which are now liberated from the context of a symmetrical rivalry. Instead, the unipole is expected to engage in more general issues from which it will improve its general position or reduce pressures against itself. This does not imply that the unipole will completely avoid the selection of friends and enemies. Its instrumental position, however, will differ, and one of the important traps, pressures on the structure, from the unipole's point of view is that it is exhausted by its sole responsibility for the whole system. Thus it is assumed to attempt to minimise the free riding opportunity with regard to the systemic managerial tasks. This implies hard work from the other states if their own positions are involved.

This formal assumption has no substantial impact with respect to conflict or cooperation which is the result of the hard work. Both outcomes are possible. For the other states, unipolarity means that there is no check on the great power as would have been the case in bipolarity. The increase in the number of conflicts is one likely result, but increased cooperation is also possible. From the unipole's point of view, it is an advantage that other states watch each other. The other states are not likely to form a strategic alliance against a weak great power, as they have no urgent incentive which outweighs the risks and costs, at least not until the situation becomes intolerable or a change in the relative distribution of strength, probably caused by the free riding/exhaustion dynamics, has taken place. In the long term such an alliance will be the sign of a probable decline in the unipolar arrangement in question.

From the unipole's point of view, these dynamics create a strong incentive to 'decentralise' parts of world politics. This can be done in several ways. One is to adopt a laissez-faire approach, but this will lead others into the ensuing power vacuums. Another is to select allies or partners in geographical or issue-oriented areas. Selecting partners, being privileged allied states, is an instrumental choice which contributes to the unipole's position because of a momentary coincidence of interests, in which the aligned in return receives a favourable treatment of its specific interests vis-à-vis other states. A partner is, in many ways, less reliable, because there is no major threat which binds the unipole and the partner. Rather, other states may consider a close relationship an advantage and contribute to the maintenance of the world order as they cannot change it and therefore benefit from stability while developing their capabilities. It is a matter of convenience for both for as long as the relationship endures. A partner is not deprived of incentives to resist the pole's specific and various interests, but it will probably be ready to support the pole when it is required to do so. The uncertainty fuels a constant flow of minor disagreements.

In the case of symmetrical tensions the other states will strive to engage the unipole as they have no great power alternatives. But according to the hard work dynamic, they may fail to, if no unipolar interests are at stake or if exhaustion is in effect.

Flocking

The single option also leads to flocking. In the case of conflicts touching vital great power interests, the other states will tend to flock around the great power because they have no alternative. While a state may turn to other states in case of challenges of its security, the most attractive option remains the unipole. *Firstly*, support from the unipole secures it against the risk of having to face the adversary *and* the unipole. It would be very risky for a small state to oppose other states already aligned with the unipole; a successful opposition would demand a surplus of capabilities which does not exist. *Secondly*, the unipole provides the greatest amount of additional security. *Thirdly*, states tend to search for allies outside their own neighbourhood (Walt 1990) in order not to have the additional security accompanied by too much outside interference in the domestic political life. In addition, as Kenneth Waltz has argued (1979), states tend to imitate the successful great powers and socialize to the world order in question. Both can be accomplished by developing ties with the unipole and thereby obtaining know-how, technology, and access to modelling political and organizational skills. Whether the other states succeed in getting the benefits or the protection they seek depends on the unipole's assessment. This last point is easily illustrated by comparing the unipolar option to the bipolar tendency to gather around the Soviet Union and the US. Immediately after the end of the Cold War the former Warsaw Treaty members in Eastern Europe signalled their wish to join NATO. The US, however, was reluctant to let them, but later they were granted access if US-defined conditions and interests were met. Though flocking will prevail as a tendency, it is not so that all states always will flock. They will tend to do so when security problems arise. The greater the problem, the stronger the tendency. As they always face the problem of reduced autonomy, entrapment and different interests as well, in periods of lesser urgency they may choose not to or even to distance themselves politically. There may also be a moderating factor involved regarding the incentive to flock: according to the effects of nuclear weapons (Waltz 1981), it appears reasonable to state that a threshold or real nuclear status may neutralize the incentive to flock. At least, a state's nuclear status challenges the unipole's room for manoeuvre, because a nuclear opponent – no matter how small – has to be treated more carefully than other opponents.

Here it is necessary to preempt some critical remarks about what has been described as an almost cooperative relationship between the unipole and the states which flock to it in the system. This relationship may resemble what has previously been described as the concept of 'bandwagoning' – weaker states following the stronger, running counter to the traditional neorealist hypothesis by which states form alliances against the stronger (Walt 1990). It is, however, important not to confuse bandwagoning behaviour with the polarisation process. The other states will tend to flock around the great powers in order to obtain effective security guarantees or not to be left out from a later settlement. These asymmetrical relations belong to the polarisation process. Bandwagoning is a type of alliance behaviour between equally strong partners, so-called symmetrical relations (*cf.* Morrow 1991). Asymmetrical alignment should be dealt with in terms of polarisation, whereas symmetrical alignment should be dealt with in terms of balancing. This distinction may seem a small one, and in some ways it is; bandwagoning behaviour and the polarisation process may seem alike in the political world. Analytically, the distinction is nevertheless important. If the distinction is not applied, the main neorealist hypothesis about alliances, which implies that states countervail the strong, may lead to an expectation of the immediate formation of a strong alliance against the US. The continuing existence of, for example, NATO in the post-Cold War 1990's is compatible with the theoretical statements if the distinction between symmetrical and asymmetrical alignment is made: because the other states are expected to flock. In contrast, if two or more powers rise to the level of possessing great power capabilities, these would be expected not to flock but to balance the US. More precisely, the two weaker great powers would balance the stronger.

It has already been deduced that the larger states among the other states will be quite well off, although not able to adopt a dominant position. The relationship is characterised by the unipole's attempt to avoid unnecessary conflicts, while the other states attempt to free ride on shared and collective issues. They build up and increase their interests, which will overlap in the long run and pave the way for mutual tensions. In the case of the unipole pursuing specific interests, the larger non-poles in the system face another challenge. Their interests will be hurt on a great scale, broadly and in depth, and this will aggregate, finally, to provide at least some of them with the incentive to resist the unipole, which is 'eating them up slowly', either by uniting in an attempt to balance what is a common barrier to the pursuit of their interests, or by fuelling individual efforts to match the unipole.

Hard work

What should be expected of the interrelationships of the other states in such a framework? The dynamic of hard work seems to play an important role. When the strategic interests of the great power are not at stake, the outcome of the conflicts among other states will not affect larger parts of the interstate community, nor when an issue is not on the unipole's agenda. The other states will act autonomously and balance each other. The number of symmetrical alignments among the other states will be comparatively high. They will not, as during the bipolar period, be aligned to different great powers, which were almost automatically involved in local conflicts, directly or indirectly. This involvement made, to a large extent, the formation of symmetrical alliances among the other states redundant: the guarantees from a great power were far more effective and often less intrusive in daily political life. In a situation with only one weak great power, it will be more difficult for the other states only to rely on asymmetrical alignment. Consequently, the small powers are exposed to hard work and will tend to align with each other or cooperate in order to secure their positions.

The other states will tend to form a relatively great number of symmetrical alignments in order to enhance security against each other on matters which do not affect the strategic interests or managerial efforts of the great power. They may fear that they cannot rely on the unipole. On the other hand, if some other states do enter into conflict, they may face one of three unipolar responses: if their conflict is assessed by the unipole as inferior or not worth the cost, they will have to fight it out by themselves. Alternatively, the unipole may encourage the parties to end the conflict by encouraging an intervention by one or more of its partners. Or, finally, in specific cases where the unipole's interests including major managerial tasks are at stake or in the case of low costs, the unipole will intervene.

As mentioned above, in the case of conflicts touching vital great power interests, other states will tend to flock around the great power because they have no alternative. Opposing the others already aligned with it would be a very risky affair. The other states are prone to adapt to these conditions because they strive to survive and, if possible, to improve their international position.

*   *   *

In summary, the relationship between the unipole and the other states can be characterised as other states' flocking (unipolarisation) as well as attempts to avoid dominance and entrapment, the single option, the incentives to hard work (towards cooperation as well as conflict), high regional activity, decentralisation, and the unipole's quest for facilitating management. The other states will balance each other in the light of these dynamics. Adaptation will prevail because of functional similarity.

SYSTEMIC TRANSFORMATION

According to neorealism, systemic transformation takes place when the relative distribution of strength is altered and then equilibrium is restored, most likely by means of war, hot or cold. Following essentially unit-based developments of strength, systems are continuously transformed. This stimulates curiosity about how, when and why the transformation process occurs, its effects and the way it fertilises the ground for all those minor decisions which finally aggregate to make up a new world order. As already mentioned with regard to structural predictions, it is not possible to deduce the specific circumstances which bring about systemic transformation. But it is possible to deduce and to support the deductions with empirical/ historical evidence in order to provide a statement on the transformation where unit-level interactions and structural causes meet. The statement is proposed below.

Systemic change leads to realignment

When looking at history and the consequences of previous transformations of the international system, it is remarkable that all the transformations were followed by either outbreaks of wars among other states, or by civil wars: this can be illustrated by the aftermath of World War I, where, for example, Great Britain and France partitioned the Middle Eastern part of the dissolving Ottoman Empire, or the aftermath of the Second World War, where Germany was divided and new states appeared in Europe as well as in the so-called Third World. Unrest also followed the Cold War, in spite of its peaceful termination.

From the point of view of neorealist theory, where relations of strength are vital in international affairs, the unrest is not surprising. By definition, the relative distribution of aggregate capabilities implies a systemic change. The importance of relations of strength is not confined to the changing great powers in question, but apply to the whole system. Systemic change leads to realignment because alignment is linked to the distribution of strength and power balancing, and as a consequence systemic change penetrates all parts of the system and spreads downwards. This is the point of departure for dealing with transformation itself.

The consequent realignment may take place asymmetrically as well as symmetrically. Alignment comes in many forms (see e.g. Singer and Small 1967): formal alliances, guarantees, security cooperation or other different kinds of support, mainly military, economical and/or political, to a party, which is thereby provided with the means to enhance its position vis-à-vis others. When the reasons for particular alignments disappear, the alignments are endangered. Some will disappear while other may continue in light of the new challenges, which may be different but still common for the aligned parties.

As for the case of asymmetrical alignment, one or more great powers may have retreated while the surviving power(s) reassesses its smaller aligned partners. Reassessment may lead to realignment or to the change of existing alignment. In international subsystems, other states will still balance each other, but a new system provides different opportunities for adding strength by means of great power assistance. As a result, balancing takes place within a changed framework and is characterised by the common tendency to polarisation and by different patterns brought about by the realignment and the consequent change in the relative positions within the subsystem.

When an international system is transformed, all the parties which benefited from the former arrangement and from the loser's (or losers') position(s) are weakened in the first place. A number of other states will lose support and external ally (allies). On the other hand, the emerging arrangement will provide other states with new options for alliance and support, which entail a strengthening of position. Among those strengthened may be some of those immediately weakened because of a reassessment by the surviving pole(s) or assessment by a new one (or new ones). The small units are thus provided with better or worse options for pursuing their sometimes conflicting interests. The change of mutual power positions prepares the ground for fighting wars, for trials of strength and for the creation of new spheres of interest among the other states. Power vacuums also arise when a losing great power, or its now weakened proxies, retreat. The filling of the vacuum leads to trials of strength. On the other hand, the changed positions may also lead to the ending of conflicts: settlements which were not attainable because of a previous stalemate may now be.

Besides, the transformation situation brings about fear, a breakdown in the channels of communication, and the sowing of the seeds of miscalculations. These factors similar to the high-risk factors which follow internal revolutions (Walt 1992), and they are consistent with the basic neorealist notion that the risk of war increases if the relations of strength are unclear (Waltz 1979 and 1988). In the light of the anarchical self-help condition, states are bound to act primarily in the name of security. They never fully know what their potential adversary thinks or plans, so the increased risk of miscalculation and overreaction may trigger a war given the innate anarchical insecurity (Waltz 1979).

In some states which were heavily dependent on the previous international context, the internal order may break down. Such outbreaks of internal disorder should be explained by either of two dynamics: first, if an external threat, which is a larger threat to domestic groups than the threats they pose to each other, disappears, the domestic groups lose their incentive to act or live together and to minimise mutual insecurity. They will, instead, turn their efforts into competition. Second, some groups which were previously restricted in the pursuit of their interests by the tension among the great powers, and were supported by one or both of those great powers, are now set free to act in another context. As with interstate relations, which may be subject to the rise of new conflicts as well as new settlements, internal orders are also subject to both kind of impacts. While some orders turn into civil war or secessionist efforts, some (dis)orders remain at rest, because the parties face a strengthened external environment.

The number of states may also change. Some will break down because of internal disorder and be subject to external occupation; others will be break down and perish because of the loss of external support. On the other hand, some groups may benefit from a weakening of their state vis-à-vis others and exploit the opportunity to become independent; or the victorious part may divide losing states. Finally, some other states may unite in order to prevent a threat from larger, external parties; or they may reunify because a previous partition has lost its power basis. Altogether, the number of states is strongly challenged by fusion as well as fission in the case of systemic transformation. Similarly, issues formerly politicised between the great powers of the dissolving system are liberated in the case of a systemic change. On the other hand, new issues may arise linked to the new world order.

The above mentioned types of development can be empirically identified as having followed every change among the great powers since the Treaty of Westphalia. The pattern is clear. It was already recognised by Lloyd George who, after the conclusion of the Versailles treaty, remarked in his somewhat grandiose powerful style: "When the big ones make peace, the pygmies start to fight". Above, this pattern was incorporated in the neorealist approach. The structural redistribution of capabilities causes a series of effects, most strongly in the very aftermath of the change.

It is not possible beforehand to state exactly what will be affected by this domino-like effect. It is evident, however, that patterns linked to the disappearing system and those being connected to the emerging one are particularly prone, also within the international subsystems as the distribution of capabilities and the equilibria are changing throughout the system. Other states often base their position on external guarantees. These positions and conditions may change with the number of great powers. Guarantors and guaranteed neighbours disappear; new ones appear and new conditions emerge. The implication is a succession of events which will trigger a response from the new leading actors. The responses in this short, but chaotic, period of transformation are all undertaken within the new structural condition, and they make up the specific attributes of the new system.

What has been gained by adding this perspective on the transformation process to the basic neorealist assumptions? Firstly, it is now possible to link the systems together. Secondly, it has provided a theoretical answer to why some periods of international politics are so turbulent. Thirdly, it is now possible theoretically to make a distinction between effects caused by a specific polarity and those of the systemic transformation itself. The importance of making the latter distinction can be illustrated by the following example: if it is asked whether the conflict in Bosnia and Herzegovina following the collapse of Yugoslavia in the 1990's is a unipolar effect or not, the distinction makes a difference. Using the statement on systemic transformation, rather than the one on unipolarity, in order to grasp the effect of the change itself, it must be concluded that the cause of the conflict was an effect of the systemic change – the break down of bipolarity. On the other hand, from a neorealist perspective, the responses to the conflict should be analysed in terms of unipolarity and the specific reactions should be seen as indicators of the specific dynamics of the new system.

The expanded neorealist approach used here can be reduced to the statement on systemic transformation, which can be applied to both the international system as a whole and to selected parts of it, as all parts of the international system expectedly are affected though not necessarily to the same extent:

- When an international system breaks down, the restoration of equilibria will lead to asymmetrical as well as symmetrical realignment, outbreaks of conflicts/settling of other conflicts internationally and internally, challenges to the number and composition of states, and new issues.

In the aftermath of any systemic transformation, a number of states tend to be formed, perish or reorganised and so does the composition of the groups of states.[5] Since the end of the Cold War, many new states have been formed while others have had to adjust. State building processes are usually high risk processes insofar as domestic power structures have not fully developed and coup d'états, or at least frequent and dramatic political changes, may occur. In the case of unipolarity, the international implications are different from those under bipolarity. No state is subject to zero-summing as the unipole's concern is not whether a change in government or the formation of a new state will add a proxy or an allied partner to the competing pole. The question is rather about management and whether or not to intervene.

THE END OF THE COLD WAR

Having dealt with the dynamics of transformation in general, it is time to focus on the actual transformation of bipolarity into unipolarity. For analytical reasons, it is necessary to have a coherent view of when and how this transformation took place. Consequently, the following considerations are included even though they for other reasons may appear to be an *excoursis*.

The former Soviet Union was in general decline at least from the beginning of the 1970's but it was still able to maintain its position as a superpower until the end of the 1980's, and all the actors in the international system treated the Soviet Union as a superpower, particularly during the tensions of the mid-1980's. There is no doubt either, that the Soviet Union was the weaker of the two superpowers. But in terms of bipolarity, any absolute difference of strength between the poles does not change the dynamics: there were two ambitious superpowers competing globally and both able to attract other states into their spheres of influence (bipolarisation). The differences in strength, however, was important in the long run, because two antagonists inevitably have to clash (Waltz 1979).

The US and the Soviet Union had a unique way of demonstrating their strength and a method for countervailing each other's strength never seen in the history before: their stocks of nuclear weapons. Though the superpowers had the weapons, they were only used for their military purpose when the US bombed Japan in August 1945. However, they were accorded a symbolic role in the game of mutual deterrence, which matured during the following forty years. The capacity was the very symbol of the superpowers' position. It showed all other states in the international system that challenging those in possession of these weapons was impossible because of their superior strength (Heurlin 1986); they signalled. But they also became a barometer within the superpowers' mutual relationship (Hansen 1991). Besides deterring the other, the development of nuclear weapons, both in terms of quantity and quality, became the essence of the Cold War. The barometer could be read by either protagonist, which could subsequently counter the moves by the adversary.

During previous periods, the transformation of the international system tended to occur in the aftermath of a war fought between the great powers or their potential challengers. As mentioned above, nuclear weapons changed this. The devastating potential of nuclear weapons deprived their possessors of any incentive to start a mutual war and to risk an escalation. Nuclear weapons implied the possibility of destroying any desired object within the system of international relations, and included the possible annihilation through retaliation of the owners themselves. Thus the weapons, although being a unit-level phenomenon, provided another mode for the system's transformation (Waltz 1981). But nuclear weapons did not change the basic structural dynamics, nor did they obstruct the actual transformation. The Cold War was fought, but on a very different sort of battlefield. The main battles were fought at the negotiating table in Geneva where the two superpowers tested each other out: arms control was the primary, political, theatre. In addition, the historical context allowed for proxi-battles. Based on this thinking, the final phase of the Cold War and its conclusion is interpreted as follows (cf. Hansen 1991).

The Soviet policy appeared to be based on the aim of being recognised as equal to the US, the stronger of the two after their common emergence as superpowers in the aftermath of the Second World War. The US position was clearly superior until the end of the 1960's: its second strike capability (i.e., ability to retalitate a nuclear strike) made it the clear number one if measured by quality, though the Soviet Union had succeeded in achieving a quantitative edge. Because the US was superior in qualitative terms the number of weapons was less important. The number, however, became crucial, when, in 1968, the Soviet Union also obtained a second strike capability. The new Soviet capability changed the balance and a few years later the Soviet ambition of achieving some kind of parity was fulfilled: the Strategic Arms Limitations Talks (SALT) resulted in a formal agreement with the principle of strategic parity at the core of the nuclear balance. SALT I was signed in 1972 and consisted of three elements: limitations on strategic arms; Basic Principles which was a code of conduct for handling the nuclear weapons in which the US and the Soviet Union promised each other not to seek nuclear superiority; and the Anti-Ballistic Missile (ABM) Treaty which intended to protect the declared parity from challenges. Only five years later, when the still unratified SALT II was agreed upon, it became obvious that the SALT process had not been built on 'equal' intentions. The (stronger) US had participated in limiting mutual armament in order to release resources for dealing with other problems. Besides, the US expected the Soviet Union to temper its ambitions when parity was acknowledged in one specific area of the nuclear weapons. At that time the US did not regard nuclear superiority as attainable, and even for the US, it was a costly project to develop a first strike capability, which would deprive the opponent of the means to retalitate.

The Soviet Union acted differently. It continued to arm at a higher, faster rate, and it also tried to use the recognition of parity as a means to increase its influence in other areas, not least the Third World. The Soviet Union, which has been labelled the one-dimensional super-power, apparently used the SALT process to compensate for what it lacked. The Soviet approach opposed and undermined the US reasons for recognising the parity. As a response, the US began what could be labelled a Cold War offensive. The offensive began about 1980 and, in retrospect, it can be described as an action in two successive phases: first, the US tried to control the Soviet approach by signalling its will and capacity to arm; second, it tried to win the Cold War by disarming the Soviet Union (Hansen 1991:48). After the Geneva talks on arms control broke down in the winter of 1983, when the Soviet Union left and rejected negotiations about NATO's double decision, the US continued to demonstrate its strength which had marked the launch of the offensive. In the years in between, the US apparently did not regard the Soviet Union an equal adversary as symbolised by SALT I, nor that it should be in front of the US, as the Soviet Union might had signalled it was striving for by its the high rate of armament. The Soviet Union had tried to maintain and expand its status as an equal superpower by means of nuclear policy. Now the US began to use the Soviet Union's own approach, disarmament, to fight this status. Analytically speaking, the policy of containment was developed into a policy of rolling back the Soviet Union (Hansen 1991).

The American policy of strength had qualitative as well as quantitative dimensions; earlier Soviet gains were also targeted. First, the Soviet Union should not perceive itself or act as equal in Europe, which, strategically, was the central regional theatre. The US signalled this by the deployment of medium range weapons in Europe. As for the offensive strategic area, the MX missile and the smaller, more flexible Midgetman missile were deployed. The first phase of the US attack on the Soviet position was not successful, however, insofar as US aims were concerned. The US then took a qualitative initiative in the Cold War, the kind of initiative which had been ruled out by the ABM Treaty. The Strategic Defense Initiative (SDI) was launched. The US claimed that the SDI was compatible with ABM Treaty provisions, but the technological development of the components for SDI had exceeded the provisions. President Reagan's SDI speech in 1983 demonstrated that the US now had the will and the capacity to escalate the political nuclear struggle to a new qualitative level which was beyond the reach of the Soviet Union. The US demands in the negotiations implied that the Soviet Union should give up quantitative superiority. If not, the US would take the qualitative step. The Soviet Union, however, was not yet ready to give up the superpower status which it had sought to preserve precisely by means of nuclear weapons. That it was not ready to do so was evident in arms control negotiations, where the Soviet Union tried to use its combination of forces as a bargaining chip, and also tried to save its sizable Intercontinental Ballistic Missile (ICBM) force, which the US considered to be the major threat.

The SDI speech, however, made the Soviet Union return to the negotiations; it seemed as though the Soviet Union had given up all aspirations of becoming the strongest superpower, as well as most of its aspirations of becoming equal to the US. Instead it would devote its efforts to maintaining its position as a superpower – to maintain a position in world politics which was, at least, superior to the other states. In the negotiations, this aim prevented the Soviet Union from making concessions on current US demands. A retreat on the positions which the Soviet Union had itself demanded when negotiating SALT I, would undermine the Soviet status it still aimed to maintain. On the other hand, the US was firmly determined to break out of the stalemate. So President Reagan declared in May 1986 that the US no longer felt committed to the SALT regime (Reagan 1986). Until then, the US had always stressed that even though SALT II was not ratified and that this was the Soviet Union's fault, the US would act within its limits. Two days later the US administration elaborated on Reagan's declaration by announcing that the SALT regimes were dead. These statements were important because SALT had symbolised US acknowledgement of Soviet parity – although when signing SALT, the US had stressed the nuclear parity, while the Soviet Union had stressed parity.

From the end of the 1970's, support for SALT principles had been central in the exchange of signals between the superpowers. It was a fundamental hallmark of the Cold War, therefore, when the US distanced itself from the principles and redefined its aim from containment of the Soviet Union to an offensive aim: to roll back the Soviet Union from its position as a superpower. The US then added a new weapon to its Cold War offensive, now at its peak: disarmament. Disarmament would be based on the US Strategic Arms Reduction Talks (START) and the Intermediate-range Nuclear Forces (INF) proposals, which had been put forward at the end of 1985 and which had paved the way for the American execution of the SALT regime. As opposed to SALT, the START and INF proposals would lead to actual reductions; under START, the target was approximately a 50 percent reduction of the Soviet force. The US demanded, simply, that the Soviet Union should disarm itself by means of traditional Soviet disarmament policy rather than pursue American arms control policy. The Soviet Union had continually demanded disarmament, while the US had demanded arms control right up until the demand for the double zero-option and reductions of the strategic weapons instead of limitations on the development of the capacities. The US increased its disarmament demands while threatening to abandon the strategic parity agreed on in the Basic Principles of SALT 1, and was thus heading towards a position as the superior nuclear power. The strategy was successful and at the Reykjavik summit in 1987, the Soviet Union was ready to make at least a tactical retreat. Soviet diplomats accepted the INF proposal by which the superpowers should disarm the central nuclear theatre, Europe, leaving the US as the winner. However, the Soviet Union still had an opportunity for a potential reconstruction of their former position by putting its precious weapons into a new political framework, 'The New Thinking', which had been developed during the previous years. The prospects for a Soviet return to the nuclear rivalry were modest, however, because the new generation of weapons, based on space research and micro-technology, posed a tremendous development problem for the Soviet Union. Major technological progress was needed, and such progress apparently demanded a total change of Soviet society.

Nevertheless the Soviet Union held on to its participation in the arms control process and its superpower position by maintaining its demand for a linkage between START reductions of strategic weapons and limitations in SDI, which it claimed was a violation of the ABM Treaty. The US, on the other hand, gave priority to START, because it included intercontinental ballistic missiles (ICBMs) which had been an important element of the American offensive. The US had identified a window of vulnerability for the US ICBM force (Minuteman III in soft silos). The force was considered vulnerable to a general strike by the Soviet ICBM force. The identification of the window reflected US frustration at the Soviet interpretation of SALT, which was seen as a defection from the rules of the game and, indeed, a challenge to US leadership inside the rivalry. Although both parties had a solid second strike capability, the Soviet Union was, approaching a quantitative edge within a selected category – the category which the superpowers had agreed on as central in the SALT process. This, in combination with the Soviet demand that the US remained at its actual qualitative level and halted the SDI project, was unacceptable to the US. So, the US continued to arm, fought for its right to develop the SDI, still on the drawing board, and demanded disarmament.

On September 21, 1989 the Soviet Foreign Minister, Eduard Shevardnadze, handed a letter to President Bush in Washington. Shevardnadze said that the Soviet Union would give up its claims on how the US developed SDI, and the Soviet Union no longer considered SDI an obstacle to a START treaty. Thus, the Soviet Union accepted that the US could have something nuclear that was outside its own reach and which would prevent it from maintaining the state of parity (Hansen 1991). According to this interpretation, the Soviet Union surrendered not only prevailing arms control regime in favour of a purely US solution, but it also gave up its superpower position, acknowledging the US as the only superpower. It was doing so in terms of the definition of superpower rivalry which the Soviet Union itself had put forward and which had been recognised by SALT I.

The bipolar Cold War thus came to an end. Many factors were involved, and it is evident that the decline of aggregate Soviet capabilities and particularly the Soviet economy and economic organisation played a major role.[6] It is evident, too, that the end of the Cold War was a process, and that the end took place at different times in different parts of the world and regarding various issues. The final battle between the two bipolar rivals, however, is interpreted to have taken a specific form, and nuclear weapons were the basis of the peaceful termination. When successive systems are analysed, as is done here, it is necessary to identify the time when the systemic transformation and structural change took place. According to this interpretation, the bipolar system finally broke down in September 1989 after what has been interpreted here as a Soviet surrender.

THE NUMBER OF POLES

The next question to be considered is whether or not the actual distribution of strength after 1989 can be described as being unipolar. How strong, after all, is the US? As already mentioned above, this problem is an empirical one and is not of relevance to the working out of the model. According to Waltz, a pole is a state that possesses a strong aggregate capability relative to other states. To carry out the identification, a process of exclusion is applied; in neorealist theory a superpower must score on all main capabilities (Waltz 1979). It need not necessarily be number one in each, but should be in most and it must not have severe disadvantages.

The states usually referred to as being large, besides the US, are Russia, Japan, China, Germany and sometimes the EU (India will probably be taken into consideration soon because of its progress in many areas). None of these states qualify as superpowers, however: Russia is still suffering from the internal collapse of 1990–91 and is facing severe economic problems. Japan is obviously not convincing militarily; this also holds for Germany. The EU still lacks political cohesion and the ability to act collectively. These states and the EU possess superpower potentials, but during the 1990's, they did not qualify under Waltz' original criteria (1979). The assessment of the aggregate Chinese capabilities is, however, more difficult. China qualifies on several criteria: territorial size, population, political cohesion, vast military forces and equipment. But in economic terms, China is still rated a relatively poor country, although its economy is large in absolute terms. There is no doubt that China possesses considerable resources and has superpower potential as a single gigantic state, if it does not disintegrate because the process of modernisation of the economy may led to a set back in internal cohesion, and provided the economy improves. The result, however, is that the US is the only state in the world which qualified in 1989 (and the following ten years) on all capabilities, thereby distancing it from the other states. The assumption made from the very beginning about US unipolarity is, therefore, justified.

An often heard critique should be addressed, namely that of 'but there are a lot of things that the US cannot do and American policy is often unsuccessful'. Agreed on! A unipole is not omnipotent, there is no guarantee that it pursues a wise and successful policy, and it will often, intentionally or unintentionally harm the interests of other states or groups and trigger resistance. Still, the unipole possesses special characteristics and a power edge compared to other states which arguably makes a diffence to international politics.

SUMMARY: THE MODEL AND THE CHANGE

Above a theoretical model of unipolarity was elaborated. It was done in order to provide the classical neorealist theory with a model for cases where there is only one great power in existence. As assumed – and argued by a method of exclusion – this is exactly the case from 1989 onwards. It was also argued that the transformation from bi- to unipolarity took place in September 1989. Because of nuclearity the antagonist rivalry was terminated by a US Cold War offensive. The model is held to be essential for the empirical analysis which is to follow.

It was stated that the systemic transformation itself brings about turbulence throughout the system. The turbulence is assumed to affect all parts of interstate life, which are regarded as essential from a neorealist point of view. The statement says that a systemic change will lead to realignment, changes in conflicts and issues, and a challenge to the number of states in existence. Consequently, previous patterns of conflict and cooperation are challenged. As for the general unipolar dynamics, it was argued that unipolarity contains no symmetrical great power balancing, but that balancing will work among the other states, and that the unipole will continuously balance between the external and the internal use of its resources. The main statements (hypotheses) about unipolar international systems and the effects of unipolarity on the conditions by which states help themselves and interact summarize as follows:

- Unipolarity is a robust, but not necessarily durable variation of polarity. Balancing among all powers functions as issue-related balancing of the unipole, but not symmetrical great power balancing, and so does the unipole's own balancing of its resources. Great power wars will not occur because there is a lack of equal adversaries

80

- The other states have a single option only for great power guarantees in the case of unipolarity. This weakens their bargaining power vis-à-vis the unipole, and it gives them an incentive to flock around the unipole if necessary. They will tend to flock (unipolarisation) when faced with strategic security needs, or if the unipole's agenda demands polarization. A nuclearised or nuclear threshold status may reduce a state's incentive to flock
- The other states need to work hard and carry a comparatively bigger burden with respect to enhancing their security. Regional symmetrical activity, including cooperation as well as conflict, will be high.
- The unipole has to undertake managerial tasks, but it will try to share these burdens with others, primarily regional 'partners'. The unipole is challenged by the risk of exhaustion due to its managerial tasks as well as by others' free-riding and growth; on the other hand, it puts its position at risk in the event of a laissez faire attitude. The unipole is in a unique position to define the agenda of world affairs.
- From 1989 to date, international politics should be analysed in terms of unipolarity, with the US as the unipole, and with nuclearity tempering conflicts. The US position as the unipole and its policy make up the US World Order.

Chapter 5

The US World Order

The theoretical characteristics constitute the general position of the US as a *unipole* from the termination of the Cold War in the Autumn of 1989. In addition, the US policy and priorities constitute the specific characteristics of the *US* unipole, which are dealt with below. The general and specific characteristics are summarised by the analytical concept of 'US World Order', which reflects both the two characteristics: it reflects the unipolar position of the, and the political priorities and interests, which the US has chosen to pursue.

The US approach to international politics was transformed between 1989 and 1994. The Reagan Administration's core formula of 'Realism, Strength and Dialogue' at the end of the Cold War was substituted in the Summer of 1989 by President Bush's 'It is time to go beyond Containment' (Bush 1989). The shift represents the first phase of the challenge to the bipolar antagonism by the emergence of the US unipolarity. Only about a year after, there came another evident turning point. The Iraqi invasion of Kuwait demanded international management and triggered a US response. The response made the unipolar American position manifest and obvious, and paved the way for major policy changes. Part of the response was the emergence of a US principle for a New World Order. "Don't bully your neighbour", said President Bush after the Iraqi invasion of Kuwait, declaring that interstate aggression was not to be tolerated after 1989. In the Autumn of 1989, President Bush also declared 'a new world order' to be a US aim (Bush 1989a). In 1994, the US took a further step with the national strategy for 'Engagement and Enlargement'. This is interpreted as the US committing itself explicitly to undertake managerial efforts arising from its unipolar position, and making explicit that it aimed to lead the world.

US actions in the first ten post-Cold War years correspond to a three-phase development: at the outset, the US let the Cold War norms and antagonisms disintegrate and tried to bring the Soviet Union into its one-world concept, supporting its former enemy in order to prevent total chaos within the losing empire. In the second phase, the New World Order phase, the US manifested its position by leading the full-scale, UN approved, force projection into the Gulf area; and in the third and, so far, last phase, it began to build up the 'New' according to American aims and using a unipole's relative freedom of action. This phase included an extention of US alignment into the former Soviet empire by the process of enlarging NATO with former Warsaw Pact members.

Below, the US post-Cold War Strategy is analysed in the light of this process of emerging and becoming recognised as a unipole. Firstly, the focus is on the general, international US policy. Secondly, the US Middle East policy is dealt with.

THE US INTERNATIONAL POLICY IN GENERAL

Before the Iraqi invasion of Kuwait, the US had concentrated on adjusting itself to the end of the Cold War and to the absence of the superpower rivalry, which had dominated the US international and foreign policy since 1945. The US response was briefly encapsulated by President Bush, who already in the summer of 1989 declared that the time had come to "go beyond Containment and to integrate the Soviet Union into the community of states" (Bush 1989); this indicated that the Soviet Union was no longer an overwhelming threat and that the former division into blocs was no longer the US view of the world. In the beginning, the concept of 'going beyond Containment' was rather unclear, and focused mostly on what had ceased to be a problem. The only explicit ingredients of the concept besides disentanglement from the antagonism was the notion of cooperation between the Soviet Union and the US, non-proliferation, and some minor priorities such as fighting drug-trafficking and terrorism. The US did not declare any objectives with regard to major international changes; no signals indicated the world to be different, except for the end of the antagonism.

US actions immediately before 1989, in general, supported the vague Bush notion of Beyond Containment, and the prevailing characteristic of these actions was restraint. The US-Soviet relations in years from 1987 to 1989 were detente-like and characterized by a softening compared to the previous years. With respect to Eurasian developments, where major changes took place from 1989, the US approved or at least did not act against them. The only notable action was the aid to the Soviet Union, whose decline the US regarded as dangerous, lest internal unrest explode and split up the vast and nuclearised loser uncontrollably. West of the Soviet Union, another striking event was the reunification of West and East Germany. As this was in harmony with one of the US Cold War objectives; the reunification was regarded as something natural, which the surrounding world could hardly prevent anyway. In other places, dramatic developments took place, too. The Yemens declared their unification in the spring of 1990 and the US merely took notice of this. President Bush accompanied the signals by a series of diplomatic efforts which gave priority to cautiously dealing with the immediate repercussions of the Soviet retreat in Europe. While the relationship to the former Eastern Bloc was improved and developed, NATO was still reserved for its existing members until January 1994, where President Clinton committed the US to an enlargement of NATO.

In addition to these external priorities, the Bush Administration addressed the internal American situation. It did not do so in a comprehensive way or with a new programme, which would convince the voters in the following elections. Yet, the Administration did highlight the need to reorganise the US, which up to then had been locked into a state of cold war. And though the Bush Administration's attempts did not convince the American voters in the later election, it did fuel some fear abroad that the US was returning to 'isolationism'. The general US approach towards other states during this first post-Cold War phase was based on an effort to maintain the relationship to its friends and allies, while it sought to cope with former enemies in a common world lacking the communist threat. At the same time, the US focus was primarily on Europe and the Eurasian development. Consequently, the combination of the US signals and geographic focus was likely to be perceived by the former Soviet allies and proxies outside Europe that everything would be as it was before except for their own positions, which would be weakened by the lack of Soviet aid and security guarantees.

The engagement in, and successful outcome of, Operation Desert Storm dramatically encouraged the emerging American policy. During the military build-up and after Desert Storm, President Bush declared that the US now opted for the 'New World Order' and saw a possibility to implement the vision. The US understanding of this Order was, besides freedom from the need to contain the Soviet Union, and the already declared aims of fighting terrorism and drug-trafficking, freedom from aggression, non-proliferation of nuclear weapons, and the advance of the free market and liberal democracy, now had the highest priority. When Iraq invaded Kuwait in August 1990, the US Administration had to face the first post-Cold War test of its position. All over the world, there were doubts about whether the US would actually resort to armed force. It did so, however, when Iraq did not comply with US demands as expressed, mainly through the United Nations.

After the Gulf War, the development of US objectives and statements accelerated. In July 1994 the White House produced "A National Security Strategy of Engagement and Enlargement" (the White House 1994). The strategy, which here is called the 'Engagement and Enlargement stragegy', gave priority to three central goals: to sustain US security with military force, to bolster US economic revitalisation, and to promote democracy abroad (Op.cit.:Preface). It was also stated that the major security challenges to the US were regional conflicts and the proliferation of weapons of mass destructions (Ibid.).

In addition to making its aims and the challenges clear, the White House committed the US to a specific global role as described by the very title of the paper: "engagement" committed the US internationally and the rest of the world was made subject to an "enlargement" of the US world order; i.e., the "community of free market democracies" (the White House 1994:5). The strategy reflects a US perception of itself which had developed during the first five years after 1989, a perception which had gradually become more self-confident.

The basis for this strategy was laid about a year after Operation Desert Storm. The US was described as being in a "unique" position, as being able to "change the world", and called as "the strongest nation on earth" in the State of the Union Address (White House 1992). The concept of New World Order was still important, but in addition a sense of the US leadership position had developed.[1] The latter was fully formulated in the Engagement and Enlargement strategy (White House 1994). The paper clearly stated that the US interests could not be maintained adequately without global leadership. In the White House paper on the strategy, the reasons given for this were that the external orientation of the US economy is heavily dependent on free market opportunities abroad, which demand that the US stimulate the free market globally; and that the promotion of democracy abroad is also necessary in order to prevent friction and to consolidate the stable conditions for the pursuit of the US interests (Op.cit.:16, 19). The way to pursue engagement and enlargement was developed in the US 'Integrated Regional Approaches'. Priority was given to the expansion of cooperation with cooperative states/groups of states, committed to the US world order by different means, such as the Partnership For Peace programme and NATO.

Since then the cooperative dimensions were further stratified during the middle of the 1990's, and, in addition, to the challenges identified in the Engagement and Enlargement strategy, potential enemies and hostile powers were also identified. These had two things in common: their opposition to the world order and their being on the threshold of nuclearisation or capacities of other WMD-weapons. In the first half of the 1990's especially Iran and Iraq in the Middle east were subject to US critique and measures and, to a lesser extent, so was Libya. In Asia, especially North Korea was subject, being labelled a so-called rogue state.

The regional approach was supported by planning for major regional contingencies, the identification of potentially hostile powers, and a strong mainly military overseas presence facilitated by the network of cooperation. It also comprised a new kind of burden sharing. The US emphasised its demand for participation of other states in the solution of regional conflicts, as was the case in the Balkan wars. In theoretical terms, the unipolar American managerial approach reflects the incentives to prevent free-riding and to encourage hard work.

As for the US military positions, the Pentagon was working out the new US contingency plans in light of the nuclear disarmament, which followed the two comprehensive treaties worked out with the Soviet Union during the last years of the Cold War, INF and START. While nuclear weapons were destroyed, weapons systems phased out and SDI was replaced by a new research programme, the *Win-Win* strategy was adopted as part of the reorganisation. The reorganisation of the US defence had already been announced in 1990 by President Bush in a speech at the Aspen Institute. Later, the Secretary of Defense, Dick Cheney, interpreted the proposal as a shift of direction; from focusing on the worst case to focusing on the most likely case (quoted in Tritten 1992:12). This was a top-down reorganisation of the defence strategy and force structure (Op.cit.:27), with an emphasis on a regional approach. Two years later, the strategy was further developed by the Bottom-Up Review presented by the Pentagon. The review elaborated the building of force structure and capacity to win two major regional conflicts fought simultaneously (hence the label 'Win-Win').

The reasoning behind this strategy was that there existed no main threat that could be compared to the Soviet Union, but that the US instead should be prepared for regional conflicts arising independently in different areas; in practice, this was envisaged as fighting one and being capable of deterring another at the same time (The Military Balance 1994–5:13).

In December 1991, the North Atlantic Council of Cooperation (NACC) held its inaugural meeting. 25 countries participated initially, but as NACC membership was open to all Eurasian states, it came to include all the members of the former Warsaw Treaty Organisation, even Russia. In January 1994, NATO adopted the US Partnership For Peace programme, which was offered to the same states which were NACC members, but on conditions that were harder to meet. In 1994, the US also signalled that it now considered NATO open to the East European states on some, not yet stated, conditions. Different, but as intensive, efforts to pursue integrated regional approaches were carried out in the New Pacific Community for East Asia and the Pacific, and by NAFTA for north American cooperation. The regional approach was complemented with a statement about the need to "ensure US influence over and participation in collective decision-making" (White House 1994:6). All the regional efforts may be interpreted to serve to establish cores, which adhere and contribute to the consolidation of the US world order.

The US also made specific and considerable efforts to halt the horizontal proliferation of nuclear weapons: partly by boosting the Non-Proliferation-Treaty regime, partly by squeezing the threshold states opposing the US world order. In addition, efforts were made to advance the implementation of the disarmament treaties with the Soviet Union, now Russia, and also with the now independent, former Soviet republics. The US even promoted the comprehensive test-ban from 1995.

During the development of the strategy and concepts, the Republican Bush Administration had been replaced by the Democratic Clinton Administration, elected not least because of its comprehensive programme for internal American reforms. During Clinton's election campaign, major differences to Bush's foreign approach appeared: for example, the challenge to China's internal rule in the beginning of the presidency. After the election, however, no major changes in approach took place; nor did any occur since the mid-term elections of 1994, which resulted in Republican control of Congress. President Clinton entered the presidency devoted to internal US affairs. The programme included health reform, administrative reform, and a package of law and order initiatives.

Some even regarded the policy as the beginning of a new US isolationism. However, while the military budget was cut and the military posture was restructured to meet the new challenges according to the Bottom Up Review and, from 1997, the Quadrennial Defense Review, the commitment was not reduced. In its first years the Clinton Administration developed its external policy into a strong commitment to global American leadership: "The Cold War may be over, but the need for American Leadership abroad remains as strong as ever. I am committed to building a new public consensus to sustain our active engagement abroad" (White House 1994:Preface).

The post-Cold War US international policy developed during the first five unipolar years into a complex of policies which were clearly distinct from those of bipolarity. The following five years the policy was continued but it was characterized by also *unilateral* action (the airstrikes against Iraq and the initiatives against Yugoslavia during the Kosovo-crisis are illustrating examples) and an active role in terms of international management. Examples are the NATO enlargement, the role as mediator in a series of conflicts and crises and the commitment to dealing with the Balkan conflicts. In sum, the policy was characterised as follows:

- The containment of the Soviet Union was replaced by enlargement of the US World Order and a commitment to US leadership and engagement.
- The bipolar American view of the world as divided into pro-Soviet and pro-US states was replaced by the view of a division of states following or opposing the US.
- Overseas alignments were reassessed according to the new opportunities to pursue US interests. Some alignments were maintained because they were still valuable but for new reasons, others were replaced or just cancelled.
- Priority was given to the enhancement of regional security in order to facilitate the pursuit of the US interests – the socalled Integrated Regional Approaches. This reflects a geographical rather than an antagonist approach to world affairs.
- The regional approach comprised the creation of stable pro-US cores as well as increasing demands for burden sharing: decen-

tralisation and encouragement of what is interpreted as hard work in order to prevent free riding and US exhaustion.
- The US challenged the proliferation of weapons of mass destruction, especially by states opposing other aspects of the US World Order.
- A readiness to act unilaterally and to undertake managerial affairs was developed.

US AND THE MIDDLE EAST

US policy towards the Middle East between the Autumn of 1989 and the Iraqi invasion of Kuwait in August 1990 was a prolongation of the policy from the last years of the Cold War: a continuation of efforts to initiate negotiations between Israel and the Palestinians as the first step towards an Israeli-Arab settlement. This, and securing the oil supply, were the US priorities in the area. Although the peace efforts were overshadowed by the US preoccupation with other parts of the world and downgraded accordingly, they continued, encouraged by the Soviet withdrawal from Afghanistan in 1988–89 and the softening of Soviet Union positions on other regional matters, as Mikhail Gorbachev's assurances that the Soviet would now cooperate with the US to solve regional conflicts.

The Bush Administration tried to put pressure on the PLO in order to pave the way for negotiations between Palestinians outside the PLO and the Shamir Government in Israel (Quandt 1993:390). Although some minor progress took place regarding the PLO's position towards the negotiations (Op.cit.:390–1), the US did not succeed in persuading Shamir's government.

On the other hand, the dialogue between the US and the PLO was disrupted by the Palestinian Liberation Front's attempted terrorist attack on the beach at Tel Aviv. The precondition for dialogue had been the unciation to terrorism by the PLO National Council in Algiers in November 1988. In the spring of 1990 the peace process had, therefore, become deadlocked. In the meantime, Iraq was making its way onto the agenda. In the course of the Iraq-Iran War, Iraq, though receiving economical support from more Arab countries, had become isolated in Middle East politics and now began its efforts to break the isolation. The first Iraqi steps were quite moderate, and even though still tougher positions vis-a-vis Israel and the US were to appear during the spring of 1990, the US chose to interpret the Iraqi positions as purely tactical.

Already from 1989, however, Middle Eastern problems were subject to US reassessment within Central Command, which had replaced the controversial Rapid Deployment Force. Central Command assessed the most urgent threat to come from Iraq, and it drew up a new contingency plan (Trainor 1992:199). The identification of the Iraqi threat, however, was not welcomed by the State Department, which had given assurances that Iraq was not an enemy (Ibid.). The State Department relied on earlier assessments and practical experiences during the last phase of bipolarity, when the US-Iraqi relationship had improved during the course of the fighting of the Iran-Iraq War.

The US State Department's assessments were based on reports from its bipolar allies in the area. Egypt's President Hosni Mubarak was keen to persuade the US that Iraq was not an enemy, and Egyptian actions confirmed his view: Egypt and Iraq had joined the Arab Cooperation Council (ACC) together. Besides, Iraq seemed to have changed its strategy to a more moderate one. These reports were welcomed, given the US preoccupation with Europe and the decline of the Soviet Union. James Baker, then US Secretary of State, was aware, however, of the possibilities for progressing towards a solution of the Arab-Israeli conflict. During the Gorbachev years, the Soviet Union had shown some willingness to rethink conflicts in the Third World, and the withdrawal from Afghanistan was a clear proof of the 'New Thinking' policy. None of the parties involved, however, seemed to assess the situation in the same way as Baker. The PLO was departing from the opening positions it had made immediately before the end of the Cold War, and the Likud government in Israel was determined not to make any concessions concerning the occupied territories. The combination of the dramatic Eurasian development, the rather positive US assessment of Iraqi intentions, which should be seen against the background that Iraq was perceived to be the most likely aggressor, if any (Trainor 1992:199), and the dull prospects produced by the lack of cooperative will of the parties in the Arab-Israeli conflict, provided the conditions for the US to focus its attention on other areas and urgent issues in the immediate post-Cold War period. It was important, however, that the US did not cancel its commitment to the peace process.

Before the Iraqi invasion, the US approach to the Middle East was characterised by being a low priority compared to other issues and areas. A deadlock in the peace process and a set-back in the US-Iraqi relationship were not considered to be too serious by the US. The

Middle East was by and large left to itself. However, it was, as were all other areas, indirectly subject to the general US approach on non-proliferation, etc. But the US saw the international agenda as being most urgent elsewhere and gave priority to the strategic relationship with the Soviet Union, to dealing with the events in Europe, and to care for its cooperation with the Third World where the Soviet Union was involved (Garthoff 1994).

The Iraqi invasion dramatically triggered a renewal of the US policy. Shortly after the end of Operation Desert Storm, President Bush presented the new approach whose main aim was to secure peace and stability in the area as well as the oil supply. The strategy gave priority to the Gulf Area through a US reliance on GCC, a US naval presence and a commitment to non-proliferation of weapons of mass destruction; to a reinvigoration of the Arab-Israeli peace process; and to regional economical development (Hunter 1993:65). The US thus committed itself to a period of activity in the area in order to manage and to make progress towards long term US objectives. It initiated the Madrid process and kept it going, it continued to confront Iraq, to put some pressure at Iran, to cooperate with the Southern Gulf States, primarily Saudi Arabia, to encourage economic and some security cooperation in the Maghreb and it sought to build regional cores. All these initiatives are dealt with in the following chapters. In 1994, the approach and the objectives were stated as part of the Engagement and Enlargement Doctrine, and this policy was maintained also during the following five years. To summarise, the US Middle East policy during the 1990's was characterized by the following elements:

- The pursuit of "a comprehensive breakthrough to Middle East peace, assuring the security of Israel and our Arab friends".
- The maintenance of "the free flow of oil at reasonable prices".
- The implementation of "a strategy of dual containment of Iraq and Iran as long as those states pose a threat to U.S. interests, to other states in the region, and to their own citizens". (All quoted from White House 1994:25.)

The US concern for the oil supply was still an important element in the post-1989 US policy as had been before. The two other elements reflected a new emphasis: whereas during bipolarity the US encouraged peace talks in the Arab-Israeli conflict provided the security of Israel was ensured, it was now actively committing itself to the peace process and the security not only of Israel but of its Arab allies as well. As for the US' policy towards Iraq and Iran, this was qualified into 'dual containment'.

Before proceeding to the empirical part of this analysis, three points about the US approach must be emphasised. *Firstly*, the US approach was developing throughout the period in question. Most importantly, there was a clear difference between the US approach before and after Operation Desert Storm. Before Desert Storm, neither the US position nor its post-Cold War strategy had been clarified, while afterwards its position became manifest and the strategy developed. *Secondly*, the global strategy was developed and clarified according to the Engagement and Enlargement Doctrine, together with the Integrated Regional approach. *Thirdly*, the US strategy towards the Middle East became part of an integrated regional approach, which is interpreted to be essentially about the creation of regional cores. Its specific priorities as far as the Middle East was concerned included: a commitment to peace process, to securing the supply of oil, and to putting pressure on nuclear/WMD threshold states which oppose the US World Order.

The American Way

The purpose of this chapter was to portray a few but important features of the specific US way to act as a unipole. As stated in chapter 3, a unipole should not be considered omnipotent, and it is evident that it faces many problems vis-à-vis the other states, not least when trying to implement its policy. The other states might fear dominance and loss of autonomy, and conflicting interests provide problems. During the late 1990's some US actions were subject to a decline in international support but the US chose to pursue its policy. In the specific case of the American unipolarity, the spread of free market capitalism and liberal democray creates seriously challenges to many states and groups; e.g. in the Middle East this is probably an important factor behing the rise of radical political islam. Yet the unipole deeply affect the balance of power in the Middle Eastern subsystem, and consequently it is crucial to consider the unipole's specific policy and agenda which the other states may not agree with but can hardly disregard.

Chapter 6

The Unification of Yemen

The reorganisation of the post-bipolar Middle East began in a quiet and peaceful way with the Yemeni declaration of unification.[1] In November 1989, the two Yemens entered into an agreement on later unification and on the constitutional arrangements for a single state. The single state project was to merge the Arab Republic of Yemen (YAR) in the north with a population of 9.2 million and 38,500 in the armed forces, and the large territory to the south, the People's Democratic Republic of Yemen (PDRY), with a population of 2.3 million and 27,500 in the armed forces (The Military Balance 1990–1:121). In accordance with the 1989 agreement YAR and the PDRY declared their actual unification on 22 May 1990 and made San'a (in the north) the capital.

Already in the Spring of 1988 the leaders of the Yemen had begun to discuss a possible merger. By the end of 1989, it was agreed on: Unity Day was scheduled for November 1990. But it was brought forward six months of unexpected progress in the negotiations (The Middle East, July 1990:5). From May 1990 a 30 month transition period began. Within that period, the laws, economies, organisations and infrastructures had to be prepared for the merger. Shortly after Unity Day, the army commands were unified and later the Air Forces and the Navy, but parallel armed forces and state structures, however, were preserved until the summer of 1994, when the former YAR leadership in the North won the civil

Although the two Yemens had occasionally clashed during the 1970's and the 1980's, each of them had promoted their will to merge throughout the years. This was done in spite of the different internal arrangements of the two, differences were partly of tribal nature, and partly based on a traditional concept of society in the North and a modern (socialist) concept in the South, respectively. For example, intense efforts at unification were carried out, unsuccessfully, by the leaders of each Yemen, Al-Hamdi (YAR) and Rubayyi Ali (PDRY), at the end of the 1970's.

Unification, when it came, was quite surprise, however. It was received calmly, and almost unnoticed outside its near neighbourhood. However, the Southern and Northern Gulf states were carefully following the development and the formation of a new major power. Saudi Arabia had most at stake: Saudi Arabia and YAR had unresolved border issues, and Saudi Arabia was fearing a unification with a revolutionary leadership. Iraq and Iran were both interested in influence at the Peninsula.

The history of the Yemeni states has been one of unrest in many respects. Great powers have fought over their territories; they themselves have had mutual clashes, internal upheavals and civil wars. During bipolarity, both the Yemens were seriously influenced by the superpower rivalry, and when it ended their situations changed dramatically. PDRY had been strongly supported by the Soviet Union, which regarded the PDRY as a useful ally in its attempts to get a foothold in the Red Sea area and the Arabian Peninsula. Moreover, both the Yemens had benefited from the superpowers' rivalry: neither of the superpowers wanted to see a unified or both of the two Yemens falling into the hands of the other one. When the Soviet Union began to reduce its commitments in the Third World, during the Gorbachev leadership, its ambitions in the Red Sea area were also reduced. As the Yemens received still less support from the Soviet, the US made corresponding cuts. In the beginning, it was not absolutely clear if this was just another Cold War fluctuation, or something new. As the situation in the Yemens became rapidly worse, they both responded quickly. Negotiations began and, within a short while, the new unified state, the Republic of Yemen, was a fact.

The new constitution of the Republic of Yemen led to what was called the first real democratic experiment in the Middle East. Elections were held and the government of the Republic of Yemen was carefully composed of representatives from each of the former states. During the first years, the Air Forces and Air Defences were put under one command, and the Navy was concentrated in Aden (Military Balance 191–1992:123). The armies, however, were not fully integrated or put under joint command. Instead, armed force units from each side were stationed on the other's territory (Strategic Survey 1994–1995:156).

While two armies actually still existed, the new republic had, in 1990, succeeded in unifying politically, and the Republic of Yemen was from then on represented in the United Nations and the Arab League, and joined the ACC, in which the Republic of Yemen replaced the YAR. In 1993 general elections were held, and have been characterized as 'fair although with problems', the problems primarily related to anonymity which was difficult to maintain because of widespread illiteracy (Andersen 1994:110–11). Four years after the unification, however, an intense civil war broke out between the North and South and during the summer of 1994, the North, which was by far the stronger of the two, took control and finally established an effective monopoly of power.

The key words when analysing the unification of Yemen is thus the asymmetrical dealignment, the following subsystemic challenges, and the internal power struggle.

THE YEMENS AND THE US-SOVIET RIVALRY

Historically the Yemens were particularly exposed to the great powers' pursuit of their external interests, due to their strategic position with respect to the Red Sea, the Horn of Africa and the Gulf. Great Britain succeeded in occupying the South in 1839 through its Egyptian suzerain, Muhammad Ali, while their Ottoman competitor occupied the North in 1872. After World War I and the defeat of the Ottoman Empire, the North gained sovereignty under the rule of Imam Yahya of the Zaydi Shi'ites, while the South was declared a British protectorate in 1937. During occupation, however, neither of the two great powers succeeded in gaining control with parts of Yemeni territory. Not least the mountains in the North prevented the great powers from occupying several cities in spite of intense efforts, and although the Hadramaut region bordering Saudi Arabia became part of Great Britain's Eastern Aden Protectorate actual control was hardly achieved (Andersen 1994).

The end of World War II led to a loosening of European influence and, eventually, to the end of the British protectorates. The British left South Yemen rather late, and full and independent sovereignty was not a fact until 1967. Then the Marxist, National Liberation Front gained control and declared the People's Republic of South Yemen (PRSY), renamed, only three years later, the People's Democratic Republic of Yemen (PDRY). In the meantime, the North had suffered an internal rebellion which ended the Zaydi rule and began the life of the Yemen Arab Republic (YAR). The coup had been carried out by a pro-Soviet group in the army. At the very beginning YAR appealed for

Soviet support, needed because Saudi Arabia was supporting efforts to have the imamate restored (Page 1985:5), but which the Soviet Union was not willing or able to fully provide. Instead the Soviet Union left direct intervention to Egypt, which was not able to bring about any solution and this led to resistance to Egyptian as well as Soviet influence. A new political strategy was forced through in YAR and a new government formed in San'a (Op.cit.:6). YAR then developed a pro-Western course, contrary to, after an initial period of hesitation, the pro-Soviet inclination of the new PRDY.

When the PDRY approached the Soviet Union, it was welcomed. The Soviet Union, then in a period of expansion, aimed to create a stronghold on the Horn of African and in the Southern part of the Arabian Peninsula (Golan 1990: Ch.15); it had been looking for allies and proxies. It had initially supported North Yemen but the relationship had deteriorated and the North Yemen was turning to the West. At that time the relationship between the Yemens was characterised by confrontation, and the Soviet Union also had to chose between them. From the end of the 1960's, Soviet military aid to PRSY (later PDRY) rapidly increased, while aid to YAR was stopped (Page 1985:157). The Soviet Union and the PDRY then signed a Treaty on Friendship and Cooperation. The alignment contributed to a broadening of the Soviet sphere and provided it with the opportunity to have bases, naval and air facilities in Aden, and to make use of the Socotra Island south of PDRY.

For the Soviet Union the PDRY alignment was a strong asset. The location near the Horn of Africa and the military facilities were of substantial benefit. The PDRY had been weakened by its struggle to avoid being dominated by the Northern centre of the Imamate and its subsystemic isolation vis-à-vis the moderate, conservative, oil-rich states made the alignment an opportunity.

Although the Soviet Union supported the PDRY, it was reluctant to alienate the North, which would invite Western influence, and the Soviet foothold at the Peninsula was weak. Fearing that the North would fall directly into the hands of the US, the Soviet Union did not cease, fully, to support the YAR, and a few years later the YAR and the Soviet Union also signed a Friendship Treaty, which was based on the original treaty with the North when it had been ruled by the Zaydis

The US also supported both of the Yemens, although to a much lesser extent and primarily the North. It came in the form of political support, economic aid and arms sales, but no direct military assistance. The US aimed at preventing full Soviet control of either of the Yemens. Soviet indfluence in both Yemens would have been extremely problematic for the US, as the implication would be an actual encirclement of the strategic US allied state of Saudiarabia; with Iraq to the North. The Yemens were located on strategic straits, they supplied Saudi Arabia with a substantial part of its labour force, and they were able to put pressure at Riyadh (Page 1985). In this light, the separation was a favourable state of affairs for the US. A unified Yemen, if supported by the Soviet Union, would be the only real threat to Saudi Arabia on the Arabian Peninsula, and Saudi Arabia was the key oil country and the one on which the Americans relied. Saudi Arabia had, since the late fifties, aligned (tacitly) with the US, which in return had a strong proxy on the Peninsula. The US did not totally exclude the Yemeni question from the antagonism and supported the North as a major donor – although compared to other states at a relatively low scale. US support was also given because of the radical political nature of the South. During the Cold War the US had, in general, given support to regimes at risk of communist takeover.

Altogether, during bipolarity the two Yemens had been on the periphery of superpower rivalry in the Middle East, and then gradually become part of it. The Yemens became a battlefield for the proxies, where adjacent Arab states interfered on each side during the civil wars in the 1960's in support of one or other side (Egypt supported the southern republicans, while Saudi Arabia supported the northern tribal traditionalists) in state-to-state clashes.

After the Reagan offensive in the Cold War the positions became fixed. New shifts were unimaginable: the PDRY was considered the pro-Soviet, while the North was neutral and, mostly because it was not pro-Soviet, considered the pro-Western. The PDRY was the only party which had external military advisors and facilities, acquired since it had turned to the Soviet Union. However, the Gorbachev Doctrine, which followed the US offensive, entailed a decrease in Soviet support for the PDRY.

The Soviet Union gave up its ambitions in the Red Sea area as part of the Gorbachev Doctrine. First, economic aid to the PDRY was reduced, and then the military presence was phased out, but not until after the systemic change did the Soviet Union completely end its commitment. Similarly, superpower support to the YAR was cut. The YAR had received much less than the PDRY (partly from the Soviet Union, partly from the US).

For the two Yemens the bipolar superpower policies were beneficial. Both parties gained economically and had the possibility to acquire modern military equipment. Moreover, the South secured independence, which would have been hard to upheld by its own means against the superior North. It gave the two the opportunity to pursue and realise different strategies for their internal arrangements and they were able to improve their separate positions within the subsystem.

The Yemeni separation was zero-summed in that a single Yemeni state could not be won by either superpower. If it fell into the US camp, the Soviet Union would be deprived of its only foothold in the Peninsula, and if it turned to the Soviet camp, this would, from a US view, have represented a challenge to Saudi Arabia and US positions. Neither did the superpowers want to antagonize both of the two Yemens.

Yemeni bipolar history was turbulent but specific in character: it was marked the availability of two alternative great power guarantees which made changes between them a possibility, as the shifts proved, and also strengthened the bargaining position of the Yemens because of the superpowers' attempts to prevent either Yemen from fleeing into the arms of the other. Bipolarisation also increased as the Cold War intensified and eventually fixed the superpower affiliations.

The bipolar arrangement had further advantages for the Yemeni positions within the subsystem. It made both of them safe, it provided both of them with support when the oil-rich states were strengthened during the1970's, and it made the existence of two different states a possibility. The PDRY benefited most. It was the weaker of the Yemens, and as a consequence it gained most in terms of autonomy. A unified Yemen might have been able to balance Saudi Arabian dominance of the Arabian Peninsula, but the option was ruled out during bipolarity. Instead, the superpower rivalry prevented Saudi dominance of the Yemens.

The Cold war did not create the separation between the Yemens, but the conditions froze a separation. The PDRY's dealignment from the Soviet Union changed this situation and both the Yemens were facing new challenges.

THE SOVIET RETREAT AND THE CHOICE OF THE YEMENS

After the beginning of withdrawal of Soviet support, and the decrease of the lesser US support, the two Yemens had to reconsider their situation. The North was the stronger, but separately they were both weak vis-à-vis Saudi Arabia. Together, however, they would be quite strong. The Yemens were economically weak, and both were lacking oil reserves compared to other Gulf states. Only in 1986 oil production began increased in YAR, and joint exploration with PDRY was initiated in the border area; but before then the Yemens had been poor in oil.

In 1988 and the beginning of 1989 is was not clear whether the Cold War was ending, but it was clear that the Soviet Union and the United States were tempering their rivalry in the Middle East, and that the Soviet support was strongly decreasing. Both the Yemens were therefore subject to weaking in respect to their asymmetrical relations and the double option resulting from the bipolar rivalry. Asymmetrically, there were weakened, too. Saudi Arabia was still an important US ally because of its importance for the oil supply, and in spite of their own problems Iraq and Iran were much stronger than the Yemens. Therefore, the Yemens had the weakening caused by the ending of the Cold War in common, as well as they were both subject to weakening of the related subsystemic impact. Compared to each other, YAR was the stronger in terms of aggregate capabilities. In addition, PDRY was losing more because of its previous support from the Soviet Union, and because it was even less integrated in the subsystem.

From the YAR point of view, in this situation unification seemed a wise choice. It had no need to fear control by the South because of its own strength, but it would add the South's oil resources, better educated labour force, and harbour facility and thereby increase the ability to increase its security and gain influence in the area. The PDRY found itself left between Saudi Arabia and the YAR. It faced Northern dominance if it merged, but Saudi Arabian dominance if it did not. Besides, the PDRY had not only lost its economic support and security guarantee, it had also become alone and isolated. It was a radical, Marxist state, although substantial *perestroika* reforms were carried out in Aden (Kostiner 1996:6), and it was not member of the ACC as YAR had just become. In the light of these circumstances, the PDRY quickly opted for the lesser of these evils: unification. The unification was thus carried out in the light of the subsystemic changes and challenges which followed the end of bipolarity. The unification itself, however, also brought about changes of power within the subsystem, which particularly affected Saudi Arabia.

When the Republic of Yemen was declared it was recognised by the US and welcomed by the Soviet Union. It was also officially approved of by Saudi Arabia, and King Fahd stated that it had always supported Yemeni unity, and now "supports it, totally, without limit". Saudi Arabia was, however, deeply concerned about unification because it created one strong Yemen, and because the new republic joined the ACC which might help advance Iraqi and Egyptian influence in the Peninsula. For its part, the Republic of Yemen was not convinced that Saudi Arabia was going to support the unification project without reservation.

Shortly afterwards, the Gulf Conflict seriously affected the relationship between Saudi Arabia and the Republic of Yemen, and all the traditional conflicts (border definition, Yemeni claims on the Asir and Najran provinces, and Saudi Arabian interference in religious and tribal matters) were aggravated in the first years of the Republic of Yemen's existence (Strategic Survey 1994–95:158).

When the civil war broke out, and it seemed as if a return to separate Yemens was an option, Saudi Arabia's anti-unification actions became more obvious; but the US calmed Saudi Arabia and the interstate relationship.

THE 1994 CIVIL WAR

In the very beginning of the Republic of Yemen's existence, everything seemed to work well.[2] The Republic of Yemen was the first state in the Peninsula to commit itself formally to democratisation, including a multiparty system and general elections (The Middle East, Dec. 1992:9–11). Elections were held (the North was represented by General People's Congress (GPC), which had ruled YAR, and the Yemeni Alliance for Reform (al-Islah); the South was represented by the former PDRY ruling party, the Yemen Socialist Party (YSP)). The elections were praised as having been fairly conducted (Middle East, June 1993:16); but the Republic of Yemen was careful not to let the democratisation intimidate its Saudi Arabian neighbour in the light of their fragile relationship: "Other people may have something to learn from our example, but we are not looking to teach them anything. We are not in the business of exporting democracy", as Vice President al Beidh said before the elections (Op.cit.:17). The democratic development prior to the civil war was appreciated by the US. US officials stated, however, that the elections were only one step towards democracy, more had to be taken.

The Republic of Yemen had joined the ACC as one member upon unification. The YAR was the original Yemeni representative but was substituted by the Republic of Yemen without any problems. To both the YAR and the Republic of Yemen, the ACC represented a way out of isolation, a way to balance Saudi Arabia by adding Egyptian and the Iraqi strength, and a way to stand up against the oil-rich sheikdoms. The other ACC members also appreciated the addition of YAR, later the Republic of Yemen, which gave more weight to the ACC because of the admittance to the Red Sea ports and the numerous Yemeni population. Egypt and Jordan, however, feared that Saudi Arabia, with which they both tried to be on good terms, would see the Republic of Yemen's inclusion as a problem. Consequently, they tried to calm Saudi Arabia by positive signalling (Heikal 1993:123).

Shortly after the The Republic of Yemen was declared, Iraq invaded Kuwait. The ACC was split: Egypt fought in the Coalition against Iraq, Jordan was 'neutral' and considered to be siding with Iraq, and the The Republic of Yemen did not participate in any sanctions before the end of Operation Desert Storm. The Republic of Yemen's policy was one of abstention. This position reflected the Republic of Yemen's assessment that Iraq was at that time the worst enemy, but one that pursued the traditional Yemeni interests of balancing Saudi Arabia and Arab oil wealth. The Republic of Yemen abstained, however, in the votes at the Arab summits; it did not support Iraq, oppose the mainstream positions, or express reservations.

The Republic of Yemen's abstention on Iraq had the practical consequence of support for Iraq, and it should also be seen in the light of the Republic of Yemen's seat on the UN Security Council during the Gulf Conflict. Its Security Council seat made it impossible for the Republic of Yemen to pursue its interests in a low profile way: the US worked hard to gain support for its proposals, or at least not to have them opposed. In this connection it is important that the Republic of Yemen also expressed its position in the Security Council by abstention, and thereby did not confront the US directly. Also in the Arab League the Republic of Yemen chose to abstain, both when the Arab foreign ministers met on 3 August 1990 and condemned the invasion, and when the question of sending troops against Iraq was dealt with in the Arab League. Later the Republic of Yemen moderated its position. It stressed that it supported the Iraqi people not the regime; and in January 1990 it promoted a peace initiative in order to improve its image (The Middle East, May 1991:26).

The fear of Saudi Arabian dominance of the Peninsula had been one of the reasons for the unification. The Iraqi invasion did not threaten the Republic of Yemen but provided an opportunity to balance its neighbour. It also provided the Republic of Yemen with the opportunity to pursue another aim: to equalise the relations between the oil-rich and the poorer states, like the Republic of Yemen. This aim had also been important in the unification of the Yemen. Republic of Yemen's position of abstention was ill-received in Saudi Arabia, which regarded it as a threat to the international consensus against the invasion of Kuwait and thus as support of Iraq (Ibid.); Saudi Arabia immediately expelled about 50 Yemeni diplomats and about 300,000 Yemeni migrant workers. More followed later, and it has been estimated that up to 700,000 Yemenis had to return (The Military Balance 1992–3:126). This inflow was very hard on the Republic of Yemen economy which was not at all suited to absorbing the migrants, and which had relied on them as workers remittances (and aid from the rich Gulf states) as its main source of hard currency. It has been estimated that the Yemeni attempt to realise its newly discovered oil potential reduced but not offset the economic consequences of its Gulf conflict position (The Middle East, Dec. 1991:38). The Yemeni economy was in deep enough trouble: inflation at 100 % a year and unemployment at 35 % (Ibid.).

The increasing economic decline probably contributed to the outbreak of the civil war. It was, however, mostly a struggle about the internal control of the Republic of Yemen, reflecting the lack of political preparation for the unification (Kostiner 1996:18). In the Autumn of 1993 tensions increased between the North and the South. A new Presidential Council was to be elected, but Vice-President al Bid, a YSP member, did not attend the election meeting but remained in Aden (Keesings 39:10:39711). However, he was elected at the October 1993 meeting, which he did not attend, but he was not sworn in (Keesings 39.10.39711). His absence indicated the rising tensions.

During the following six months, a power base was build-up in the South and a rebellion was prepared. The GPC prepared the North to counter the rebellion, which eventually arose in the spring. An attempt at conciliation in February had turned out to be unsuccessful. In the beginning of May 1994, a civil war broke out between the once partitioned North and South Yemen. The civil war lead to severe human casualties and material losses. As the leader of the South, al Bid led the preparations for the rebellion against the North, which was accused of dominance and a selfishness about the recent oil riches. When the military commands were eventually split, each part still had its forces as the parallel structures had been maintained.

While the North feared a rebellion by the South, the South feared the North was planning to eliminate its influence and the initial response was an attempt to deter this by the use of force (IISS 1995:157). The North was not deterred, and general fighting broke out. The fighting took place between the armies of the formerly partitioned North and South Yemens, respectively. In late May, the South declared its secession from the Republic of Yemen and formed its own presidential council.

The South's secessionist attempt had little support. Saudi Arabia, mainly, was engaged on behalf of the South. When the civil war broke out, the Saudis were quick to side with the South in spite of its Marxist past and old wounds. Saudi Arabia tried to work for recognition and to involve the UN on the side of the weaker South. This was not surprising in the light of Saudi Arabia's positions concerning the unification and of its fear that a strengthened Yemen would pursue Yemeni claims to the Azir and the Najran oasis, but also its own specific territorial claims. Shortly after the Yemeni unification Saudi Arabia had tried to raise the question of the Saudi-Yemeni border. The line had been demarcated by the 1934 Ta'if Agreement, which despite some unclearness had been adhered to. Recently discovered Yemeni oil reserves happened to be located within the unclear zone, and as early as 1991–92 Saudi Arabia had begun a political offensive to state its claims to the zone.

The US State Department was brought into the affair when Saudi Arabia addressed American companies (Schofield, 1994:26). The US intervened, telling Saudi Arabia that its claims in the zone were not recognised (Ibid.). After the US position had been made clear, some negotiations between the Republic of Yemen and Saudi Arabia took place, and the latter seemed to abandon its renewed claims. In 1994 the Ta'if Accords expired and border clashes erupted. The parties negotiated again and the matter was settled by a prolongation of the Ta'if definitions in a Memorandum of Understanding dated February 1995 and the setting up of joint commissions (Strategic Survey 1994–95:158).

When Saudi Arabia supported the South's attempt at secession, it succeeded in raising the problem in the Security Council. A resolution was adopted which called for "an immediate cease-fire", recommended that its implementation should be "acceptable to both sides ... preferably involving countries of the region" (SC Resolution, 1994). The North, which was about to achieve total control, and had most to lose, claimed that the problem was an internal Yemeni one.

When the North achieved control at the beginning of July 1994, the South's leaders escaped to Saudi Arabia via Oman.

The Civil War went on for three months until the North's army succeeded in besieging the southern capital and the centre of the resistance, Aden. After crushing its opponent's elite and its troops, the North took control of the defeated Southern army. The South's attempts to realign again, this time with Saudi Arabia, had come too late.

After the end of the fighting, a new government was announced. It comprised more ministers (a rise from six to nine) from the al-Islah, indicating a strengthening of the political Islamic movement (Keesings 40.10.40256), present not only in the North, but which had also to some extent substituted Marxist ideology in the South.

In the subsystem, the civil war put an end to the then debate on future security cooperation in the Arabian Peninsula which had arisen after the immediate controversies of the Republic of Yemen's Gulf War position. It what been debated whether or not the Republic of Yemen should be included in the GCC, but the talks were abruptly ended by the civil war.

UNITING THE REPUBLIC

PDRY and YAR unified into the Republic of Yemen after asymmetrical changes and dealigment which also brought about subsystemic changes: both the Yemens were weakened by the ending of the bipolar rivalry, and PDRY in particular was weakened by the decline of the Soviet Union. The related symmetrical changes in the subsystem implied further weakening of both parties, primarily in relation to Saudi Arabia but also to the Northern Gulfstates. The systemic change thus provides the background for the response of the Yemeni states: the merger of 1990, and the unification is therefore considered an outcome caused by the systemic change.

When responding to its subsystemic weakening, South Yemen could not turn to any other pole in order to obtain the guarantees and backing it needed against North Yemen and Saudi Arabia. Although Saudi Arabia was supporting the South during its secessionist attempt, the Sauda Arabia could also turn into a dominant neighbour, and it had territorial claims against the South. Neither could the North rely on continuing US support, because the reason for that support, the containment of Soviet influence, had vanished. For the North, therefore, the prospects and the ability to secure its position were also weakened, not least with regard to Saudi Arabia. The merger provided North Yemen with an opportunity to strengthen itself as well as depriving Saudi Arabia of influence in the South.

The Yemeni unification broke with the bipolar patterns of conflict and cooperation in the sense that the two states, priviously belonging to different asymmetric and asymmetric camps turned into the closest form of cooperation: fusion. The mutual competition was subordinated the new challenges.

In the context of unipolarity the Yemeni weakening was serious, as they had to work hard symmetrically, and the single option implied that they could hardly rely on alternative great power support. In the case of the unifications of the Yemens, therefore, the unipolar impact was identifiable. The theoretical statements on the single option and the hard work explain the unification in the light of the subsystemic changes and redistributions of strength in addition to the asymmetrical de-alignment. The Republic of Yemen was not one of the Middle Eastern states which flocked around the US. It was also on the 'wrong' side during the Gulf conflict in 1990–1, but it did not directly oppose the US World Order. Rather, the Yemeni position was a balancing act against Saudi Arabia. The Republic of Yemen, however, carefully expressed that the unification did not represent any kind of threat to Saudi Arabia. When Saudi Arabia tried to renew its claims against the northern part of South Yemen, the The Republic of Yemen appealed to the US, which chose to support stability by not backing these demands of its ally, Saudi Arabia

Although the new Yemen is fragile, unification did take place, and the civil war in 1994 did not bring it to an end. The civil war led to internal rule by the stronger part, the North (and to some strengthening of the political islamist movements). The civil war thus completed the unification in the sense that a monopoly of violence was established in the new state. It also created the basis for another South secessionist movement, but the South's organisational and military capacity was crushed during the fighting. Saudi Arabia supported the South politically, but no external power intervened. Neither did any when the Yemens United, and the US even expressed a sympathetic attitude.

Chapter 7

Iraq's Invasion of Kuwait

Saddam Hussein ordered some 100.000 Iraqi troops into Kuwait on August 2, 1990. Kuwait was conquered militarily in a few hours and annexed after a week. When the invasion took place, Iraqi troops had already been deployed at the border, and the two countries had been arguing for months about the partition of the oil revenues, quotas and prices. Iraq accused Kuwait of selfish overproduction resulting in lower prices, and claimed that the Kuwaiti oil policy had led to heavy Iraqi losses. The al-Rumaylah issue was highlighted as Iraq claimed that "part of the surplus oil Kuwait was dumping on the world oil market was stolen from the Iraqi al-Rumaylah oil field" (Aziz 1990:22). Iraq also claimed that Kuwait (and others) had been free-riding during the 1980–88 war between Iraq and Iran. Saddam Hussein publicly declared that Iraq had fought the war on behalf of all the Southern Gulf States (and the whole Arab world) and had succeeded in checking Iran and keeping its ambitions down. In return, Iraq now expected the other states – not least Kuwait – to help restore Iraq's war damaged economy.

The Iraqi claims to Kuwait are presented in Freedman and Karsh (1993:47ff) with a reference to two key sources: The letter of July 15/ 16, 1990 which the Iraqi Vice Prime Minister and Foreign Minister Tariq Aziz sent to the General Secretary of the Arab League Chadli Klibi for distribution among the Leagues' memberstates (Aziz 1990). The letter elaborated on the issues forwarded by Saddam Hussein in his speech of the 22nd anniversary of the July 17 Revolution (Hussein July 1990). In Saddam Husseins speech Kuwait was not mentioned explicitly and specific claims or demands were not presented. The speech focused on the Iraqi situation, the Iraqi loss of 14 billions dollars a year following the low oil prices, and outlines a confrontation between Arabs and Israel. Tariq Aziz' letter comprised direct accusations against Kuwait, specific issues and calls for Arab states to lead the dissidents, Kuwait and the United Arab Emirates, into a pan-Arab direction. Specifically, Aziz stated, this could be done by raising the oil price to more than 25 dollars per barrel, to completely remission of the Iraqi debt obtained during the Iran-Iraq war, and to implement an Arab plan of compensating for Iraqi war-related losses and damages. The Iraqi claims were thus primarily of economic character except from the emphasis on the al-Rumaylah issue, and they publicly summarised a series of claims continuously promoted during the first half of 1990 behind closed doors in different Arab fora (Freedman and Karsh 1993:21ff).

The first official Iraqi announcements about the invasion said that its purpose was to change the unjust order in the Arabian Peninsula, and that Kuwait had been cheating in the negotiations on oil prices. Kuwait was annexed after one week and on August 28 declared the 19th Iraqi governorate; Iraq claimed that it had an original right to include also Kuwait and that the two areas had been artificially kept apart for years.[1] Two weeks after the invasion, the cause of the Palestinians was introduced into the Iraqi reasoning. By introducing a 'linkage' between Iraqi and Israeli occupation, Saddam Hussein tried to challenge Arab stances towards the invasion of Kuwait and win legitimacy (Freedman and Karsh 1993:102).

The Iraqi aggression was only the second major international event in the Middle East after the end of bipolarity, but it definitely fuelled the speed and extent of the Middle East transformation. When the invasion took place, the Soviet Union still existed. It had, however, retreated from its superpower position in September 1989; it was now suffering from domestic troubles and its external influence was further in decline. Immediately after the end of the Cold War, the bipolar international order was breaking down and the US had to take many decisions on a new basis. It was most intensely preoccupied by Eurasian developments. The US had to deal with a nuclearised loser in a state of dissolution and with a Europe in motion (cf. Chapter 4). The US post-Cold War policy, including the concept of the New World Order, was only at the drawing board stage. The Middle Eastern problems and issues were not exactly shelved, but American attention and priorities were elsewhere. The unification of the Yemens three months earlier had passed almost unnoticed. Ironically, the Middle East would soon become the very place of the first military trial of strength after the Cold War.

According to the statement on outcomes of systemic change (cf. Chapter 3), one should expect an increased risk of war in the aftermath of the disappearance of an international system: partly because trials of strength occur during the process of restoring balances of power; and partly because the uncertainty and the lack of transparency cause an increased risk of miscalculation, which may lead states into war. Consequently, two matters become important and become the focal points: firstly, Iraq's international position and responses to the changing international relations of strength prior to the invasion, and, secondly, Iraq's calculations regarding the risk of the US interference in the case of an invasion. Finally the unipolar impact is discussed.

IRAQ AND THE SUBSYSTEMIC BALANCE OF POWER

The Soviet retreat was a challenge to (and later became the end of) the Soviet-Iraqi alignment, and it therefore threatened to weaken the Iraqi position within the subsystem. This weakening looked likely to cause severe long-term damage to Iraq being about to restore itself after the war against Iran, and to regain its position within the subsystem. Iraq had already been exposed to the effects of the declining Soviet commitment as well as to the vanishing of external support, also from the West, related to its warfare against Iran that ended with the cease-fire.

Iraq is one of the larger and resource-rich states in the Middle East, and it has been subject to continuous superpower attention. After the Second World War the Western camp made Iraq a cornerstone in its attempt to influence the region through the Baghdad Pact. But Iraq left the Pact and became a Soviet client as the Cold War intensified and spread horizontally; its alignment with the Soviet Union was formalised by the 1972 Treaty of Friendship and Cooperation. Within the relationship the Soviet Union showed tolerance and leniency regarding Iraq's often 'independent' policy, partly because of Iraq's proximity to the Soviet Union, and partly because the other states around Iraq, except for Iraq's rival, Syria, were all attracted to the West (Golan 1990). During this phase Iraq was a prominent member of the subsystemic radical camp and regarded as hostile by the US. The close alignment with the Soviet Union lasted until the end of the 1970's, when the Iranian revolution and the Iraqi response brought about a change of the Iraqi position within the subsystem, as well as a change in the policies of the superpowers. Moscow became more careful and the US became more interested. Then the Soviet-Iraqi alignment loosened, but it did not end.

In 1980 Iraq invaded Iran. The war caused both superpowers to reconsider their relations to Iraq. The Soviet Union was uneasy about the unrest close to its borders, but acted according to two priorities: the primary one was to avoid escalation into and within the superpower relationship (Heller 1988). The US had made clear in the Carter Doctrine on the US commitment to the stability of the Gulf area that no Soviet moves there would be tolerated. The implication was, therefore, that the position of the Soviet Union towards the war and its parties became subordinate to avoiding a confrontation with the US. The second Soviet priority was that neither of the belligerents should achieve a decisive outcome, which would deeply disturb the Soviet standing in the area. If Islamic-revolutionary Iran won, the Soviet Union would face troubles with its Southwestern republics comprising major muslim populations, and if Iraq won the area would become extremely volatile within a nuclearised superpower rivalry. In the first phase of the war the Soviet Union thus pursued a 'hedging strategy' (Moltz and Ross 1990) which was also aimed at maintaining Soviet influence in the Arab world. Though the continuing unrest was a problem, it was better than a decisive outcome, or escalation. (Heller 1988). This led the Soviet Union to support Iraq throughout the war on a low scale, increasing its assistance now and then after Iranian offensives. At the same time the Soviet Union attempted not to alienate Iran, and a rapprochement with Teheran and the opportunity to halt US influence by improving Soviet-Iranian relations was not ruled out even in the light of the Soviet-Iraqi alignment (Moltz and Ross 1990). The Soviet Union was thus ready to contribute to prolonging the conflict and preventing either side from gaining a decisive victory. It supported Iraq because it appeared to be the weaker party at the end of the first years of the war, when a large scale Iranian counter-offensive was launched, especially after 1982 when the war was taken into Iraq.

The US also feared an Iranian victory. When the revolutionaries took power in Teheran, they clearly disentangled Iran from its former superpower ally, the US, but they also distanced Iran from the Soviet Union. This double disentanglement from the bipolar order paved the way for a challenge to the privileged positions of both the US and the Soviet Union as superpowers. Like the Soviet Union, the US did not opt for an Iraqi victory, which might be followed by regional turmoil and drag the superpowers into a dangerous and escalating conflict. Because of the relative weakness of Iraq and the extremist positions of Iran, the US began to support Iraq in spite of their former animosity and of continued Iraqi membership of the radical camp. From the Summer of 1981, when Iran advanced, the US government began to support Iraq, and the support continued (Hubel 1995). Among other things, the US did not prevent exports of technology to Baghdad, intelligence about Iranian deployments and potential targets was delivered to Iraq. At the same time the US did not want to push Iran towards the Soviet Union (Op.cit.:60–61), and attempted to maintain a series of options as long as the outcome was indecisive. The US tolerated the war as long as the war was weakening both parties which both were more or less hostile to the West, and did not escalate, and as long as US-allied or the oil supply were not endangered (Op.cit.:65). Regarding the central dimension, US policy was thus similar to that of its antagonist, the Soviet Union: Iraq was given most support, but a decisive victory to either party was evaded.

When applying the theoretical framework for explanation, it is not surprising that the two superpowers had similar approaches: their fear of escalation moderated their zero-summing. Iran's challenge to the bipolar order, in the light of its size and strength, also contributed to producing similar approaches, because it might be able to act in a way which prevented the United States and the Soviet Union from controlling the development of the war. As a result, the US and the Soviet Union succeeded in preventing the Iran-Iraq conflict from exacerbating their mutual competition. They did, however, also contribute to prolong the conflict, mainly through their support to Iraq. In spite of that support, Iraq had to face the probability that its attack on Iran in 1980 might turn into a defeat: Iran was bigger and stronger, and, before the attack, Iraq had apperantly overestimated the internal chaos of the revolution. In 1988 a cease-fire was agreed on terms that were very only slightly favourable to Iraq, and peace negotiations began in Geneva.

During the 1980's Iraq was preoccupied by the war, and its relations to the other states in the area were developed in order to facilitate this major task. For example, its position towards Egypt had been softened in spite of Iraq's immediate condemnation of the Camp David Accords, as had its positions towards the conservative Gulf states. The other way around, after the Iraqi attack on Iran the Southern Gulf States, especially, had passed the buck to Iraq to check Iranian ambitions; though they did support Iraq financially. The war between Iraq and Iran was dangerously close to them and caused serious concern but still, with the two major regional powers at war with each other, the Southern Gulf States had greater opportunities to act and less reason to be concerned about the potential threats against themselves from either Iraq or Iraq. For Iraq the war implied a binding of resources, damages and a growing politicial isolation within the subsystem.

The ceasefire agreement with Iran enabled Iraq to divert resources and military power to other purposes. It is important to note, however, that after the cease-fire the two states did not make progress towards a resolution of their mutual conflict and were still on collision course until the summer of 1990, when Iraq's attack on Kuwait changed the situation. To close the conflict, Iraq then offered quite large concessions to Iran, including all the minor Iraqi gains and demands from the war: Iraq acknowledged Iranian sovereignty over the eastern side of the Shatt al Arab, agreed to withdraw its remaining troops and to exchange prisoners of war, and recognised the 1975 Algiers Accord on the borders. The final agreement was announced on November 16, 1990.

The ceasefire led to a subsystemic strengthening of Iraq in the short term because of the closure of an important front. But Iraq was facing the long term prospect of a weakening if nothing was done to overcome the material costs of the war and the economic deprivation of its civilian population; and the increased cooperation between other states in the region not involved in the Gulf War might also lead to a change adverse for Iraq in the subsystemic relations of strength.

During the Iran-Iraq War several other states in the Middle East had entered into or prepared cooperation. The Southern Gulf States had set up the GCC, which remained in operation after the end of the fighting between Iran and Iraq. The countries of the North African coast were, at that time, preparing to form the Arab Maghreb Union (UMA). Iraq had to begun to manoeuvre behind the scenes. It was not easy. The other states saw Iraq as a strong, potential threat and left Iraq isolated. Iraq began to look for allies in order to break out of this isolation, and its policy towards its moderate dating from the last phase of the war was further developed neighbours (Karsh and Rautsi 1991:200–205). New problems had arisen for Iraq immediately after the cease-fire: Saddam Hussein had to restore Iraq's position in the subsystem and to end its isolation, but the possibilities for this were limited because of the others' fear of the Iraqi military capacity: in spite of the losses related to the war against Iran, Iraq had received arms and new technology. Therefore, it was still among the strongest military powers in the Middle East.

The effects of Mikhail Gorbachev's inclusion of a Soviet Middle East policy in the New Thinking had also begun to appear, and from about 1990 the impact of the New Thinking began to unfold (Moltz and Ross 1990). The policy meant serious cuts and a withdrawal from earlier Soviet positions, and led to a weakening of the Soviet proxies. The full retreat of the Soviet Union led, quite simply, to a regional reshuffling of strength. Within a subsystem, such a reshuffling leads to an adjustment of the balance of power. The apparently emerging power vacuum – and the inability of either Syria or Egypt to fill the vacuum – as well as as the Iraqi problems and isolation, provided the background for the Iraqi moves.

THE IRAQI RESPONSE

How did Iraq respond to the new situation and how did it perceive the international political context? Iraq was very active between 1988 and 1990; the government made intense diplomatic efforts. One theme about the post-Cold War world permeated Iraqi actions and was present in speeches and declarations: that dominance by the US and the US proxies was threatening the Arab World. The Iraqi thesis was presented from Baghdad, and at successive Arab summits and meetings in the recently formed Arab Cooperation Council (ACC), the main fora chosen by Iraq.

During the first half of the period Iraqi actions were based on Iraq's expressed understanding of itself as a kind of an Arab leader. The Iraqi aspiration was not only wishful thinking but was supported by Iraq's military capability and Iraq being on guard regarding regional non-Arab threats. Whatever the perceptions and motives, however, it is clear that Iraq relied on an extrovert, though not offensive, strategy between 1988 and February 1990. Iraq's diplomatic activity during 1989 included the formation of the ACC and the conclusion of non-aggression treaties with Saudi Arabia and Bahrain. Iraq was also promoting a non-radical, cooperative policy, which included advocacy of the full return of Egypt into the Arab League framework. Iraq found itself in confrontation only with Syria, e.g. at the Arab League summit in Casablanca in November, 1989, but this did not affect its general reputation as becoming a more moderate state, because Syria had also belonged to radical camp.

In February 1989, Iraq and its closest partner, Jordan, took the initiative to forming a third regional block, the ACC. Besides Iraq and Jordan, the two other ACC member states were Yemen[2] and Egypt. By pooling their assets they might all be able to enhance their regional positions. For Iraq, the formation of the ACC was a means of ending its isolation (Karsh and Rautsi 1991:200–5). It also provided Iraq with some backing against a potentially rebuilt Iran, it was a way of isolating Syria and of gathering influence against the richer countries' GCC (Heikal 1993: Ch.7). Finally, Iraq saw the ACC as in instrument in the promotion of the Palestinian cause (Karsh and Rautsi 1991:200). Iraqi interests in promoting the ACC were obvious: by unifying those countries left over from the first round of grouping, Iraq could increase its ability to counter all its potential enemies and competitors, Iran, Syria, Israel and the Southern Gulf States. Egypt had its vast manpower and central position, but because it was suffering from severe economic problems, Iraq did not fear Egyptian dominance within the cooperative framework (Heikal 1993:120–1).

Iraq's moves, not least in the ACC initiative, were carefully watched by its neighbours. In spite of Saudi Arabia's discontent with Yemeni membership, the ACC was considered by the other Arab states to reflect a continuation of the Iraqi cooperative strategy, a cessation of its radicalness, and a willingness to relate to the moderate camp (Bulloch and Morris 1991:86). The signing of the Saudi-Iraqi treaty on mutual non-aggression one month later, though it seemed to reflect some Saudi uneasiness, also demonstrated that the Iraqi diplomacy had been persuasive.

Iraq's only political clash during 1989 was with Syria, and inspired by Syria's rival Ba'th Party. Iraq was concerned about its relations with Syria. The common Soviet guarantee and their shared radicalness had so far prevented Iraqi-Syrian conflicts. But now that the relationship was freed from the constraints of this guarantee, it needed Iraqi attention. At the Arab summit in Casablanca in 1989 animosity between the two states was openly expressed. Syria and Egypt had a rapprochement, precisely one of Iraq's fears and a reason for giving priority to the formation of the ACC. And a tough debate took place on the Lebanese Civil War, with Syria supporting the government side and Iraq supporting General Aoun's Christian militia. Later, Syria boycotted the May 1990 summit in Baghdad to show its disagreement with the main subject on the agenda which had been chosen by Iraq: 'Threats to Arab National Security', in particular the struggle against Zionism (Heikal 1993:200–15). In the light of its weak position, this was not the time for Syria to confront Israel.

Although the other Arab states seemed to welcome Iraq's moderate and integrative policy, they did not give up their own interests, and they were concerned about the oil issue. None of the oil-rich countries seemed to be willing to pay back Iraq for the costs of the war against Iran by changing their oil policies or facilitate Iraq's reconstruction by any other means. Nor did they show any willingness to accept any kind of Iraqi leadership of the Arab World or parts of it. It became obvious that Iraq's policy was not advancing its aims, and from the beginning of 1990 Iraq changed its strategy.

The unsuccessful 1989 integrative strategy was replaced by an offensive one, which emphasised division: Iraq's signals became more confrontational, not only towards the extra-Arab world but also towards the oil rich Arab states. Iraq offered to head one part of the Arab world against the other, a division defined by oil wealth and/or pro-US positions.

The changed Iraqi approach also led to a clearer and more direct focus on the oil policy. This was no longer considered an issue to be solved in the spirit of cooperation. Iraq now claimed the Southern Gulf States were ignoring its past efforts against Iran, and probably assessed that it was unlikely that they would willingly give any compensation on the scale wanted by Iraq.

The first indication of the new 'aggravated strategy' emerged at the ACC's Amman meeting in February 1990. Iraq strongly attacked the US. Egypt and Jordan tried to compensate by making long and mild speeches on the American connection, and President Mubarak stressed the importance of continued US commitment to the region. Iraq criticised US control of the oil market – an indirect attack at the Southern Gulf States, with which Iraq had so far attempted to improve relations while emphazising Iraqi claims about their oil policies. Iraq also pointed to the strength of the US and the danger it presented to Arab identity and integrity.

On April 2, 1990 Saddam Hussein made his well-known speech warning Israel against any move (FBIS-NES-90–064, 030490:32–35), and which was interpreted as a threat of a subsequent retaliation. The speech, although ambiguous and complex, included further signals. Iraq not only signalled strength and the will to strike, but it was also emphazised that this was a defensive option, an intention to retaliate only if attacked by Israel: "By God, we will make fire eat up half of Israel if it tried against Iraq" (Op.cit.:35). Saddam Hussein stressed that Iraq was not developing nuclear weapons, thus signalling that Iraq did not invite any preventive or preemptive strikes (like Israel's 1981 attack on the Tammuz nuclear plant in Osirak), but he also stressed that Iraq already had the chemical capability to retaliate. Finally, he said that Iraq should not be considered a threat; his speech included an assurance that Iraq would not attack anyone. The speech reflected the Iraqi fear of US and US proxy dominance, but it also showed that Iraq would resist this dominance from a position of strength ("Give us a strong back, not a light weight"). Possibly, Iraq attempted to boost confidence among the ACC memberstates and the internal oppositions in the US affiliated Arab states, in Iraq's ability to head the 'real' Arabs, and to promote the Palestinian cause and the unresolved post-1967 issues by antogonizing Israel.[3]

One month later, in May 1990, Iraq hosted the Baghdad summit of the Arab League. The title of the summit was 'Threats to Arab National Security'. One of the main themes was the Israeli threat; another was the threat of the West against the Arab world; and a third was the development of the region. From the Iraqi point of view, the third theme covered economic equalisation between the rich Southern Gulf States and less wealthy Arab states.[4] Iraq was, however, rather isolated at the summit: only the PLO and Jordan supported central Iraqi positions. After the Baghdad summit Iraq totally gave up any lingering remnants of the integrative and cooperative strategy. Its aggravated strategy even turned into an offensive position. Throughout the change, however, the Iraqi expression of how to understand the post-Cold War Middle Eastern situation was maintained.

Firstly, clear and explicit references to the new global situation and the changed relations of strength were repeatedly made. The US was labelled the only superpower: 'The US has emerged in a superior position in international politics' on the ACC Amman meeting February, 1990 (Dannreuther 1992:14). This view was elaborated at the Baghdad summit.

Secondly, the new US position had two consequences for the Middle East: 'US control of the oil market' (the Amman summit, February 1990; Cooley 1991:126), and a strengthening of Western proxies. The states which had once depended on Soviet support and guarantees were now weakened vis-à-vis the pro-Western states, and the most important obstacle to further US influence had gone because of the Soviet decline. Saddam Hussein declared that Iraq feared that US proxies intended to benefit. Iraq pointed especially to Israel but also to the oil-rich Gulf states.

Thirdly, Iraq expressed the fear that the US would have a free hand in the absence of the Soviet power and inhibit Arab identity and integrity. Saddam Hussein concluded that Western progress represented a threat to Iraq. The US might use Israel to halt the Iraqi missile programme and damage Iraqi military capacity (Dannreuther

1992:13). The fear was expressed when Saddam Hussein warned Israel directly against any action in April 1990.

The three changes would obstruct or slow down the postwar reconstruction of Iraq. Saddam Hussein stressed that the position of oil-rich states in the Gulf region now were improved; these moderate Gulf states had formerly been checked by the radical camp, now in dissolution because of the weakening of each of the former Soviet proxies, most notably Syria. Iraq was seriously concerned by the prospect of the Gulf States' oil policy going unchallenged; their preferences for low prices and large quotas contradicted the Iraqi wish for high prices of the crude oil to provide revenue for Iraq's reconstruction.

In summary, Iraq appeared to recognize the following three related elements to characterize the post 1989 Middle East:

- The US was the only superpower, which meant:
- A weakening of the radical camp and a strengthening of US allies, respectively, in the region; and,
- That the new relations of strength thus might bring about intolerable benefits to Iraq's regional competitors and adversaries, most notably Israel and the rich oil states, which would obstruct Iraq's reconstruction.

Iraq, as shown, anticipated a dominant US position following the end of the Cold War. US interests, however, were seen as being pursued through US regional aligments. The interests and regional connections were assessed to be unchanged. The indications points at an Iraqi perception of a continuation of the pre-1989 regional patterns only affected by the Soviet disengagement and thus halved, and by the end of superpower rivalry: the US allies then would gain while the former Soviet client states would be dramatically weakened.

Iraq's strategy, now aggravated, was still unsuccessful. But no one seemed to regard Iraq as an immediate threat. Iraq, nonetheless, had an incentive and an opportunity to develop an even more confrontational new strategy, as the problems were still there and very little had been achieved so far. It did so during Spring 1990, drawing on its understanding of the international environment and of its own position. That appreciation remained basically unchanged as far as it concerned the US position, Iraqi aims and the relationship with the other Arab States, but Iraq was now changing its methods. Iraq became increasingly direct and tough in its policy and claims toward the Southern Gulf States concerning the oil issue. Meanwhile it was building up the military threat against Kuwait. This took place in light of a deteriorating relationship with the US at the rhetorical level, but the Iraqi leadership apparently still calculated with US leniency.

The ACC, which had originally been seen by Iraq as an instrument to break its isolation, was now being exploited during the military build of a military threat against Kuwait. The ACC was used as a forum for promoting Iraqi claims against Kuwait. At the Amman summit in February 1990, Saddam Hussein had put forward Iraq's claims and asked the ACC co-leaders, King Hussein and President Mubarak, to communicate them to the Gulf States (Karsh and Rautsi 1991a:21). Another Iraqi initiative was the establishment, at the Baghdad summit in 1989, of a close link to the PLO. Iraq and the PLO lacked friends and opportunities to pursue their interests; the PLO had also suffered from the Soviet retreat from the region. It was part of Mikhail Gorbachev's reorganisation of the Soviet Union's regional policy to attempt to cooperate with the US, and the PLO might become a loser in such a game. Iraq offered to lead Arab backing of the Palestinian cause, and attempted to benefit from the weak position of the PLO to get more influence within the Organisation by means of being the Arab state willing to support the PLO and promote its political cause. Putting emphasis on the Palestinian problem held additional potential political benefits for Iraq. If the Arab states within the ACC were further committed to the Palestinians, Iraq might count on its fellow Arab states to be forced into supporting an invasion by their domestic oppositions in favour of the Palestinian cause. If this was the case, at least three Arab states could be pacified when Iraq took action.

What turned out to be the actual, positive result of the ACC 'cover' was, from the Iraqi perspective, that the moderate nature of the ACC in terms of the membership of the pro-Western states of Jordan's and Egypt did contribute to calm to outside world prior to the invasion. Even though Iraq's efforts in 1989 regarding the formation of the ACC did not fulfil Iraq's purpose of breaking out of isolation, the ACC served to convince not least the US that Iraq should not be antagonised. The ACC and other Iraqi political initiatives thereby became part of preparing the ground for later Iraqi actions.

Iraq had become politically isolated within the subsystem during the war against Iran although Saudi Arabia, Kuwait, and the Emirates had provided Iraq with substantial financial contributions in order to secure the Iraqi ability to resist Iranian advance. At the same time, however, the Southern Gulf States had benefitted from the Iraqi political and military preoccupation with the war although the war was fought dangerously near to them and did cause concern. As long as neither of the two big Gulf States seemed to be winning, the war had been quite satisfactory from the point of view of the other states: as long as Iraq and Iran were fighting and weakening each other, the other states did need to worry too much about them. Now the two were back on the scene after the war, and the regional distribution of power had changed. They chose two different ways of restoring their positions.

Iran turned inwards and began to repair the societal damages of the war (Amirahmadhi 1991) and the first years of 'radical fundamentalism' were replaced by 'realistic Islam' (Ramazani 1991). Iraq was, on the other hand, inclined to an externally based strategy to secure its position. Saddam Hussein's wish to improve Iraq's international position was not surprising. Economically, Iraq was substantially weakened at the turn of the decade. Eight years of war against Iran had drained the state of resources, domestic affairs had been neglected, and the task of restoring the country was enormous. Simultaneously, international developments in oil production and price had been to Iraq's disadvantage, and oil came close to being its only source of income, amounting to about 95 % of its foreign exchange earnings. The economic and political situation in Iraq had reached the lowest point, only the military capability was still an asset. Worse still, the prospects for improvement were close to zero given the Soviet retreat. The subsystemic relations of strength which followed did not favour Iraq and limited its options for restoring its position. A power vacuum followed the Soviet retreat, and Iraq feared that US allies would fill it, if they were not countered; but no individual state was ready to take the lead in doing so.

These factors appear to be the background for the Iraqi pressure on Kuwait and the Iraqi decision to stage a military operation against Kuwait. The invasion became a possibility because it seemed that the potential gains were certainly high, while the costs and risks were modest. From the Iraqi point of view, the potential gains from a successful invasion would be that it could ignore its vast debt to Kuwait, profit from Kuwait's substantial and high quality oil reserves, and could expand its territory to include strategic entry into the Persian Gulf. Control of Kuwaiti oil reserves would also bring Iraq right into the centre of the decision-making process on the oil production levels and prices. The effect would be a generally improved position in the region: who would dare to stand up against an expanded Iraq which had shown its capacity and will to pursue its interests by military means? Against the possible gains were the risks. Iraq would risk a confrontation with the superpower which would probably lead to another Iraqi defeat. Given the probability of defeat in such a confrontation, the basic Iraqi calculation had to be one about the likelihood of a US intervention. The calculations are dealt with below; here it suffices to say that an external intervention was the only immediate risk to Iraq, given the subsystemic arrangement and Iraqi military capacity – Iraq had the capacity to invade and occupy. It has been estimated that Iraq had a standing army of at least 800,000 troops, the majority with combat experience from the Iranian front, and sufficient materiel, but of a kind which was suited, mainly, to land operations. Iraq had a regionally strong but globally poor air capacity and an inferior naval capacity. Kuwait had no effective deterrent capacity on its own nor with regional partners. Kuwait was a member of the GCC, but the member states were all military weak, the strongest being Saudi Arabia. The GCC had no real great power within its ranks; although it had good relations with the US, there were no formal links, and the GCC itself was inferior to Iraq in terms of military capabilities. Consequently, the deterrent effect was absent. Besides, the GCC countries had been suffering from internal disputes after the end of the Iran-Iraq War (Hunter 1991). Kuwait's situation in the spring of 1990 was characterised, therefore, by the lack of a deterrent capacity and insufficient alliances in order to prevent aggression.

Before the crisis escalated into armed conflict, Kuwait and Iraq had been negotiating over the oil dispute. The Iraqi demands were: remission of its debt to Kuwait, a cut in Kuwaiti oil production to raise prices to at least 25 dollars per barrel, and agreement to exploit two Kuwaiti oil fields. The Kuwaiti answer was no; none of the Iraqi demands were to be met. The Al Sabah government did not react as if Iraq was seriously considering a military attack. Though it was clear that Iraq sincerely wanted Kuwait to change its oil policy, Kuwait appeared to perceive Iraq to be bluffing militarily even when it deployed the troops on the border, or to fear that a favourable approach to the Iraqi demands would only lead to further demands.[5] Kuwait maintained its positions and a firm stance in the negotiations. As Iraq could not obtain any concessions by way of bargaining, the troops were ordered to go ahead. The Iraqi military might was far superior and the invasion was carefully planned: Kuwait was taken overnight.

THE CALCULATIONS

It is evident that Iraq had the capacity to invade and control Kuwait, the motives for doing so, and an immediate reason: the rejection of its demands in the negotiations. Less evident is why Iraq calculated on the presence of an additional but necessary condition: the opportunity to act without interference from external powers. Kuwait belonged to the American camp, albeit not in terms of having formal seucrity guarantees, and it had been protected a few years earlier by the reflagging of its oil tankers under the US flag. The reflagging, however, had only been obtained after several difficulties and Kuwaiti applications to the Soviet Union.

All the evidence points to an Iraqi miscalculation of the likelihood, as well as of the risk, of foreign interference. When Iraq decided to send its troops across the Kuwaiti border, its decision was probably based on a conviction that the US would take a neutral stand and not interfere in internal Arab affairs. Saddam Hussein told US Ambasador Glaspie during their talks late in July that the US would not accept the scale of losses (ten thousand men a day) that Iraq would in such a conflict. That such Iraqi calculations and considerations took place is shown by Freedman and Karsh (1993:50–60). The US had sent confusing signals during the crisis before the invasion and had tried appease as well as to threaten Iraq (Op.cit.:58), and this was later revealed in the Congressional hearings on the talks between Ambasador Glaspie and Saddam Hussein, too.

That Iraq had counted on appeasement being the dominant aspect was made clear during the post-war hearings in the US Congress which revealed the content of the meetings between the US Ambassador and Saddam Hussein during the escalation of the conflict in the course of July 1990. The evidence points to an Iraqi conviction of US leniency. In support of this interpretation of the Iraqi conviction, two facts should be emphasised: the US had forwarded a 'no-position' stand on the Iraq-Kuwait dispute at the meeting between Saddam Hussein and Ambassador Glaspie on July 25, 1990, and had even expressed satisfaction with the preferred Iraqi oil price (Cooley 1991: 127–8). That is, the Iraqi demands appeared fair enough to the US diplomat while she still conveyed a message of US restraint from interfering. The assurances broadcasted in July, made by Assistant Secretary of State for Middle East Affairs, John Kelly, that the Southern Gulf States and the US had no formal defence treaties were also strong signals of appeasement to Iraq (Ibid.).

Furthermore, four indirect circumstances were probably supporting Iraq's conviction. Firstly, the obvious way in which the US was preoccupied in Europe with the German reunification and the dissolution of the Soviet empire provided grounds for doubt that the US could cope with another major problem. Secondly, the US rapprochement to Iraq during the Iraq-Iran war was mistakenly projected onto the new situation. Iraq counted on American geopolitical interests, and an earlier idea about moderating Iraqi behaviour by economic and diplomatic means, converting into acceptance in practice of Iraq's actions (Trainor 1992:198). Thirdly, as the two Yemens unified, the only external reactions had been relatively insignificant declarations of approval. It seemed, therefore, as if the end of the superpower rivalry had left regional matters to the region. Fourthly, the Iraqi communication of its perception of the post-Cold War order was that US proxies would gain but that the US was losing interest in the Middle East in general, and the fact that the Kuwaiti relationship to the US was flawed.

As for the reaction of other Arab states on an invasion, there seem to have been a certain optimism in Baghdad. Firstly, Iraq probably counted on a successful invasion which would have exceeded any Arab reaction. Secondly, it was likely that Iraq's fellow Arabs would not to support any great power intervention but emphasize Arab integrity. Thirdly, Iraq was preparing to divide the potential critics through the formation of the ACC. Altogether, Saddam Hussein had reasons to expect only verbal protests from only some of the Arab states (Mylroie 1993:125[6]). With the US expected to remain neutral, the path appeared to be open, and the Iraqi order to invade Kuwait was issued. After the invasion it was revealed that Iraq had miscalculated American incentives to react and interfere.

IRAQ AND THE EMERGENCE OF UNIPOLARITY

The Iraqi invasion of Kuwait was considered above in the light of the theoretical statements on the effects of systemic change leading to realignment as well as in the light of Iraq's changed subsystemic relations of strength and the risk of misperception.

Iraq's relations to the Soviet Union had loosened, the Soviet Union's status as a guarantor ceased to exist, and its support to Iraq was reduced (bringing about de-alignment); this represented a break with bipolar patterns. As a result, Iraq's position in the subsystem was weakened, and a power vacuum appeared as the Soviet Union retreated.

Iraq's first response consisted of a cooperative strategy and the creation of the ACC. Both efforts turned out to be unsuccessful as far as the Iraqi objectives were concerned. Instead, Iraq chose to rely on a gradually more offensive strategy which eventually led to the invasion of Kuwait. The potential gains from the invasion and Iraq's isolation within the subsystem provided the background for the invasion. Iraq's understanding of the changed relations of strength, the fear that US hegemony and that of its proxies would fill the power vacuum left by the Soviet Union, paved the way. Iraq's military capacity made the invasion an option.

The statement on the outcomes of systemic transformation provides the explanation of why the risk of Iraqi invasion was present, not least because of the inclination to miscalculate international relations. The invasion of Kuwait was apparently perceived to be a solution to the Iraqi problemes, and the risk of American interference in the regional dispute was miscalculated. It was demonstrated above that there are strong indications that the calculation was based on an assessment of US post-Cold war priorities, alignment policy and signals which recognized the US position as the only superpower but that this implied, only, a strengthening of US allies in the region alongside the declining direct superpower attention. Saddam Hussein referred to these changes in many important speeches. However, while this added to the Iraqi problems, the important thing concerning the Iraqi response was that Iraq counted on non-interference. As it became obvious later, such a calculation of the risk of American interference and of the emergence of a superpower-free region was erroneous.

It is thus clear that the systemic change of 1989 from bipolarity into unipolarity brought about an expected outcom, one of war, in the case of Iraq's invasion of Kuwait, and a connection between miscalculation and changed relations of strength have been demonstrated. The occurrence of something new took place in case of the belligerent action.

With respect to a break with bipolar patterns the invasion points at the Iraqi dealignment from the Soviet Union, the subsystemic realignments and the invasion itself. Arab countries had not attempted to conquer each other across the camps, and although Iraq had previously made claims to Kuwait it had not taken any military measures during bipolarity.[7]

Unipolarity had not been manifested, and the Iraqi aggression against Kuwait took place in the blur of the transformation period.

However, the single option indeed framed the Iraqi moves in the absence of Iraq's loss of its former asymmetrical alignment and the rivalry between the US and the Soviet Union. The invasion also pointed to the presence of the hard work condition. Iraq acted in accordance with the expected need of states to care for their international position, i.e., security, regionally and at a ground of increased regional activity. It is not surprising that the unipolar impact of flocking was absent as the US position had still not been manifested. At that time, it was not an issue.

The Iraqi problems concerning obtaining a renewed role within the subsystem and strengthening its position were not solved by means of the invasion. After the invasion, the annexation of Kuwait lead to a trial of strength which clarified and manifested 'the US World Order' and its consequences for the Middle East. Thoughout the 1990'es, however, Iraq and the US remained at a course of collision, and Iraq's problems domestically as well as internationally became even worse as a result of the unsuccessful war against the international coalition, and the UN-sanctions imposed after the conclusion of operation Desert Storm. Iraq tried continuously to halt the sanctions, and this led to more crises with a culmination in the winther 1997–98. The Gulf war and the crises are dealt with in Chapter 10.

Chapter 8

The Formation of the International Coalition

The first US reaction to the Iraqi invasion was clear: its main message to Iraq was that it had to withdraw; whether the US would use military, or political and economic means to achieve this was less clear. The US assumed leadership and began to organise Operation Desert Shield, which included a projection of US forces into the area. It also led the build up of a broad international Coalition against Iraq under the United Nations. The declared immediate US immediate purpose was to deter and prevent Iraq from further aggression in the area, against Saudi Arabia; and to put strong pressure on Iraq to make it withdraw from Kuwait, mainly through the US-proposed and UN-approved sanctions.

In the first week after the invasion, and a few days after the Desert Shield initiative, President Bush declared that the overall US objective 'is to see Saddam Hussein get out' and 'to have the rightful regime of Kuwait back in place'.[1] He stressed, however, that the US mission was 'wholly defensive'. On the same day, 8 August 1990, Saddam Hussein declared that Iraq had annexed Kuwait as its 19th govenorate. Thereafter, US efforts to bring about international support for its objectives intensified.

The Coalition was put together during early autumn 1990 under clear and explicit US leadership. A total of at least 36 countries joined,[2] and the group included former Soviet allies and clients, pro-US states, and some which had once been affiliated to the Non-Aligned Movement. Members of the military force which the Coalition would assemble, the Multilateral Force (MLF), would include democracies, dictatorships, rich and poor countries and representatives from all continents, even some volunteers from the Afghan Mujahedin movement. Amongst those allied against Iraq were a number of Arab states: Morocco, Egypt, Syria, Saudi Arabia, Oman, Bahrain, Qatar, the United Arab Emirates and, of course, Kuwait, represented by the exiled

Al Sabah government. This broad gathering represented a break with the bipolar patterns, symmetrical as well as asymmetrical, not least as far as the Middle East subsystem was concerned.

The Arab participation was extensive and remarkable for other reasons, too. Firstly, because the once loyal Soviet ally and radical state, Syria, was in the Coalition. Secondly, because the major Arab countries responded positively and publicly in spite of the presence, in their countries, of anti-imperialist and anti-American movements. There was a fear that these governments might withdraw from the Coalition to avoid being overthrown for their stance alongside the US. But none of the Arab states left the Coalition and eventually, some of them even participated in Operation Desert Storm, putting their reputations and the Arab brotherhood at risk, and exposing themselves to internal tensions. Their decisions to join the Coalition thus implied the beginning of a new and public relationship to the US – compared to that in the bipolar state of affairs.

Although several of the participating Arab states had tacitly aligned with the US as early as the end of the 1950'es, the new relationship broke with the content of the bipolar relationship in other important ways. Before, they had been reluctant to see any foreign (including US) troops on their soil; they had avoided to have US bases; and the mutual security framework of the Southern Gulf States, the Gulf Cooperation Council (GCC), did not have any formal links to the US, in spite of strong bonds (Acharya 1992).[3] Although strongly inclined to the West, they had so far carefully avoided too open and direct commitments.

Unlike the Southern Gulf States in the GCC, Syria had been a Soviet proxy, and a radical state in the sense that it epoused Arab socialism and belonged the various rejectionist fronts against Israel. Syrian participation was the most obvious and striking break with bipolar patterns.

The Arab states apperantly saw no alternative but to act as they did. They could not agree on how to conduct a military intervention against Iraq. This pointed to the need for a great power around which to 'flock'. They could not ask the Soviet Union, disengaged and preoccupied by domestic troubles, and since they could neither force Iraq back on their own, they could only resort to the 'single option' of the US. Thus their participation is explained by the theoretical statements on flocking, and on the single option. Realignment paved the way: the options of the major Arab states were halved, and former Soviet allies – like Syria – had a new offer.

The flocking had advantages in addition to being the only option. A great power can provide definitive pressure from 'above'; and encouraging a great power's efforts against aggression could serve as long term protection for the other (smaller) states. The other states in turn might later be rewarded for their support by the great power(s). When affiliating to the superpower, the other states were also able to balance their power or to opt for alternative gains. This behaviour is to be expected across different international systems, even though the options and limitations differ depending on the specific structure of the given system. The functioning of the subsystem is, as stated in Chapter 3, depending on the dynamics of the international system.

The unipole, on the other hand, responds to challenges to its vital interests and to conflicts, which may affect a major part of interstate life and the community. This dynamic forms the basis of its assessment of potential asymmetrical allies. Given the recent systemic transformation, the US unipole was expected to reassess its allies according to its now different role and aims. Management also includes to take conflicts and to react when important international norms are broken.

Analytically, this approach leads to two points of focus at the strategical level concerning the 'followers' and the 'leader' (called so according to Cooper et. al. (1991)). The first is the strategic options and actions of the 'followers': what could they hope to gain by following, and how did they change their strategies in order to join? The second is the behaviour of the leader in terms of unipolar management: what kind of interests led the to US respond to a crisis in an area, from where its antagonistic adversary had already departed?

THE PARTICIPATION

At the most general level Iraq's conquest and annexation of Kuwait brought about a regional redistribution of relative strength in favour of Iraq: Iraq added to its own the territory, oil wells and wealth of Kuwait, while other states in the region were subject to no such changes (Kuwait apart, of course). The notion about the balancing of power leads to the expectation that the other states will counter (the strengthened) Iraq. This was obviously what the majority of states did. Christensen and Snyder (1990) have pointed to the ever present possibility that each state will either pass the buck or pursue a 'chain gang' strategy when the balancing of power takes place.[4] Some states did pass the buck, but the core group formed a chain gang with the US. No state declared formal support for Iraq, although Jordan (and other geographically more remote Arab states like the Republic of Yemen chose to remain neutral and work for an 'Arab solution'.

With respect to the behaviour of the members of the coalition, it has been shown that almost all the participating states in the Middle East adhered to, in analytical terms, a balancing behaviour (Garnham 1991) within the emerging, unipolar framework. The particular form of power-balancing-power in the case of Iraq's conquest of Kuwait was characterized by the fact that the conditions in which it was done had changed: the Arab states did not, as is usually the case, balance in regional terms alone, but this time the majority also flocked around the only superpower available.

Traditionally Syria has opposed Iraq. Their respective Baa'th parties rival; they have pursued overlapping interests (the use of the Euphrates River, the struggle in Lebanon); and Syria feared that Iraq was trying to succeed Egypt as the leading Arab state (a fear which also led Syria to support Iran during the 1980–8 War, even though it angered some of Syria's other, economic, supporters on the Arabian Peninsula). Iraqi aggression brought about a fear in Syria that Iraq was about to achieve such a leadership. Syria had not in the least been soothed by Iraq's positions at the preceding summits (see Chapter 7).

After the Soviet retreat, Syria was extremely vulnerable in case of an improvement in Iraq's position; Syria no longer had any superpower backing and its own possibilities had been weakened by the cuts in Soviet military assistance, weaponry, technology and advice. Iraq, in contrast, had built up its military capacity during the war against Iran with external support although it also suffered from the decline of Soviet backing. For Syria, the Coalition thus appeared to be a useful instrument against its strong neighbour, and its participation reflected an act of balancing.

When the invasion took place, Syria was in a difficult subsystemic position. Iraqi efforts to break out of isolation after the war against Iran had included the formation of the ACC. This transmitted the isolation to Syria, which then became the only major, and centrally situated, Arab power not belonging to any of the blocs. This, its loss of the Soviet backing and chronic lack of oil, meant that Syria's situation had become very difficult. These troubles had been anticipated, especially during the second half of the 1980's; Syria had reduced its ambitions, and the dream of Greater Syria had been given up (Ajami 1992:142). Syria was, therefore, too weak to fill the power vacuum or to pursue any adventurous aims.

By joining the Coalition and the US, Syria could hope for some kind of new superpower backing at to come at acceptable terms with the US. Having been on a collision course, Syria now had the opportunity to get on better terms with the US. Besides, cooperation with the US could pave the way for loans and a lifting of the economic sanction which had followed Syria's black-listing for supporting terrorism. For its part, Syria could add to the American project of gathering the coalition: Syria could add its Arab-Islamic image, considered to be very important by Saudi Arabia and the US, to the Coalition. For the US that image would be important in securing general credibility in dealing with the whole world rather than a part of it as opposed to bipolarity. It was important to the US that the coalition did not appear as kind of anti-Arab neo-imperialism.

Syria was surprisingly quick to join the Coalition, and the first Syrian troops arrived in Saudi Arabia as part of the operation Desert Shield on 21 August 1990. President Hafiz Asad was careful when giving the reasons for joining the coalition. He declared that Syria had sent troops for specific reasons: the fulfilment of a promise to King Fahd of territorial defence, to protect holy places, as security against the fragmentation of the Arab world, and as an alternative to foreign troops in the Gulf (Lesch 1991:42).

In the Western camp it was feared that the Syrian shift might be too dramatic, and that internal opposition in Syria would prevent it from joining the Coalition properly or might later force it out. This did not happen, and President Asad publicly explained the Syrian reason for joining the Multilateral Force (MLF) and for accepting US presence in the area: "But the issue is not that of foreign troops ... the problem is the occupation of Kuwait" (quoted from Freedman and Karsh 1993:97).

The decision to join the MLF was by no means a popular one and the opposition to the Asad leadership was considerably strengthened. There were large pro-Iraqi demonstrations, especially in the Eastern part of Syria (Joffe 1993:188). This did not affect the new Syrian course, however; and Syria remained a loyal member of the coalition throughout the conflict (see Chapter 9).

The unipolar order had left Syria with one choice, which it immediately opted for, even though it was not facing any direct or urgent threat from Iraq. Syria flocked and affiliated to the superpower, which it had formerly opposed, and it joined its subsystemic, moderate (now former) adversaries against its former co-radical, Iraq.

Egypt had been a stable member of the Western camp since the Camp David Accords in 1978. It is less surprising, therefore, that Egypt chose to join the Coalition – even though it was also a member of the ACC. However, two circumstances make the Egyptian choice less obvious than it immediately appears. Firstly, political islam had gained ground in the domestic political arena. Though the Muslim Brotherhood had changed its strategy in favour of moderation and had thereby become a more acceptable choice for many non-extreme Egyptians, who were dissatisfied with the results achieved under President Mubarak, militant Islamic groups had emerged and were able to attract the radical opposition. Political Islam – highly anti-American – was thus going forwards. This development was reflected in demonstrations, as in Syria, against Egyptian participation in the Coalition; the anti-Mubarak camps profited politically. Secondly, Egypt was in a better position than Syria to care for its own interests: partly because of a generally stronger position, and partly because Egyptian interests to some extent overlapped with those of Iraq. Iraqi expansion was not necessarily a negative development for Egypt which had given up ambitions of Arab leadership for the foreseeable future; and it could have benefitted from (Iraqi) pressure on the oil states in the Southern Gulf region – this had been part of the Egyptian reasoning for joining the ACC in 1989 (Heikal 1993). However, Egyptian interests strongly favoured a stable environment in which to resolve its serious economic problems, and any considerable strengthening of Iraq would have destabilised that environment.

Shortly after the formation of the ACC, Iraqi rhetoric became sharper. Saddam Hussein gave speeches against the US in an offensive style, and President Mubarak had tried to neutralise them. At the ACC summit in Amman in February 1990, President Mubarak felt the need to distance himself from Iraqi criticism of the US, and he stressed the necessity of US engagement in Middle Eastern peace (Heikal 1993:156–7). The ACC membership was soon disregarded by Iraq after the invasion. Egypt felt betrayed and exploited by Iraq: it seemed that the ACC had been held together by Egypt while Iraq prepared the invasion; and that Iraq had used the ACC to borrow the credibility of a moderate state.

These circumstances provided Egypt with an incentive to 'pass the buck' and let other states perform the balancing. On the contrary, however, it joined the Coalition at an early stage. Egypt was still dependent on US commitment to peace and preferred US engagement in the area to Iraqi leadership of it, and its overall needs favoured external rest and internal development. It needed, quite simply, continuous superpower backing for the foreseeable future. By joining the Coalition, Egypt showed the US that it was a credible ally in a volatile region and thereby still worth the effort. In return, the US showed that Egypt could count on the benefits of future superpower backing. Besides, Egypt made palpable gains by joining. It received major economic transfers from the US and the possibility of more. In spite of the domestic obstacles and the subsystemic problems, Egypt decided quickly that it would ally the US and contribute to US-led initiatives.

Did Egypt pursue a strategy of balancing? Yes: although it might have opted for another balancing strategy *vis-à-vis* the Gulf states, it balanced Iraq and thereby contributed to maintain the regional *status quo*, which it agreed with at the time. Egypt was not prepared to pick up its old, ambitious role, but it would not let Iraq have the leadership either.

West of Egypt only Morocco joined the Coalition. The Moroccan story is similar to that of Egypt and Syria in that domestic troubles followed the decision to join. Morocco, because of its geographical remoteness from the conflict, was not threatened by Iraq at all, and would hardly have suffered any material or political losses by a successful Iraqi annexation of Kuwait. Morocco, however, sought and obtained the available superpower backing against its neighbour Algeria. A US appreciation of decisive Moroccan control of Western Sahara, disputed by Algeria, Libya and the Western Saharan Polisario, would be an asset. The question of Western Sahara had been politicised, albeit to a low degree, during the bipolar period: Soviet proxies supported the Polisario Liberation Front against pro-Western Morocco. Morocco's behaviour is thus explained by flocking to the unipole, hard work and the subsystemic balancing of two neighbours.

The Southern Gulf states of Saudi Arabia, Oman, Bahrain, Qatar and the United Arab Emirates lay close to the strengthened and expanded Iraq. Even though their mutual relationships had tradition-ally been uneasy, and characterised by disputes on border issues and oil lines and by the fear of total Saudi Arabian dominance of the Peninsula, they stood together as they had done during the Iran-Iraq War a few years earlier. None of these states had ever espoused Arab socialism; they were all conservative states. They were also 'moderate' states, especially after 1973 when the quadrupling of the oil prices boosted their positions (Oman apart). Similarly, they were pro-Western states throughout the bipolar period. The only exception was

Kuwait's flirtation with the Soviet Union during the reflagging dispute: Kuwait persuaded the Soviet Union to charter three tankers. The break with bipolar patterns was not, given their Western orientation, their superpower affiliation. What was new was that they openly and publicly admitted their affiliation. The rulers of the Southern Gulf States had more than any others legitimised their rule by reference to Islamic and Arab values in the aftermath of the two World Wars: they were anti-imperialist and pro-Islam. By challenging their internal opposition, these governments put their very existence at risk. They faced a dilemma with respect to their choice of alignment: national interests versus the elites' quest to survive in power. National interests were given priority – and in spite of this, the elites survived in power for at least the following decade.

During the bipolar period they had avoided the dilemma. The US had been careful not to pressure the oil states into a realignment eastwards, and it had tried to ensure the survival of the kingdoms/ emirates in order not to risk communist takeovers. In this case, however, the dynamics of the double option were no longer present to free the states from hard work. They had nowhere else to go: they were exposed to the policy of the only superpower in existence, a superpower on which they had to rely and which they needed. The invasion and the formation of the Coalition was a moment of truth for the Gulf states, as was seen in Saudi considerations before the acceptance of American troops. It has been shown how the Fahd government tried to bargain with the US and to oppose its strategy, but also that this opposition was mainly due to a fear of being abandoned at a later stage. Saudi Arabia feared that the US would send an inadequate number of troops, spoiling the government's Islamic legitimacy without providing enough protection. Riyadh wanted troops on a large scale (L. Freedman and Karsh 1993:87).

The US was becoming increasingly aware that the question of Islamic legitimacy might become a serious problem and it sought to ease the task of the states in question. The US fear was no longer one of Communist takeovers, but of the instability and isolation of these states from the US World Order. US concern about this was demonstrated, for example, in its efforts to provide Desert Shield and the Coalition with Arab credibility (which was also important to the US in order to obtain general credibility); the very name of Operation Desert Shield was probably conceived because of its associations and resemblance to the name of the GCC's military force

– the Peninsular Shield Force; and the US exclusion of Israel from the Coalition had the same logic.

In the case of all the Southern Gulf States flocking and subsystemic balancing would seem best to describe best their commitment to the Coalition. Furthermore, 'chain-ganging' replaced 'buck-passing' as a description of their respective decisions to join the Coalition rather than give it tacit support. This replacement was probably due to the Kuwaiti experience and shows the effects of the hard work condition.

The only case which one might have expected to flock (because it was already aligned to the US), but which did not, is Jordan.[5] Why did one of the weakest Arab states choose to stand outside the Coalition? The relationship between Jordan and Iraq had developed and improved during the 1980'es, and it was at it height when the two states were forming the ACC. At the summits Jordan supported Iraq; the economic interaction increased; and military cooperation developed to include a joint Jordanian-Iraqi air squadron.

Before this intensification of the relationship, Jordan had been affected by a series of external developments and pressures: from the middle of the 1980'es, after the end of the oil boom, the amount of Arab oil money given to Jordan declined by one-third (Garfinkle 1993:298). The US Cold War offensive, which had given further priority to Israel, also made Jordan worried about the potential peace process initiative. It was feared that Israel, from its privileged position, would 'take it all'. In order to keep the dialogue going, the US Administration had excluded from the peace initiative agenda the major issues of a process: final status issues and the role of the Arab (Garfinkle 1991:298). The Palestinian upheaval the *Intifada* had deepened Jordan's concern about the potential spread of the upheaval, even to the East Bank, (Garfinkle 1993:302), and of an escalation involving Israel. Given the privileged Israeli status and Jordan's economic weakening, in Jordan's search for a strong ally, Iraq was the obvious candidate (Baram 1991:55).

Iraqi-Jordanian cooperation reached its peak in 1989–90. When Iraq invaded Kuwait, Jordan expressed understanding of Iraq's moves at the Arab summit in Cairo. However, Jordan rejected the annexation of Kuwait and stressed that the Emir was the lawful ruler (Lesch 1991:45). Nevertheless, Jordan countered all steps to make Iraq withdraw (Garnham 1991:73), refused to join the Coalition and expressed reservations about the Arab vote to send troops to oppose Iraq. The close Jordanian-Iraqi cooperation before the invasion leads one to focus on whether Jordan may have miscalculated the Iraqi opportunity as did Iraq itself. Within the Hashemite leadership there was reportedly discussion of which gains Jordan should opt for after the invasion. Whether or not it miscalculated, Jordan did not grasp the opportunity to change when the US made its position clear. Jordan changed its assessment of the situation, however, and tried hard, but unsuccessfully, in bilateral efforts to make Iraq comply with international demands – and withdraw. The policy reflected Jordan's tradional aim for a role as mediator, and its efforts to bring about an Arab solution.

From its position of extreme weakness, Jordan was trapped: if Iraq were successful (which required the US not to intervene), it would easily be able to occupy Jordan if Jordan were regarded by Iraq as a problem. On the other hand, Jordan, because of its weakness, would not be able to make any decisive contribution to force Iraq to withdraw from Kuwait or to restrain it from further steps. In these circumstances, it is not surprising that Jordan was joining Iraq and passing the buck. It opted for a neutral status, but that status was not feasible given the Coalition's attempt to isolate (and later fight) Iraq. Nevertheless, Jordan's choice points to a balancing of Israel. This was apparently based on the same calculations as Iraq's about the subsystemic relations of strength: the privileged status of the US ally, Israel, was unconditionally projected onto the new situation. From the Jordanian point of view, therefore, loyalty to Iraqi was a way of sustaining Jordan's international position.

It has also been a traditional Jordanian priority not to get entangled in conflicts with its neighbours but to remain on good terms with them (Hamarneh 1992), as well as to resist external intervention in Arab affairs. These aspects were also present during the Gulf conflict.

A group of Arab states geographically distant from the theatre did not join the Coalition. As early as the very day of the invasion, Libya and the The Republic of Yemen abstained from supporting a resolution adopted at the emergency session of the Arab League Council in Cairo called for by Kuwait. Along with Jordan Mauritania and Sudan expressed 'reservations'. The resolution condemned the invasion and demanded an immediate Iraqi withdrawal. At the Arab League summit on 10 August 1990, the decision on sending troops to oppose Iraq was on the agenda. The same group of states abstained or expressed reservations; Libya voted against. It is interesting to note, however, that Libya, following its no-vote, scaled down its criticism of Western behaviour and condemned the 'irresponsible actions' of Saddam Hussein (Garnham 1991:77).

The smaller countries which abstained or expressed reservations, had in common that they were all situated far from Iraq. None of them would have been seriously affected if the eastern Arab balance of power had tilted in favour of Iraq. Besides, they were all aware that the major Arab states depended on a US commitment and a contribution to that balance. Before the summits, Egypt, for example, had been very active diplomatically and had tried to persuade the distant Arab states. Obviously, the positions of these states would hardly affect the general Arab or the leverage on Iraq. Besides, none of them was subject to the same pressure to enter the Coalition as was Jordan – or some of the states which actually joined.

East of the conflict centre, Iran could have attempted a common Iraqi-Iranian challenge to the US. But it chose to oppose the invasion - and the external military presence in the Persian Gulf. Iran let the Coalition balance Iraq, even though it did not flock, and Iran only challenged the US World Order at the rhetorical level and not in practice.

Israel did not participate in the Coalition. This was the first time Israel had abstained from taking direct action itself in the case of a threat. It had to subordinate itself to the new conditions as well. Israel was eager to see the Coalition work. The US kept a distance from Israel in the opening days of the invasion: it made no open contact during the first 48 hours after the invasion, and political contacts thereafter were kept to a minimum (Pimlott 1992:50–51). Another indication of the US fear Israeli policy disturbing the cohesion of the coalition, was the Temple Mount incident on 8 October 1990. When Palestinians were killed by Israeli forces during a demonstration on the Temple Mount in Jerusalem, the US demonstrated its preference: in a marked confrontation with Israel the US supported the condemnation of Israel and the establishment of an investigation committee (cf. SC Resolution 672). The US preferred to avoid political clashes with Arab members of the Coalition (Pimlott 1992: 51).

The US considered it too risky, politically, to let Israel into the Coalition. It feared that Israeli participation would have made it difficult for the Arab states to join, and the Israeli participation was assessed to be of less political value than the Arab. At that time, the Front Line States were still upholding their declarations of war against Israel and those in question might have had second thoughts about joining the Coalition, if they were to ally or send troops in alongside their traditional enemy. The need to build up and ensure the cohesion of the Coalition, thus led to a reassessment of Israel's position, during bipolarity, as the most stable and special American ally in the region.

The formation of the Coalition represented a break with the subsystemic bipolar patterns and also something new: a realignment. It included asymmetric as well as symmetrical realignment; and it also scored well as far as its unipolar content was concerned: there was flocking behaviour.

Four of the major Arab states decided to join the MLF and later to send troops. This was definitely something new. The Arab states had never during the bipolar period sided with the US; and Syria entered the Coalition directly after having had a firm alignment to the Soviet Union. This is not to underestimate the importance of former tacit alliances with the US, such as with Saudi Arabia. But this time the alignment was open and extended. The Iraqi invasion triggered asymmetrical realignment.

As for subsystemic relations, only the GCC maintained its cohesion; the recently formed ACC dissolved and the Arab Maghreb Union (UMA) was divided, as were Arab states outside the blocs. The Republic of Yemen, Algeria, Libya and Iran did not flock, but neither did they directly oppose the US World Order. The PLO supported Iraq because of its organisational dependence on it. Jordan tried to remain neutral, a position which it was not successful in maintaining because the US regarded Jordan's position as important. Israel was in a dilemma and while 'flocking in substance', Israel did not participate in the Coalition because the general US strategy. Strategically speaking, each state partly attempted to balance a local adversary (as required by Iraq's gain in relative strength), and partly to achieve specific benefits *vis-à-vis* other states.

UNIPOLAR MANAGEMENT

At first, the process of building the Coalition seemed to be a troublesome experience for the US. The Bush Administration made great efforts to secure international support, especially from the major powers of Europe, the Soviet Union and Japan. China was also consulted many times, with the result that, though it did not actively support the military operation which ensued, it did not oppose it and it abstained in the vote in the Security Council. During the process, the US was careful to take into consideration the views of its partners. The 'deadline of goodwill' (the US offer to Iraq to extend the period within which it should withdraw from Kuwait) and the acceptance of last minute efforts by Soviet envoys are just two examples. All this is consistent with the theoretical statements on the strategical options facing a single superpower (whether an action is carried out unilaterally, multilaterally, or collectively), especially in the period of systemic change in which the US position had not been manifested. In the end, however, the Coalition was build up and acted in a unified manner and in accordance with the US goals, which is consistent with the unipolar condition as outlined.

On 3 August 1990 President Bush declared the integrity of Saudi Arabia to be of vital interest to the US. He also warned Iraq not to attack Saudi Arabia and thus committed the US to preserve involvement in the region, notwithstanding the Soviet retreat. As the supply of Middle Eastern oil was still considered to be important, and as the Middle East remained a volatile region, the new single superpower would be inclined to interfere. Simultaneously, the managers in the Pentagon and the US Armed Forces were asked to work out a plan for a military liberation of Kuwait. The plan had to meet two criteria: first, the potential operation would have to ensure that the US was not trapped in the Gulf for years in a Vietnam-like tragedy. Second, it had to carry as small a risk of American casualties as possible, so as not to antagonise the American public about the operation. The implication of the meeting of the criteria was the deployment of an adequate force, and both criteria demanded careful logistic planning and enough time for preparations.

In the meantime, the US pursued the second track of its strategy. Perhaps Iraq could be pressed into withdrawing without the use of military force. This option was pursued mainly through the UN, by sanctions and an active US diplomacy in order to create an overwhelming political front against Iraq. It has been argued that the US pursued a mixture of buying support and demonstrating its overwhelming military might (Cooper *et al.* 1990). This view does not clash with the approach elaborated here. A superpower is indeed characterised by its ability to pursue international goals by means of different instruments including economic, cultural, political and military means. From the minor states' perspective, turning towards the one (or those) who are in a superior position may bring about more palpable benefits, too. For example, Syria contributed to the MLF and was rewarded by being brought back into international diplomacy and being given a free hand in Lebanon, and Egypt profited economically. However, it is striking that the US devoted so much effort to get backing for its second strategy and the means to achieve it, even though the process eventually ended in war.

During the Autumn of 1990, when the US sent strong signals and specified its demands to Iraq and committed itself to those demands, the character of the conflict changed. The conflict turned into a trial of strength, the US showing its will to act as a classic superpower objecting to an average-sized regional power challenging the explicit signals of the superpower and refusing to comply with directly expressed demands.

MASSIVE SUPPORT

The formation of the Coalition broke with the bipolar patterns of conflict and cooperation by asymmetrical and symmetrical realignment – most notably Syria, but also the public and open affiliation of the Southern Gulf States and the non-participation of Israel; by symmetrical realignment – the reshuffling of Arab alignment between radicals and moderates; and by changed positions of the individual states. What was new was the direct cooperation of Arab states with the US against another Arab state, and the formal alignment between Arab states and a superpower. The unipolar content can be seen in the clear appearance of flocking and the single option, and also in the appearance of hard work: the states in the subsystem had to take action, they could not leave to the superpowers as during bipolarity. On the other hand, unipolar management explains the US policy, but in respect to means and ends.

Globally, the flocking even included the Soviet Union: The Soviet Union supported US-promoted UN resolutions against Iraq and international sanctions. The Soviet Union did not merely restrain itself from putting forward alternative policies, it supported the US approach. It did have a different view on the crisis, and it did try to bring about a softer international position towards Iraq, but when the US was firm, the Soviet Union followed. And China did not oppose.

As for the unipole's behaviour, the US cooperation with the Middle Eastern states is fully compatible with the theoretical statements about systemic change and unipolarity: it was done according to a US initiative and to the US definition of the Coalition's objectives, which had in turn produced a reassessment of US allies. It also reflected the unipole's incentive to manage international affairs: the US being in the best position, it had a strong incentive to avoid an emerging international order in which states began to invade and conquer each other and thereby creating disorder and instability.

As Freedman and Karsh (1993) have emphazised, the full-scale Iraqi invasion of Kuwait was a clear-cut break with the international order, and consequently it is not surprising that the international reaction was as strong as it was. The unipolar impact should not be exaggerated as the immediate response to the invasion was an 'evident' case. However, the gathering of the Coalition represented something new in terms of the broad participation, and the preceding series of realignments broke with both symmetrical and asymmetrical bipolar patterns. Finally, as argued, the unipolar security dynamics favoured the formation of the Coalition.

Iraq, however, did not withdraw from Kuwait or met the other international demands posed by the UN. The formation of the Coalition did not put enough pressure on Iraq to make it comply. From the invasioin in August 1990 to January 1991, a series of mediation attempts were carried out alongside increased pressure in the form of sanctions and the military build-up. Nontheless, Iraq rejected to withdraw from Kuwait, and in January 1991 Operation Desert Storm began. In the meantime, another event took place: the end of the Lebanese Civil War.

Chapter 9

End of the Lebanese Civil War

In Autumn 1990, while the Coalition was being put together, the civil war in Lebanon came to an end. After fifteen years of civil war, interrupted only by a few and short periods of rest, and more than 100,000 casualties, a solution was forced through. Syria, in cooperation with the Lebanese Army, took full control of the country, and the vast majority of the militias were disarmed.

The end of the war represented a break with a bipolar conflict pattern, all previous attempts to settle the conflict had been unsuccessful.[1] In October 1989 the Ta'if Accords had been agreed on but were only viable when the Syria took control.

Until the end of the Cold War, the failures to end the civil war were deeply connected with the external interference in Lebanese politics by Middle Eastern powers which thereby provided the fighting Lebanese parties with the means to continue the fightings – although the roots of the civil war were internal. However, the civil war was put into another context after 1989. What was new was that an attempt to put an end to the fightings succeeded and thereby broke with the bipolar patterns as well as the previously bipolarised issue of control with Lebanon. Syria had the opportunity to impose a solution, as the subsystemic external interference was freed from zero-summing. Consequently, the focal points are the redistribution of systemic and, therefore, subsystemic strength that changed the internal Lebanese balance of power, and the Syrian presence.

FROM THE NATIONAL PACT TO THE TA'IF ACCORDS

Lebanon was created out of the Middle Eastern reorganisations which took place after the two previous systemic changes. When the Ottomans retreated after the First World War, France took over the territory and included it in its mandate. During the Second World War

Lebanon declared independence, realised when the French troops withdraw shortly after the end of the war. The Lebanese state was based on the National Pact of 1943. This outlined the internal arrangements as well as a framework for external orientation, and was based on a compromise between the Maronites and the Sunni Muslims about the principle of the partition of power along sectarian lines and proportions (Faris 1994:17–18); the sectarian groupings also included Lebanese Shi'ite, Druze, Greek Orthodox and other groups.

The principle behind Lebanon's external orientation aimed at staying clear of a close French alliance and also an Arab merger. It has been characterised as the 'double negation', because it indicated which foreign policies were not to be pursued, rather than those which should (Salem 1994:70). In the beginning of the 1950's Lebanon also refused to join the Middle East Defence Organisation in order to avoid the nascent US influence. But a change took place, however, as Lebanon turned towards the US and accepted the Eisenhower Doctrine in 1957 to counter the now growing influence of the Soviet Union and of Nasser's Egypt (Op.cit.:74).

In the 1960's and early 1970's the internal part of the national compromise was challenged by demographic developments and social change. Demographic developments had made the sectarian system (which favoured the Christian Maronites) less representative. Socially, imbalances had grown and undermined the position of the elite, which had developed according to the carefully composed sectarian principles. Not least, however, the Lebanese arrangement was challenged as the result of external developments: the Arab defeat in the 1967 War was the beginning of turning Lebanon into a major Palestinian base. The Cairo Agreement of 1969 allowed the Palestinians to carry weapons and pursue guerilla warfare against Israel from Lebanese territory. The crushing of the Palestinian revolt in Jordan, 1970, the Black September, enforced the Palestinian building up of bases and organization in Lebanon, and the Palestinians then entered the Lebanese political scene. The Palestinians became an ally of the Lebanese opposition (Faris 1994:19–20).

The original base of the Lebanese state was thus subject to still more pressure, and the traditional internal coalitions and alignments changed. In 1974 a new Lebanese agreement on partition of power was attempted, but it did not bring about an end to the tensions. Instead, tensions mounted into what became a full-scale civil war. During 1975 at least three factors contributed to the outbreak of the violence: the government's management of workers' strikes, rightist phalangist maronites' attack on Palestinians which made the Lebanese factions choose side between the pro-Palestinian LNM and the anti-Palestinian LF, and the murder of a former member of parliament.

In 1975 Maronites, Muslims and Druze and Palestinians began to fight over the rule of Lebanon. The fighting quickly spread and the parties gathered into two coalitions: The Lebanese National Movement, the 'progressive', and the Lebanese Front, the 'conservative', (Faris 1994:20), and each side sought external allies. The fighting and the dissolution of the Lebanese state immediately attracted external interference. In 1976 Syria sent troops into Lebanon. In the first place Syria assisted the Lebanese government against the Muslim-Palestinian side. Syria's President Asad had a good personal relationship to the then Lebanese President Frangieyh and later President Sarkis, and, probably more important, Syria appeared to seek control with the Palestinians. If LNM had won, Palestinian attacks on Israel might have increased in number and so would the risk of an Israeli invasion. Nor did the prospect of ending up with two radical neighbour states, Lebanon and Iraq, appear favourable to Syria. In general, Syria had fundamental interests at stake in Lebanon. A political vacuum in Lebanon was intolerable to Syria, because it could become an avenue for Israeli or Iraqi threats to Syria.

At that time Syria was deeply concerned about Israeli strength (Salem 1994:78) and the intervention should be seen in this context. The Syrian stalemate with Israel dated from the 1967 War when the Golan Heights were occupied by Israel. The 1973 War did not change the stalemate and Syria had to sign the Golan Heights Disengagement Agreement in 1974. Given that agreement, Syria could no longer confront Israel directly, but the Lebanese civil war provided it with an indirect option (Deeb 1991:333). Lebanon also became a problem because of the emerging systemic power vacuum caused by the retreat of the Soviet Union.

However, in the first phase of the developing civil war in Lebanon, there was kind of an agreement between Syria and Israel concerning mutual recognition of security interests in Lebanon. In addition, both parties were opposing the PLO, and there were the red-line agreement between Israel and Syria in South Lebanon. Syrian non-compliance and the Israeli interventions undermined the understanding of security interests. In 1976 and 1978 the Israeli-Syrian relationship deteriorated, as Syria did not comply with the red line, and the deterioration culminated with the 1982 Israeli invasion. Syria, therefore, had a strong interest in sending forces into Lebanon.

President Asad's strategy for Syria was to stay in Lebanon and to maintain a low intensity conflict there (Ibid.) in order to weaken Israel: partly by preventing Israeli control of Lebanon through the Syrian presence, partly by binding in Israeli resources through the low intensity conflict.

In 1978–1982, however, Syria changed side in Lebanon and assisted the 'progressive front'. The commitment was not new as Syria originally had supported the LNM morally and financially. The internal situation in Lebanon in the mid-1970's, however, was complex. The Maronites were split between the government supported by Syria and the Phalangists supported by Israel, but the Maronites tilted towards the phalangists who became the powerful block. This internal, Lebanese development was accompanied by external developments as well, which favoured a change of Syria's strategy for alignment from 1978: Egyptian President Sadat's travel to Jerusalem; the increasing Israeli influence on the Maronites; and growing resistance in Syria.

Israel had reacted and tried counter Syria as early as 1978, but a fully fledged attempt was to do so was eventually carried out in 1982 with *Operation Peace for Galilee*. Israel also began to support the South Lebanon Army (SLA). In 1976 Israel had supported the creation of the SLF which was renamed SLA in 1984. Although its declared purpose was to halt the Palestinian terrorist raids on Israel from southern Lebanon, the full and ambitious purpose of Operation Peace for Galilee was not just to stop these attacks, but to drive the PLO from southern Lebanon, Syria from Lebanon, and to assist the establishment of a pro-Israeli Maronite government (Cordesman 1993:303).

The Israeli operation Peace for Galilee was carried out at the beginning of the Reagan Administration's Cold War offensive, which included the notion of a strategic alliance between the USA and Israel. Probably encouraged by this, Israel felt free to invade Lebanon. Israel did not succeed in bringing about its more ambitious purposes, but it did expand and consolidate a buffer zone in southern Lebanon and a base for its troops and for further influence. The buffer zone had been established as a result of *Operation Wisdom of Stones* in 1978. The South Lebanon Army (SLA) was strengthened in South and began to increase its role in the South Lebanese power game.

The Civil War was carried on at full pitch until 1989 and involved more and more factions as some of the original factions split in the course of the civil war and there was continuous external interference. Iran interfered with its revolutionary guards in support of the southern Shi'ite militias and it is estimated that between 1,500 and 3,000 revolutionary guards were present in Lebanon (Cordesman 1993:313)). Iranian interference, however, was on a relatively small scale. Lebanon was, in practice, parted between Israel and Syria, but in a negative way with respect to the internal conflict, as neither part was able to take full control. This gave Lebanese factions the opportunity to continue the fight, because they were supported by one or other of the two major external powers. As Israel and Syria each belonged to one of the rival superpower camps, neither of the superpowers could enforce an international solution because of zero-summing.

The PLO also became involved in the civil war. The impotence of the Lebanese government made it possible for the Palestinian movement to build up bases, social networks and an organisational infrastructure. This took place mainly in the southern Lebanon and in the Western, Muslim part of Beirut. Both places were well suited from the PLO's point of view: partly because these areas were populated by the Palestinians who had fled to Lebanon after the 1948 war, and partly because they had been important areas in the political work of the PLO. Beirut was the centre, and from southern Lebanon it was possible to carry out military operations against northern Israel. Violence was a vital part of the PLO strategy to destabilise its counterpart: if Israel felt very troubled by the violence, its government might be forced into negotiations on the occupied territories. As the PLO had become part of the Lebanese civil war, its presence and operations provided Israel with an incentive to interfere. The PLO, in the initial phase of the civil war, had been an instrument for Syrian interests, but later became an adversary.

During the 1980's Syria and Israel established and consolidated their 'partition' of Lebanon, with Syria being the major external actor. After the 1982 invasion Israel slowly withdraw to the Southern part of Lebanon. From September 1983 Israel withdraw southwards from Awali and later, in June 1985, to the buffer zone. In addition, then Lebanese President Gemayel changed side from Israel to Syria in 1984, and Syrian supported allies occasionally gained terrain: the Shiite Amal militia in Beirut. Druze PSP also gained terrain in the Shuf Mountains as did Iranian supported Hezbollah in the South.

By the end of the 1990's, however, the Soviet Union was on the retreat, and this paved the way for an international solution. The National Accord Charter was signed at a meeting of the Lebanese assembly in Ta'if, Saudi Arabia, an indication of the strengthening of the US camp vis-à-vis the Soviet (Maila 1985). In 1989 the fighting factions declared a ceasefire. The Ta'if Accords were the most successful and radical attempt to settle the civil war so far.

The agreement contained: a reorganisation of power in Lebanese politics including a reduction of the Maronite president's power and a strengthening of the government which implied a change of executive power; a strengthened representation of Muslims and Druze which implied an end to major parts of the sectarian system; an equal representation of Muslims and Christians (the Druzes were defined as a Muslim sect) in the Lebanese parliament in contrast to the previous favourization of the Christians (this meant no strenghtening of the Druzes but of the Shi'ites); and an acceptance of the Syrian presence though with a planned Syrian retreat to the Bekaa (National Accord Charter Agreement 1989). Syrian needs were also recognised and formalised in Ta'if (Drysdale 1993:287). Lebanon decisively directed its external orientation in favour of the Arab side, a strong affiliation to Syria, which represented an opening for an international solution (Maila 1994).

The Ta'if Accords were the first sign of the loosening of the Cold War patterns in Lebanon, but its implementation had to wait until a decisive redistribution of strength in Lebanese politics had taken place. The Ta'if attempt to restore the Lebanese state did not succeed immediately as General Aoun and his Christian militia refused to disarm and launched an attack against the Lebanese Forces. The fighting went on.

When Iraq invaded Kuwait, Lebanon was still partitioned, in a state of civil war; and it was still not reorganised, much as had been the case from 1975 to 1990 during which time Israel and Syria, and in more indirect ways, Iraq, Iran, and Saudi Arabia as well, had intervened in Lebanese politics to support the competing factions. The factions were, because of external support, able to counter each other just as Israel and Syria were able to prevent each other or each other's factions from taking over full control and ending the civil war.

These bipolar patterns were broken in the Autumn of 1990 when, in October, Syrian and Lebanese forces definitively defeated the Aoun militia. After that the pro-Syrian Lebanese Government disarmed all except for Hizbollah and the SLA, and the civil war came to an end.

During bipolarity many ceasefires were declared and peace plans worked out, but none of them lasted or created internal peace. In the long term it remains uncertain whether or not the 1990 settlement will endure, but it came into being and has lasted longer than any previous attempt – it lasted throughout the 1990's, and this is definitely something new. It was also new that the former Soviet proxy, Syria, could, unrestrained, launch the October strikes and gain control; it was an action approved by the US and Israel did not react.

Syria remained in post-civil war Lebanon: More than 30,000 troops occupied about two thirds of the country. Lebanese foreign policy was directed from Damascus, and the reconstruction of the Lebanese state was strongly influenced by the Syrian presence. The Israeli zone in the south continued to exist, however.

SYRIA AND THE END OF THE CIVIL WAR

Syria had vital interests in Lebanon since its very formation. Syria was present in Lebanon since 1976, and throughout the civil war it expanded its position there. The intervention of its forces in October 1990, however, produced a qualitative change in that presence. After General Aoun's militia had been crushed, Syria backed the Lebanese Army in disarming and pacifying the vast majority of the militias.

Syria intervened and brought the civil war to an end in the context of the Gulf Conflict in 1990–91. Firstly, the US had reassessed Syria after its participation in the Desert Operations and saw it as being able to play a constructive role in the settling of the conflicts in the Levant, which presupposed an end to the Lebanese civil war. The US, therefore, allowed Syria to end the fighting (Freedman and Karsh 1993:97). The US acceptance was decisive because it prevented the Syrian solution causing a clash with Israel; and the approach was possible because the Soviet Union had retreated from the competition in the area. Secondly, Syrian efforts were helped by the fact, that the PLO had suffered not only from the Soviet retreat, but also from the consequences of the Iraqi aggression and from its own role in the Gulf Conflict. The PLO had lost its backing from Saudi Arabia and the other rich Gulf States, and Iraq was now unable to support the Palestinians. None of the Palestinian factions were, therefore, in a position to be able to play a major role in the Lebanese conflict. This both changed the Lebanese balance and eased the way for Syrian intervention (Brynen 1994:91), in terms of simple strength and legitimacy.

For Israel, the Syrian presence in Lebanon had pros and cons. On the one hand, the solution was not trusted because an adversary had gained control: Israel declared that it would not discuss its own presence in southern Lebanon until 'other foreign' forces have withdrawn. On the other hand, it may turn out to be beneficial to Israel in the longer term, if the solution contributes to the emergence of a stable Lebanese state which is able to maintain its integrity and make peace with Israel.

After the end of the civil war a series of reforms began in Lebanon: the army was reorganised with Syrian support; elections were held in 1992 and 1996; an investment plan was designed; exiled Lebanese began returning home, and closed plants, like the oil refinery in Tripoli, were reopened. Even Hezbollah and its subgroups, like Islamic Jihad, began quite early to adapt. In 1991 they began to release Western hostages. Similarly, the Iranian revolutionary guards were withdrawn.

During the 1990's Lebanon was being rebuilt under vassal status. In May 1991 Lebanon and Syria signed a Treaty on Brotherhood, Cooperation and Coordination. The treaty allowed Syria to deploy forces in Lebanon and to deal with threats to its interests (Cordesman 1993:304). The treaty was followed by the September 1991 Pact of Defence and Security. In its peace negotiations with Israel, the Lebanese approach was almost identical with the Syrian. Lebanon, though, is especially concerned about its water supply, the Litani River, and Palestinian refugees. The PLO, however, in an already weakened position was substantially damaged by the Syrian action. It was forced to retreat from its major bases, and only a few factions continued to train and organise in the Bekaa Valley.

Syria indicated that it will withdraw from Lebanon when the state is stabilised (cf. the Ta'if Accords), but this is a question still open to Syrian interpretation. Israel, on the other hand, declared that it will not retreat from its buffer zone until Syria is out. David Levy, then Israel's Minister of Foreign Affairs, said in 1991 that 'other foreign forces' were also to be pulled out, and a Treaty between Lebanon and Israel would also have to be signed if Israel were to retreat (Middle East Sept. 1991:9). Since then, the debate about Israeli withdrawal from Lebanon has increased in Israel. After a series of heavy Israeli casualties in the middle of the 1990's, demands became still stronger in Israel concerning a withdrawal. By the end of the 1990's, all major Israeli political parties were promoting withdrawal from Lebanon, although on different terms and with different schedules. During the negotiations in the peace process which commenced in Madrid, 1991 Israel promoted a 'Lebanon first' argument which appeared favorable to the Lebanese government but not to Syria.

The costs of reconstructing Lebanon were immense, and although reconstructing activity in Lebanon was high and Lebanon quickly attracted substantial foreign investment, the social tensions were not eliminated. A remaining problem was that the Palestinians in the South of Lebanon so far has been the 'stepchild' of all the participants in the peace process.

THE LEBANESE CHALLENGE

As the US gathered support for the Coaltion and Operation Desert Shield, Syria was quick to respond and join.[2] Syrian control of Lebanon was a consequence of its participation in the desert operations against Iraq.

As kind of a reward for the Syrian contribution, the US gave it a free hand in Lebanon. For the US there were advantages to a Syrian solution: A Middle Eastern problem would be removed in the middle of a much larger unfolding problem. Lebanon would no longer be in a position to tempt Israel and Syria to fight each other over its control. Lebanon could be part of the peace process when some internal order had been established. Syria had proof that the US did pay off its supporters. Syria's incentive to nurture friendly relations with Iran was reduced. Lebanon might get a chance to rebuild itself as a state.

At the time Syria acted, the US had committed itself to work for a settlement of the Palestine problem and the Arab-Israeli conflict in order to counter the linkage made by Saddam Hussein's linkage between Kuwait and the Palestinians. If the US were to achieve a successful settlement, Syria necessarily had to be part of the process. Syrian progress towards control in Lebanon, however, no longer meant a Soviet gain. The Lebanese civil war had been delinked from the bipolar zero-sum game in its proxy form.

The US-Syrian relationship thus reflected a unipolar content: Syria flocked to the US; the US reassessed the Middle Eastern states and now found Syria usable; the US wanted to put an end to minor conflicts – including the Lebanese civil war, which was also a proxy-struggle. The single option meant that US approval was necessary as well as sufficient for Syria, and acceptable to Israel.

As with so many other political initiatives during the course of the Gulf conflict, Israel did not actively participate. It maintained the buffer zone and the US saw no need to change this and accepted it as vital to Israeli security, especially in the case of total Syrian control over the rest of Lebanon.

The external changes also brought about a shift in the balance in Lebanon: The 'progressive' opposition, which had originally had aligned with the Palestinians, was weakened, as were the factions opposing an Arab-Syrian affiliation. Instead the way was paved for an international, US-approved solution in which Syria became the broker.

All in all, the end of the Lebanese civil war in 1990 contained a break with bipolar patterns and a unipolar impact.

Chapter 10

Operation Desert Storm

On the night of January 16, 1991 Operation Desert Storm was launched: US and Coalition air forces began to attack Iraqi forces in Iraq and Kuwait, as well as targets in Iraq; and they kept on bombing for six weeks. The stated objective of the operation was to force Iraq to withdraw from Kuwait, and it was carried out in accordance with the UN Security Council Resolution 678 of November 29, which authorised the use of "all necessary means" to bring about the withdrawal (SC-Resolution 678).

From the date of the US-sponsored resolution up to the night of the invasion, a series of last-minute efforts at mediation and increasing the pressure on Iraq were undertaken. Eventually, a deadline of January 15, was issued: if Iraq had not withdrawn from Kuwait by the deadline, military action could begin. Iraq made no attempt to retreat and did not obey the deadline, which had run out the day before the war began.

The UN resolutions had made clear demands on Iraq, requiring full compliance. As Iraq had still not complied, even after almost six-weeks of air strikes which had inflicted substantial damage on the country, a ground offensive began on February 23, 1991.

In military terms, the ground offensive succeeded after only two days. Iraqi troops surrendered to Coalition forces in huge numbers (an estimated 25,000 or more in two days), and Iraq signalled that it was withdrawing.

On February 26, Iraq formally announced its withdrawal and began a full retreat. A day later the US imposed a unilateral ceasefire: the war was over. Iraq would not escape UN sanctions, because it had failed to comply fully with a number of secondary issues, but the massive, military action was complete. The US and the Coalition victory was overwhelming; the difference in relative losses (defined as tanks lost, prisoners taken, and casualties) was one to a thousand in favour of the winning side (Perry 1992:242). They had quickly and totally achieved their primary objectives.

According to the analytical framework proposed here, Operation Desert Storm was a trial of strength following the departure of Soviet influence from the region and brought about a new balance of power. The invasion of Kuwait, which had led to the war, had been triggered by the Iraqi (mis)calculation of a sufficiently low risk of external interference, (see Chapter 6).

The US had two alternatives to the operation: it could have, albeit with regret, ignored the Iraqi occupation; or it could have pursued the chosen objective by other means such as an intensification of the sanctions and their maintenance for a longer period. Calls for these alternatives were not lacking during Autumn 1990. Other states, politicians and analysts were advocating them, not least within the US itself.

When the operation was launched, however, it was approved by the UN as well as the US Congress; and the Coalition managed to maintain its cohesion. It did not break up when turning from the defence of Saudi Arabia by deterrence to war against Iraq, and the Arab members of the Coalition remained loyal even when it came to warfare.

Operation Desert Storm broke with the bipolar patterns by representing asymmetrical and symmetrical realignment as did the gathering of the international Coalition. It became evident, that the former superpowers were no longer in competition. The Soviet Union supported the US quest for a war mandate in the UN,[1] although it did not send combat units itself and favoured a political solution. At the subsystemic level, Desert Storm changed the previous (bipolar) Arab position which rejected external great powers fighting in the area. It also broke with the bipolar inter-Arab alignment into a radical and a moderate camps, and it broke with the former pattern of asymmetrical alignment. The two latter breaks had been anticipated and manifested already during the formation of the Coalition. The Arab participation in Operation Desert Storm was, however, not only a repetition of the different patterns of alignment, it was probably the strongest indication of what was new. The focal points regarding the warfare are the US agenda and leadership of the coalition in the 'moment of truth'. In addition, the Kurdish uprising in the north-eastern part of Iraq shortly after the end of Operation Desert Storm is an event in itself, but it also served to put the international efforts in perspective. Finally, the series of crises between Iraq and the US after the Gulf War deserves attention.

US OBJECTIVES AND AGENDA

The stated objectives of the US developed during the Desert Shield phase of Autumn 1990. The very first reaction had been to hold back: the US declared that it was not considering any military action, and that no Arab state had asked for assistance. The same day, however, President Bush condemned the invasion, calling it naked aggression, and he declared that no options were ruled in or out, and that the US would impose an extensive economic embargo on Iraq. The day after the invasion President Bush warned Iraq not to attack Saudi Arabia, whose integrity had been declared of 'vital' American interest. The US's first step had, therefore, been to 'contain' Iraqi expansion. The US eventually ended up with three objectives when taking its positions towards the Gulf crisis: to deter Iraqi aggression against Saudi Arabia; to make Iraq withdraw and restore the Emir's rule of Kuwait; and to curb the Iraqi military capacity (most notably its mass destruction capacity) in order to secure the future stability of the area.

During the first week of the crisis the US took many initiatives. Besides the embargo and the freezing of Iraqi assets, aircraft carriers were sent to the Gulf, and troops were added to the Combined Task Force still there from the Iraq-Iran War. Desert Shield was initiated, and the US negotiated with other states about their participation in the Multilateral Force (MLF). Finally, President Bush drew a line in the sand and declared the overall American objective was for Iraq to get out of Kuwait and to have the legal (Al-Sabah) government reinstalled. The US soon added to its reasons for the defence of Saudi Arabia, that an Iraqi attack would threaten the American way of life.

The first step in the US policy was to engage the UN, to draft political and economic measures against Iraq, to gather the international Coalition and to implement Operation Desert Shield. During the Autumn the US sent more, and confusing, signals about its will to use military force. On many occasions President Bush assured the US Congress that he was not preparing for war; but he also stressed that war was an option. When an additional 150,000 troops were ordered into the area on November 11, 1990, the offensive option was acknowledged for the first time as being definitely ruled in. President Bush announced the decision to give the MLF an offensive option.

In November US objectives were extended and specified through a series of US statements: Secretary of State, James Baker, said that Iraq's actions were a threat to the US economic life-line and to American jobs; and President Bush made a reference to Iraq's stock of weapons of mass destruction. These weapons were, however, to be dealt with after the withdrawal. In December the objectives were fully elaborated. Besides the defence of Saudi Arabia, which was considered to have been achieved, the US goals were: a full Iraqi withdrawal from Kuwait, the return of the Emir leadership, and the release of the Americans taken hostage by Iraq.

The second step taken by the US was to 'roll back' Iraq. At home President Bush had told the Congress that the approval of the UN Security Council Resolution 678, which authorised all member states to use all necessary means to make Iraq withdraw,was not an ultimatum but another form of pressure on Iraq. The Congress was asked late for support of a military action and gave its approval on 12 January after days of debate. After that the Administration became clear and explicit. It announced that Iraq would be living on borrowed time if did not withdraw by the January 15 deadline, and that the US would resort to military action sooner rather than later.

The third US step, which could be anticipated towards the end of the Desert Shield phase and which developed during the air campaign, was to disarm Iraq. This step was given impetus by Iraq's Scud missile attacks against Israel; the US devoted substantial efforts to the so-called 'Great Scud Hunt.' The aim of destroying Iraq's weapons of mass destruction capacity was also significantly reflected in the later UN resolutions (see SC Resolution 686 B8, B9).

The disarmament of Iraq was aimed at limiting Iraq's future options for reconstruction and the offensive restoration of its position in the region after Desert Storm. From a US point of view, the limitation contributed to maintaining the postwar stability of the area.

Another indication of the US quest for stability in the Gulf was the decision to enforce the unilateral ceasefire which ended the ground offensive and the war. The US Administration was under pressure to let US troops continue into the Iraqi heartland and to target the Iraqi leadership in a decisive way. Instead, a ceasefire was announced.

A final possible step of destroying Iraq completely, as a state, was not taken. The Kurdish uprising in Spring 1991 forced the US and the UN to interfere in some way, after all, and the result was that Iraq became in practice, though not formally, divided, by the UN safe haven for the Kurdish people guaranteed by the US.

THE LEADERSHIP AND THE COALITION

From Iraq's invasion of Kuwait to Operation Desert Storm the US carefully gathered collective support for its objectives and for the means by which it would achieve them. The Desert Shield phase and the preparation of Desert Storm were characterizedby intense American diplomatic efforts. The main elements of this collective approach were the involvement of the UN, the securing of Arab participation in the Coalition (and the non-participation of Israel), and the commitment of non-participating countries in other ways. The means by which this support was raised reflected the broad spectrum of US capability assets: some states were persuaded, some were 'bought' or convinced by economic or political gain, and some were subject to strong US pressure. Others just defined their participation as being in their own long term interest: by joining, they would contribute to secure the principle of non-invasion, or the US might assess them as credible allies, worth helping in the case of later problems.

From the Iraqi perspective, it was important to inflict as much political damage on the international coalition as possible in order to weaken its leverage, and to try to split it. It tried to do so mainly by putting pressure on the participating Arab states: partly by linking the question of Palestine to the occupation of Kuwait, which might force the Arab states to withdraw from the Coalition in order not to be exposed to internal uprisings given the popular solidarity with the Palestinians in the Arab world; and partly by trying to provoke Israel into entering the war by tempting Israel to retaliate against successive (even though not military significant) Iraqi Scud attacks. During bipolarity, Israel had adhered to the principles of countering aggression and of relying on its own military efforts; if it were to have resorted to these principles, the cohesion of the Coalition would be seriously endangered in the light of the unresolved conflict between Israel and several Arab states.

The US response to Iraq's efforts was a double one: it put strong pressure on Israel while providing it with the US Patriot air defence system, an intercept countermeasure against the Scud missiles; and in parallel (for the Arab states), the US promised to speed up the peace process as soon as the crisis was resolved. In a speech to the UN General Assembly on October 1, 1990, President Bush said that an Iraqi withdrawal might contribute to "settle the conflicts that divide the Arabs from Israel". That way the US succeeded in avoiding direct linkage, while providing its Arab allies with some internal political legitimacy to stay in the Coalition as well as it advancing its own credibility with respect to all potential Arab allies.

US references to the peace process also contributed to ease its efforts with respect to major allies outside the Arab world, such as the Soviet Union and France. These two states were the most troublesome to the US inside the Coalition: both pursued initiatives on their own and exposed the political flanks of the Coalition by promoting different positions. From an Iraqi point of view, the two were potential weak links in the Coalition chain: Iraq had had a long and close alignment to the Soviet Union; and France, traditionally, was the radical party inside the Western alliance – and had provided Iraq with substantial arms supplies during the war between Iraq and Iran.

In September 1990, the US and the Soviet Union had agreed to meet in Helsinki to discuss the crisis. Iraq immediately tried to influence Soviet policy and asked for an Iraqi-Soviet meeting as well. The Iraqi foreign minister was invited to Moscow, but the Soviet Union simultaneously signalled that it still supported US policy because Iraq's action was an aggression which the Soviet Union neither would nor could back (Freedman and Karsh 1993:163). In October, the Soviet Union decided to send a special envoy to Baghdad in order to explore the possibilities of a political solution, which lay at the centre of the Soviet policy. Yevgeny Primakov travelled to Iraq, but he did not make any breakthrough to soften Iraqi positions; nor did he when he was sent to Baghdad again during the air campaign. Similarly, France pursued a unilateral mission, trying to boost the role of the European Community, and it had plans for Algeria to act as an intermediary -because of the relations it had both to France and to Iraq (Op.cit.:264–268). France's efforts were as unsuccessful as the Soviet Union's, although Iraq attempted to make the most of them.

These unilateral efforts caused some irritation in the US administration, and they were given extensive media coverage. It was important, however, that even though the Soviet Union and France pursued some policies of their own and promoted their own profiles, they did subordinate specific interests and policies to the general, US-led project. They both supported US-sponsored Security Council resolutions: the Soviet Union supported their political content, and France contributed substantially to Operation Desert Storm from the first air attacks to the end when it sent forces deep into Iraq.

In sum, the Coalition was kept together under, and by, US leadership during Desert Storm, there was no substantial international opposition, and Iraq remained isolated. Although Iraq had continuously attempted to improve its positions by minor trials of strength during the larger trial, it did not succeed in changing US objectives or to fracture the cohesion of the Coalition.

THE KURDISH SAFE HAVEN

While the ground offensive was at its peak, media and public opinion encouraged the US to 'go to Baghdad'; not just to impose defeat on Iraq, but to topple Saddam Hussein. The US resisted this encouragement in the light of the risk of creating a chaos in Iraq in the absence of a credible opposition which could take over: chaos might lead to an Iraqi partition. A partition might lead to further instability in the area, and this was exactly what the US had tried to prevent when resorting to force against Iraq. In addition, the legitimacy of the Gulf-intervention appeared to vital to the US. The UN mandate did not include the toppling of the Iraqi leader.

President Bush signalled that there would be no US regrets, if the Iraqis themselves brought about internal changes. There was no evidence, however, that this implied support for a Kurdish rebellion. The US and the Iraqi-Kurdish leadership met regularly in the years before the conflict, but the US, while expressing understanding of the Kurdish problems, had continouosly refused to commit itself to the formation of an independent Kurdish state. A Kurdish uprising took place, however, immediately after the war.

During the Iraq-Iran war the to major Iraqi Kurdish factions, the KDP and the PUK, were on Iran's side. They were also in mutual conflict. After the Iraqi regime in a very brutal way attacked the Kurds after resources had been freed from the war,[2] they changed their strategies into one of cooperation through the Iraq Kurdistan Front, and when Iraq was shattered after the Desert Storm-defeat, a new and major uprising took place.

The US did not support the uprising. Instead it launched an initiative in early April, *Operation Provide Comfort*, which included an airlift of food, shelter and medicine (Cordesman 1993:449); the UN was involved, and the US established a no-fly zone (NFZ) which excluded Iraqi aeroplanes and, later, helicopters, too and sent troops to set up camps in the North East part of Iraq where the Kurds were seeking refuge. Iraq had to obey these pressures and sign an agreement late in April 1991 on a UN security zone, a 'safe haven', for the Kurds.

Still another civil war took place in the changing Middle East. Between 1994 and 1996 a civil war between the Kurdish factions of KDP and PUK[3] in the safe haven in Iraq. They fought about power, the control with major cities and the partition of the 'customs' revenues (Cordesman and Hashim 1997). Mediation under US auspicies led to agreement which did not last. Instead, the KDP entered into an alliance with the Iraqi regime and Iraqi forces were subsequently invited (Ibid.). The alliance won control. The US reacted by cruise missile attacks and by extending the NFZ to the 33rd parallel.

The establishment of the safe haven was conducted in order not to create a Kurdish state. On the other hand, it was also monitored to see that it remained detached from the Iraqi centre. Iraq was close, therefore, to being partitioned by the winning Coalition; it was, at least, deprived of control and sovereignty over part of its territory. Later this proved to be a vulnerability for Iraq when, in Spring 1995, Turkey carried out an eigth week long large-scale operation into the zone to prevent the organisation of attacks on Turkey by Turkish-Kurdish PKK guerillas who had established bases in the zone. Also attacks on the oil pipe-line running through the safe haven and thereby damages on Turkey's economy were of concern. Though the operation *Steel* involved the deployment of about 30,000 Turkish troops, its mission was limited and Turkey shortly afterwards began a withdrawal.[4] However, minor Turkish interventions repeatedly took place.

The Kurdish uprising and the Turkish interventions were not the only post-war troubles that occurred in Iraq. Right after the cease-fire, a shi'ite uprising in the south of Iraq took place. It was less organized than the following Kurdish uprising, and it attracted less international attention. The uprising, basically rooted in frustration over loyalty met with bad treatment, was crushed by Iraqi forces. Many fled to the Marsh areas but were followed by Iraqi forces who also attacked there and killed and relocated marsh Arabs.

The uprisings and the interventions tell the story of a state in defeat and the occurrence of internal power vacuums. The domestic troubles further added to the Iraqi decline of capalities, and its way of dealing with the uprising further antagonized Iraq internationally. In one way this points to Iraqi difficulties with and rejection of a strategy for adaptation to the new, international order. In another way it points to the state's struggle for survival. Finally it points to Iraq's status as a 'peripheral loser', both following the Cold War and Operation Desert

Storm where it was defeated but not to a degree, including change of leadership and domestic model, as many losers before have experienced. Such a status contains a risk of deadlock.

The US-Iraqi stand-off

After the Gulf War, the US-Iraqi relationship did not improve. The most important issue was the weapons of mass destruction (WMD). Iraq did not fully comply with the UN SC687 which among other things demanded the inspection and elimination of the Iraqi WMD-capacity and long-range ballistic missiles. On the other hand, the United States insisted on Iraqi compliance. Other issues in the relationship was the harsh Iraqi way to deal with the internal post-war Kurdish and Shi'ite up-risings, and the continuous potential threat against Kuwait. In more cases, intelligence reports pointed towards potential threats, indicated by Iraqi troop concentrations along the Iraqi-Kuwaiti border.

These issues led to US action in the form of increased military presence in the area, cruise missiles attacks and airstrikes. The 1996 Iraqi intervention in the Kurdish civil war in the safe haven made the US carry out cruise missile attacks in September 1996 and extend the NFZ to the 33rd parallel, and previous clashes had led the US to give priority to sponsoring the exiled Iraqi opposition. The series of military actions took place, culminating in the winter of 1997–98 when US (and British) airstrikes became a daily occurrence. The crisis erupted after a critical report by the UN special commission UNSCOM which implied that the sanctions were not to be lifted in the immediate future. Iraq expelled the UN weapons inspectors. In the first place the US increased its military presence, Iraq then seemed to obey but did not, and from early 1998 airstrikes were carried out.

The air campaign of 1997–98 was carried out according to US claims that Iraqi radars and air defence systems were targeting US surveillance planes, controlling the no fly-zones. The international support for the campaign, and for US military actions against Iraq in general, was declining. Only Great Britain participated whole-heartedly, while especially Russia, France and Arab states spoke against the actions. The US, however, insisted on its mandate to curb Iraqi non-compliance and choose to act almost unilaterally.

Unipolarity alone cannot explain why Iraq did not adapt during the 1990's. Capability-analysis and an additional concept of 'peripheral losers' may help. When looking at Iraqi capabilities in the 1990's, the development reveals a steady decline in all, relatively speaking, except for military means. Although Iraq had suffered losses in Gulf War, it was still a military strong power in the subsystem, and its WMD-capacity, of which most of the stand-off with the US centered, was a definite asset according to the assumption that other states deal more cautiously with WMD-states than with non-WMD-states. Particularly the Iraqi nuclear threshold status contained an incentive for the US to limit the Iraqi capacity before it developed into a nuclear power. While cautiousness becomes the recipe after a nuclear status, efforts to prevent this are encouraged in the case of a state being on the threshold (cf. Chapter 4).

Apparently, the Iraqi leadership balanced the equation of societal decay versus the maintenance of a WMD-capacity in favour of the latter. 'Peripheral loser' covers, in the context of the 1989 systemic change, the states which were not fully in either superpower camp or did receive support from both of them. In the Middle East the Yemens belonged to this category, and so did Iraq. Although Iraq was a radical Arab state and aligned to the Soviet Union during bipolarity, it received support from the US and the West during the war with Iran. When the Cold War ended, the peripheral loosers lost almost all support and had meagre prospects of getting specific international attention. That way, they were specifically hit by 1989. For Iraq, the new international order did not mean much else but loss of previous support and privileges and a quest for changing the specific Iraqi model, much alike the defeated Soviet model in lack of democracy and market economy. In addition, strong regional competition from the 'winners' was apparently anticipated (cf. Chapter 7). To guard Iraq's chances of survival, not least after the defeat, the WMD-capacity might thus have seemed to be the best card.

With respect to capabilities, Iraq had few assets to back its foreign policy. The military capability was the edge, while warfare and sanctions had decreased the others (Hansen 1997).[5] The capability of 'political competence' might not be convincing in the case of Iraq but in the short term it is the one of the easiest to manipulate. The diplomatic efforts of the Saddam Hussein regime during the 1990's indicate that Iraq was relying on that, alongside its military means. The regime chose a strategy in favour of intransigence[6] regarding the internationale demands and tried to split the states behind the international pressure.

Flocking behaviour is expected to be most signficant in the case of security threats against the 'flockers' (though it might occur for other reasons as well, see Chapter 3). The Iraqi threat was definitely reduced by the Gulf War defeat and the subsequent sanctions. To many states the threat was inferior to problems now created by Iraq being expelled from the international economy, and to the subsystemic neighbours the 'political absence' of a major power for such a long time became troublesome. It diminished their options for long term planning and left the subsystemic puzzle indefinite.

On the contrary, to the US unipole the Iraqi behaviour did not present lesser problems throughout the 1990's. According to the statements on unipolarity and the US world order, the US had the following 'deep' reasons to maintain a strong pressure on Iraq until full compliance was a fact – or until other international challenges demanded a re-priority of US ressources:

- Credible management implied that the US could not let a state escape demands if only the state was steadfast
- The US had decided to make an example of the Iraqi case which therefore provided a long-term political investment
- Iraq's WMD-capacity provided the US with a strong incentive to curb this before fully unfolded as WMD-capacity demands a more cautiouss approch from the manager and thereby reduces its policy options
- A WMD-capacity is especially troublesome to the manager if the WMD-state also opposes the world order as did Iraq

That the efforts against Iraq could be carried out at low costs probably added to the US determination. Finally, the absence of other major, international challenges, except for the Kosovo crisis of Spring 1999, facilitated the efforts.

In sum, the Iraq-US stand-off during the 1990's is explained by antagonistic positions towards the world order. In the case of non-adaptation neorealism points at two possible outcomes: that the weaker part subordinates at last, or that it will face serious problems, even 'death'. Since Spring 1991, Iraq has been subject (temporarily) to an amputation of the Kurdish enclave and to the loss of air control in its Shi'ite southern part. Regarding Iraq's WMD-capacity it seems as if is up to a US decision whether and when the capacity is reduced to what is an acceptable and possible[7] reduction – and the policy is also a matter of general, global priorities which may change.

THE GULF WAR

The analysis of Operation Desert Storm reveals a break with and the replacement of bipolar patterns, of symmetrical as well as asymmetrical alignments, much as took place during the formation of the international Coalition. In the case of Operation Desert Storm, the new alignment patterns had distinctly unipolar characteristics as well: the parties flocked around the US, and they carried out the US-defined objectives in a US-led coalition *even* when it came to war.

Put another way, Operation Desert Storm is fully compatible with expectations about unipolar intervention. In this, Operation Desert storm was notable in two ways: US leadership in the Desert Shield and the Desert Storm matched the expectations of a unipole in general, but also of its pursuit of a modest strategy with an emphasis on gathering support.

Firstly, the US actually intervened. This is consistent with the model's assumptions about the expected intervention of a unipole (even in spite of substantial potential costs) if strategic interests are at stake, and if a large part of the system – with the unipole right in the large centre – is affected. The Iraqi invasion of Kuwait and the potential threats against Saudi Arabia endangered the world supply of oil, and it might have given rise to a Middle Eastern challenger, if Iraq had succeeded and won a strategic centre of supply and expanded geopolitically. The effects on the oil market and on the regional order would have been immense, even without considering the longer term challenge, and the interstate community would have been affected. With so much at stake, a superpower is expected to intervene.[8]

Secondly, the specific behaviour of the US was characterised by its efforts to secure international support, especially from the major powers of Europe, the Soviet Union and Japan. A Chinese abstention in the UN and from the hostilities, was engineered. During this process of gathering support, the US took into consideration the views of its partners and accepted, for example: the deadline of goodwill, last minute efforts at a peaceful resolution, the Soviet Union's sending of envoys to Baghdad. These efforts characterise the US pursuit of a modest strategy; but it is striking, nevertheless, that the Coalition remained intact, and that the Arab states and the Soviet Union still flocked in the case of war. Operation Desert Storm revealed a US reassessment of its allies as well, in some cases negatively: although Israel was provided with the Patriot batteries, it was not allowed to enter the war even after it was attacked with the Scud missiles; and Israel obeyed.

With the implementation of the UN decision on a safe haven for the Kurdish people, Iraq was subjected after the war to an effective fission. Iraq, however, kept on testing its surroundings at a lower level. This caused the US also to resort to unilateral action three years later, its position in the Middle East having been clarified by Desert Storm: in November 1994, when Iraqi troops again concentrated on the Kuwaiti border, the US military, on its own, deterred further moves and compelled a retreat. The US also initiated unilateral action (although with the support from a smaller group of states and military support from Great Britian) during the inspection-crises of the late 1990's.

Operation Desert Storm initiated a new chapter in Middle East history: a trial of strength was carried out in the aftermath of the systemic change of 1989, and it became clear to all parties that the US was the only superpower to rely on – and the only to fear as a superpower. For its part, the US had departed from its bipolar positions on the issues and alignments in the area and was now pursuing new objectives by means of renewed relationships. While this does not rule out serious problems between the US and the Middle Eastern states, it manifested the new.

Chapter 11

The Western Saharan Cease-fire

One of the least spectacular events of the early 1990'es took place in the Western Saharan desert. Morocco seized control of the entire Western Sahara, while US peace initiatives were topped the Middle East agenda. The ceasefire and the agreement to a referendum on the long term status of the area ended the long an open struggle about Western Sahara. The referendum has still not been carried out, but it has for the first time become a serious option.

The disputed territory of Western Sahara is a former Spanish colony. In the 1960'es, Spain began to prepare its withdrawal in accordance with the 1960 UN Declaration on the Granting of Independence to Colonial Countries and Peoples. In 1974–5 two of Western Sahara's neighbours, Morocco and Mauritania, put strong pressure on Spain to withdraw, finally. The Moroccan 'Green March' in Autumn 1975 triggered the final Spanish withdrawal as well as a decisive entry into the area of Morocco and Mauritania. The two parted Western Sahara and began shortly afterwards a competition for overall control, which also included a third, neighbouring, state, Algeria. The Western Saharan movement for political independence began to resist, and after some years the competition inspired the formation of armed resistance, the Polisario.[1]

Mauritania withdrew from the competition because of its relative weakness. Morocco, already in control of the majority of the area, took over the Mauritanian part, and now faced Algeria and Polisario. The Moroccan-Algerian relationship almost turned into a war over the area, but Algeria's commitment was changed into strong political and military support (for example military bases) for the Polisario. Libya also joined in support for the Polisario with economic aid and arms (Cordesman 1993).

During the 1980'es, Morocco gained more territory, and the dispute turned into a struggle between Morocco (the stronger party) and Polisario, backed by Algeria and Libya. Although the UN sided with the Polisario on the future of the Western Saharan people and on the right of the Western Saharan people to decide their own future, the situation was deadlocked: Morocco was in control but challenged by the growing resistance of the Polisario, backed by Soviet proxies.

In 1989 the General Assembly adopted a resolution (44/88) on joint efforts between the UN and the Organisation of African Unity (OAU) to bring about a settlement (UN DPI 1991:2). This was the first time that any resolution on Western Sahara had been adopted by consensus (Ibid.). The resolution, and the consensus behind it, represented a break with the bipolar stalemate for the external parties to the conflict.

The resolution did not, however, lead to a solution but rather it triggered decisive fighting. The fighting continued for almost two years and increased in intensity. In Summer 1991 Morocco had taken the main cities of Western Sahara which had thus far been controlled by the Polisario. Morocco and the Polisario agreed to implement a ceasefire from 6 September 1991 with assistance from the UN. during the talks prior to the ceasefire in order to guarantee the integrity of the referendum. The UN also estabished the Mission for the Referendum in Western Sahara, MINURSO, which monitored the cease-fire.

The ceasefire agreement's terms were that: firstly, both parties agreed to a referendum on the area's future; secondly,they accepted a substantial number of Moroccan forces at the Western Saharan territory, but less than the number there before the ceasefire; and, thirdly, they accepted a UN Peacekeeping Force.

A decade later, the referendum had still not been carried out. Both Morocco and the Polisario have tried to postpone it to allow them to move voters into the area. Morocco has sent voters lists to the UN which included the names of Moroccan settlers; Polisario Front has claimed the right to vote for nomads and refugees in Algeria.[2] Both parties were aiming to be sure of a majority in the referendum, and were trying to manage the outcome in their own favour.

In January 1995, however, King Hassan of Morocco announced that Morocco would withdraw from Western Sahara, if the Polisario Front were to win the referendum. This was the first time that Morocco admitted, fully, the possibility of Western Sahara's independence (IBRU 1995:January). Other procedural difficulties took place as well, as when Morocco in 1994 objected to observers from the OAU.

In spite of the inclusive outcome of the ceasefire and the continuing problems about the census, the ceasefire was clearly different from the earlier bipolar patterns in the area. Firstly, Morocco was not able or allowed to take the full control before 1991: partly because it was countered by the Soviet proxies Algeria and Libya, which later decreased their involvement; and partly because the superpowers politically opposed each others stances. Secondly, because a referendum was ruled out because of superpower zero-summing: the Soviet Union had advocated the referendum, but the US had not wanted another pro-Soviet stronghold on the periphery of the Middle East.

The ceasefire, including the agreement on a referendum, thus represents a break with the bipolar patterns and something new. Its unipolar content is evident from the existence of the single option as both parties have to share the same superpower and compatibility with the US World Order in terms of the provision of a free hand to Morocco in reward of its Gulf War efforts. Hard work is reflected in the handing over of the problem to the parties by means of the UN resolution. To the US, the Western Saharan territory had lost most of its importance once Soviet attempts to include it in its sphere of interest had disappeared while Morocco was still an important ally because of its geopolitical position and relative internal stability.

Symmetrically, the question also happened to be affected by the cooperative initiatives in North Africa in the early 1990's. The creation of the UMA had brought about a momentum which demanded the participating states to rethink their mutual approaches. In the case of Moroco this included an incentive to end the Western Saharan issue. In addition, the Algerian civil war further weakened Algeria and its regional ambitions, and Libya was preoccupied by the international sanctions following the Lockerbie-affair.

Chapter 12

The Gaza-Jericho Accords

Shortly after the end of Operation Desert Storm, the US invited the parties of the Arab-Israeli conflict to talks and launched a new peace initiative. The immediate background was that President Bush in his October 1990 speech during the Desert Shield phase had encouraged the hopes that the US would re-approach the conflict. In March 1991 he told the US Congress that "We must do all that we can to close the gap between Israel and the Arab states and between Israelis and Palestinians" (Bush 1991).

The US efforts led to a formal opening of the peace process at the Madrid Conference on October 30, 1991. Compared with earlier initiatives, this one was ambitious: the US planned to settle both the Israeli-Palestinian conflict and the Arab-Israeli conflict in one process. It was the first time since the more modest Camp David attempt that such a two-pronged approach had been presented. Moreover, this time the US aimed explicitly to settle the conflicts and to reach treaties – and not merely to start a process with the aim of reducing the risk of direct warfare.

The Madrid initiative consisted of two parallel sets of talks: bilateral and multilateral talks. The bilateral talks among Israel and Jordan, Lebanon, the Palestinians and Syria, respectively, were to concentrate on topics of 'hard' security, that is to resolve previous conflicts and with the eventual aim of peace accords between the parties. The multilateral talks included all the parties and covered economic cooperation and development, environment, water, refugees, and arms control and regional security.

The US role was that of the entrepreneur. It was to outline the framework for the talks and to issue the invitations the parties, which was done during Spring 1991. Israel, Jordan, Lebanon, Syria and the PLO were invited to negotiations in Madrid. Madrid was a Mediterranean capital, but it was also the capital of Spain which had been relatively pro-Arab within the EU during the bipolar era. The Soviet Union (later Russia) was co-sponsor of the peace-process and present, but its role turned out to be one merely of political support for the US initiative. All the parties accepted the US invitation. Jordan was quick to respond, eager to compensate for its position during the Gulf Conflict, which had led to US disapproval and sanctions like the Aqaba blockade. The other former front-line Arab states (Israel's neighbouring adversaries, labelled the 'front-line states' because of their adjacency) hurried to the table, too. Israel was most reluctant.

After a period of Israeli objections and procedural demands, the talks started with the historic meeting in Madrid, the parties of the Arab-Israeli process all around the same negotiating table. Indeed, the process aimed at creating a settlement which included all the parties, an important feature of the whole setting. In this chapter, the bilateral relationship between Israel and the Palestinians is dealt with; the Arab-Israeli relationship is dealt with in the next chapter.

By the end of the 1990's the process had produced several results on its bilateral Israeli-Palestinian dimension:

- The parties' participation in the Madrid Conference on October 30, 1991
- The mutual recognition in September 1993
- The Declaration of Principles (DoP) on Palestinian autonomy and further talks, September 13, 1993 (also called the Gaza-Jericho Accords or Oslo I)
- The Cairo treaty of May 1994 on the implementation of the DoP
- The elaborated interim accord of September 28, 1995 on Israeli withdrawal from additional six West Bank cities and on division of West Bank into different categories (Oslo II)
- Agreement on Israeli troop withdrawal from 80% of Hebron (Oslo III), January 1997
- The Wye River Memorandum in October 1998, which was mainly a confirmation of earlier agreement on specific issues, including Israeli troop withdrawal, and on Palestinian infrastructure and prioners' release

In addition, many specific minor issues have been dealt with, Israeli withdrawal from the areas and redeployment have taken place, the Palestinians have gone to the polls and set up authorities. In the first phase after the signing of the DoP, the process was on schedule, although the negotiations also went through many ups and downs. From 1995/96 it slowed down and was subject to stalemate. The important thing, however, is the Israeli-Palestinian participation in the peace process, particularly the DoP, including the mutual political recognition and the achievent of the Palestinian autonomy in Gaza and part of the West Bank.

The Israeli-Palestinian talks broke a bipolar pattern from their very beginning, because both parties had up until then refused to recognize each other and negotiate. Israel had rejected negotiations with the Palestinian Liberation Organisation since its formation because of its terrorist nature and its status, which was declared to be non-representative. Israel argued that no elections had taken place among the Palestinians, why there was no reason to talk to a self-appointed group of exiled and militant Palestinians. Over time, Israel's rejection of the PLO intensified; an example of this is the criminalisation of Israeli contacts with PLO representatives in the late 1980's. The Likud governments rejected talks after 1967 given the Israeli aim of continuing their occupation: there was nothing to talk about.

The PLO adopted a similarly hard-headed line: it did not recognise the formal right of the Israeli state to exist and consequently did not recognise the legitimacy of any Israeli government. In its National Charter it stated that the Palestinian homeland should be liberated, that the "Palestine, with the boundaries it had during the British Mandate, is an indivisible territorial unit", and that the liberation "will destroy the Zionist and imperialist presence" (PLO 1968). The National Charter was upheld throughout bipolarity, although minor reinterpretations became practice since 1988, see below.

Before the Gulf War there had been some minor moderation in the PLO's position on non-recognition. The PLO had accepted, *de facto*, the existence of the Israeli state at a meeting of its National Council in Algiers in November 1988. The two crucial UN resolutions, 242 and 338, were accepted by the PLO as a potential basis for a peace process. Similarly, the PLO renounced to its stand on terrorism as a legitimate means of achieving its objectives. However, the PLO had stopped short of the final step of formal recognition.

The US responded by opening a dialogue with the PLO in Tunis, but it did not last long. In May 1990 the PLO's softer stance was undermined by an attempted terrorist attack from a speedboat on the beach at Tel Aviv by the Iraqi-supported faction, the Palestine Liberation Front.[1] Shortly after this, the Reagan Administration suspended the dialogue.

The Gulf Conflict occupied the period between the suspension of the dialogue and the Madrid Conference. In many ways, it paved the way for the Conference and the talks: in order to offset Iraq's attempt to link its invasion with the Israeli occupations, President Bush had promised to intensify US efforts on the peace process. The manifest existence of a new balance of power and a new US position encouraged the US to obtain general credibility, and it also had to economise its resources, in correspondance to the theoretical statements about a unipole always facing the trap of exhaustion.

The US, therefore, gave priority to the peace process. Although the opening conference was a success, the first phase of the bilateral, Israeli-Palestinian talks were characterised by an Israeli reluctance, expressed by Israel's concentration on the issue of the criteria for proper representation of the Palestinians.

After a series of minor trials between Israel and the US, however, the process began to work; it had been helped by the parties' talks in Oslo. The peace process had begun in Madrid, but the eventual declaration was not negotiated within the official Madrid framework.

Israel and the PLO signed up to the US initiative: both were deeply affected by the end of the Cold War and the events which followed. Israel, which at first seemed to have been left with a strengthened position, was then subject asymmetric pressure to which it did not easily adapt. On the other hand, symmetrical developments in the subsystem presened Israel with a favourable bargaing position.

The PLO had lost its Soviet superpower support and guarantees. In addition, the Palestinians had been on the losing side in the Gulf Conflict. Their situation seemed to be hopeless. However, realignment became an opportunity and an agreement was reached which brought about the first Palestinian autonomy within their so-called 'homeland'.

The background was the development in relations of strength and the unipolar dynamics.

THE DECLARATION OF PRINCIPLES

With the Madrid negotiations (which had been moved early on to Washington) apparently deadlocked after the Conference, secret negotiations between Israel and the PLO took place in Oslo. Members from each camp met informally in London in January 1993 and succeeded in initiating a process, still secret, but which later became official and continued on neutral ground in an Oslo hotel. In late August 1993 the final draft was concluded on terms agreeable to both Israel and the PLO.

Once the Oslo talks had begun, the process went through several phases, the first was the official preparatory talks from January to May 1993 which were secret. This was immediately followed by a second phase when the Israeli side decided it was time to go public. From August the third and concluding phase of the process began during which there were many minor difficulties. On August 20, the final draft was ready (Hansen 1994).

An additional but decisive step was necessary before the signing: formal and public mutual recognition. The valid signature of any accords required that the parties recognised each other, and so a few days before the signing, letters of mutual recognition were exchanged between Yasser Arafat and Yitzhak Rabin on September 9, 1993.

Even though the concrete declaration was drafted using the Oslo channel and not the Madrid framework, it had been a consequence of the Madrid process. It is not unusual for formal negotiations to be paralleled by informal channels; the key step, however, was that taken in Madrid on a US initiative, and it was significant that the leaders signed their agreement in Washington, where President Clinton, who in the meantime had become President, committed the US to the accords.

The signature of the declaration was followed, some nine months later, by the Cairo Treaty. In Cairo, the Israeli and PLO leaders met again and signed a comprehensive plan for implementing the Oslo principles. The agreement included a delineation of the Jericho area, a schedule for Israeli withdrawal and articles about the transfer of authority to, as well as the structure of, the Palestinian administration (Cairo Agreement 1994). Implementation began shortly afterwards. The agreements were challenged several times, however, by Palestinian as well as Israeli groups during the technical talks, which took place between the Oslo and Cairo accords, and later.

A dramatic episode took place in the end of February 1994 which caused the PLO to leave the talks temporarily. A militant Israeli carried out a terrorist assault in a West Bank mosque, killing more than thirty people. The PLO firmly declared that its departure from the negotiations was a pause in, and not a breaking-off of the talks. After some Israeli concessions, including the symbolic gesture of accepting international observers in Jericho, the talks were resumed. The PLO leadership had managed to deal with its internal opposition. There were other incidents, several terrorist action in Israel, and some large demonstrations, but until the early Spring 1996 the two leaderships committed themselves to the peace process and subordinated the pressure from their internal oppositions. During 1994, the border between the Gaza Strip and Israel was closed several times because of violent actions by the radical Islamic Palestinian faction of Hamas against the process. Even when closing the border, Israel maintained its contacts with the PLO and demanded stricter internal Palestinian controls. During the same period different areas of authority, such as education and public administration, were handed over to the PLO in parts of the West Bank outside the Jericho area, the only part of the West Bank covered by the Oslo agreement.

The DoP which provided the framework for the following agreement and accords consisted of three structures which also framed the changed positions of both parties. The DoP:

1 Outlined the principles of Palestinian autonomy in Gaza.
2 Anticipated the autonomy model and the Israeli military withdrawal.
3 Made some procedural points about implementation (DoP 1993).

Mutual recognition had taken place a few days before the signing and had showed that the old pattern had been broken and a new one had appeared. The past policies of non-recognition had been a signal from both parties of the distance between their positions, and that they were only prepared to think of peace and a settlement if the adversary was willing to make substantial concessions. The change thus indicated that the adversary had made a substantial concession.

Israel had agreed to withdraw from the Gaza and Jericho parts of the territories occupied in 1967, since when Arab attempts, most notably in the 1973 June War, to regain the areas had failed and Israel had succeeded in maintaining control. Official Israeli policy had been that the status of the territories was only negotiable within a comprehensive peace with the Arabs which included normal inter-state relations. During the 1980's, Israel had refused to discuss the status, but the territories were not annexed, as were the Golan Heights and East Jerusalem. Instead, the territories were subject to a comprehensive settlement plan under Yitzhak Shamir's Likud government.

As far as the Palestinians were concerned, the DoP signalled a willingness to start with an autonomy arrangement rather than a real state. This proposal was not new: the Palestinians were offered autonomy during the Camp David talks. What was new was that the PLO was recognised as a part of the solution, and that the PLO moderated its initial claims and accepted a partial solution.

In Spring 1994, the Israeli military began to withdraw from the first areas and the process of implementation of the DoP was underway. According to the DoP, the easily solvable problems were to be dealt with first, and the more difficult ones were referred to a second phase. The first phase, which concerned the Israeli withdrawal and the initiation of Palestinian autonomy had already taken place. The next phase included the main issues of the Israeli settlers (their status), the right of the Palestinian refugees (and their definition) to return to the area, the final borders, and the future of Jerusalem.

The agreement was the culmination of a series of dramatic changes of position in both camps. Within the Israeli camp the strategy of 'Land For Peace' replaced what might be called the 'occupation is safer' strategy, which emphasised strategic depth. Until the Madrid process Israel had refused to discuss withdrawal from the Gaza and the West Bank until a comprehensive peace in the area was settled, which was considered impossible. Similarly, the PLO had earlier opted for a state and not for a an autonomy arrangement. During the Camp David talks, the PLO had turned down a proposal for autonomy because it meant something short of a state and because the PLO itself was not mentioned as a player in the proposals. All of this was taken to mean that the Palestinians were not entitled to a state even at some future stage.

However, in this context the 'autonomy option' was virtually a 'state option'. The DoP did not deal explicitly with the prospects beyond the autonomy period. Implicit in it, however, was the option of the formation of an independent Palestinian state. The Declaration stated that the period of autonomy should last five years from signature, and that during this 'interim period', negotiations should begin on permanent status (Declaration of Principles 1993). Hence, the Declaration took no position on what would follow after these five years. The territory was not referred to an owner: Israel had to withdraw its troops and give up authority; the Palestinians were to take over and build up a state infrastructure. If the process continues accordingly, however, the result will be a Palestinian state.

ISRAEL, THE PLO AND THE US

Both Israel, the PLO and the US had been affected by the 1989 redistribution of strength, just as the Gulf War had produced subsequent changes in the Middle Eastern balance of power.

Israel was a privileged US ally when the Cold War came to an end. The new situation and the Gulf War challenged the previous form of the Israeli-US relationship. During the Gulf War it became clear that the US did not intend to risk a successful outcome to the War just to favour Israel. The most striking example of this was the US rejection of Israeli participation in the international Coalition. Another was the opposition against any unilateral Israeli action against Iraq. The latter entailed Israel giving up one of its most prominent and traditional principles of action in case of conflict. In spite of this reassessment of Israel, the US did not intend to disfavour Israel, in comparison with other states, and it therefore offered Israel the Patriot missile system as protection against Iraqi Scud missile attacks.[2] This led Israel to give up another of its principles: until then it had firmly resisted having foreign troops at Israeli soil, but it had to accept American troops installation of the Patriot system.

There were other examples of the US reassessment of Israel. During the first phase of the Madrid talks, Israel raised several objections and procedural demands. Some of them were agreed to, others were not. Secretary of State James Baker, showed that the US felt able to put Israel in its place when it was becoming too troublesome: on television he asked Israel's leaders to phone him at the White House when they felt able to talk in a more reasonable way, and he presented them with a telephone number. Shortly after the US peace initiative was launched, Israel sought from the US loan guarantees but the US postponed these for many months until Israel behaved. The US condemned Israel in the Security Council for the Temple Mount incident in October 1990, where Palestinians were killed. During the bipolar period the US had never sided against Israel in the Security Council.

Asymmetrically, the sitiuation after the Cold War and the Gulf War was quite favourable to Israel. The end of the Cold War had deprived the previous Soviet allies of their superpower backing and of specific support. These states were among Israel's adversaries and included Iraq, Syria and the PLO. The Gulf war further weakened Iraq and the PLO, and Israel was therefore in a favourable position.

In sum, Israel was weakened in the aymmetrical relationship with the US, which put strong pressure on Israel to participate in the Madrid conference, while it was strengthened symmetrically, which improved Israeli leverage in potential negotiations.

In the beginning, the Israeli-Palestinian talks went slowly. The primary reason for this was Israel's attempt to avoid being squeezed too much by the US in her pursuit of a New World Order. The US remained firm. Likud lost the June 1992 general elections in Israel to the Labour Party and the new government took a more positive attitude to the talks, ending the procedural troublemaking. The new Prime Minister, Yitzhak Rabin, had campaigned on Israel's willingness to make concessions. From the moment of his inauguration, this approach was advanced: Israel launched a charm offensive towards the US which was welcomed and returned; the constructions on the West Bank were frozen; negotiators were replaced in the Madrid process; and Israel's overall strategic concept was changed to 'Land for Peace' i.e. to territorial concessions in exchange for a comprehensive peace.

Internally, however, Prime Minister Rabin took a tough line from the beginning. He deported 400 Palestinians said to be Hamas supporters, terrorist sympathisers and responsible for unrest, to the Israeli buffer zone in Lebanon. This strengthened his image, domestically, as a strong patriot.

The Declaration of Principles stated that Israeli military forces should withdraw from the areas it had mentioned. This was hard for Israel. Since their occupation in 1967, the territories had been an integral part of the Israeli defence strategy of adding 'strategic depth' to the country. They had also been a symbol of Israeli strength vis-à-vis the Arabs and they were Israel's ultimate bargaining chip in a long term comprehensive peace. The settlement policy would cause domestic difficulties in the case of a withdrawal: more than 130,000 settlers were living on the West Bank at the time of the first Madrid meeting. And after the waves of immigration from the former Soviet Union, Israel's problems of space and population had severely increased. The occupation was, however, a costly affair, not least since the Palestinian Intifada which broke out in December 1987. Though it would have been beneficial for Israel to get rid of these costs, the immigration from the Soviet Union made it even more difficult for Israel to give up the West Bank or even parts of it.

While Israel in terms of aggregate capabilities had been relative strengthened within the subsystem, it had been challenged with respect to its nuclear deterrence. Iraq and Iran had been developing their WMD-capacities, and although a gap still existed, Israel hadto take into consideration that they might achieve a nuclear capacity or WMD delivery systems within the foreseeable future. This provided Israel with an incentive to join the peace process, if not to conclude treaties, then at least to pacify minor challenges.

For the PLO the period leading up to the first meeting in Madrid had been one of weakening. In 1982 the Organisation had lost its military, social and organisational infrastructure during the Israeli-Syrian battle in Lebanon. Israel's *Operation Peace for Galilee* destroyed the Palestinian strongholds in Lebanon, and the PLO had to move to Tunis. During the 1980's, the Palestinian cause became subject to decreased attention and priority in the Arab world, and its opportunities for substantial support there had subsided. This left a room for Iraq to gain influence in the Organisation in the late 1980's. At the Baghdad Summit it was obvious that the other Arab states did not feel any strong need to forward the Palestinian question at that time, and that only Iraq, itself isolated, was prepared to do so. The Summit ended with a strong Iraqi-Palestinian approximation which developed further afterwards. The Iraqi influence on the PLO turned out to be disastrous. When Iraq lost the Gulf War, the PLO also lost. All the rich Gulf States, which had once supported the Palestinian struggle with huge economic aid now withdrew their support completely. They also sent their Palestinian workers home, creating serious financial problems for the PLO (the lack of remittances) and sapping its political support. From Kuwait alone, 300,000 Palestinian workers were expelled, and the PLO lost a strong base for social and economic activity. Last but not least, with the collapse of the Soviet Union, PLO lost its most important ally. Though the Soviet Union had scaled down its regional commitment during the years of the New Thinking, it was still the great protector of the Palestinians – supporting the rights of the PLO. When it retreated, almost no support was forthcoming for the PLO. All in all, the PLO had never been weaker than at the moment when the US called the Madrid talks. Inside the PLO, changes were anticipated at the Algiers meeting in 1988 when many positions were softened. However, the PLO was still open to state influence, and the Iraqi alignment offset the softenings.

The PLO's weak position, paradoxically, was bolstered by the US reassessment of the actors in the Middle East. The PLO came to be seen as an instrument which might help create a peace initiative: the reason to combat the Organisation had disappeared. The Intifada had politicised the Palestinians, and from a US perspective the PLO was the only Palestinian elite with the capacity and the legitimacy to calm down this popular unrest, and to represent the group in talks with Israel. The Palestinians needed representation: if not, the territories would have to be left to continued Israeli occupation or annexation. This would have upset the other parties involved and might have triggered responses based on an assessment that those in question would be better off outside the talks and outside a 'Pax Americana'. Creating a viable and comprehensive solution in the area required a compromise on the territories, which would have the effect of boosting US credibility towards the Arab World and allow the former front-line states to rely on American guarantees if they joined in the proposed solution.

The most urgent US reason for bringing in the PLO, however, was connected to the US positions during the build-up to Desert Storm. Saddam Hussein had tried to link the invasion of Kuwait to the Palestinian problem. The Western bloc had refused to do so, but in October 1990, President Bush declared that although the two issues should definitely not be linked, the problem of Palestine would soon be addressed. This declaration made it easier for the Arab governments to participate in the Multilateral Force. After the war, the US had to fulfil its promise in order to obtain general credibility, and also in its quest for stability.

Israel had been strengthened, relatively, at the subsystemic level, by the Gulf War. Iraq was materially and politically weakened and its weapons of mass destruction capability was broken. Similarly, Iraq's support for the Palestinians was crushed because Iraq did not have the resources; and the PLO had also lost its support from the rich Southern Gulf States.

That Israel was making more trouble for the US designed process than the PLO is no wonder. Israel was by far the stronger of the two parties, it was the one having to give up advantages and try to minimise its losses. But it was also clear, when the Shamir Government tested the Americans, that the outcomes did not favour Israel. Such trial of strength also occurred during the late 1990's.

The DoP was signed on September 13, 1993 in front of the world's media. President Clinton expressed his happiness at this "great occasion of history and hope" (Clinton 1993), and American Secretary of State, Warren Christopher committed the US to guarantee the outcome and its support for the endeavours of the actors: "The United States is committed to a comprehensive peace between Israel and all of its Arab neighbours ... This Israeli-Palestinian agreement cannot be permitted to fail" (Christopher 1993).

The systemic change of 1989 had provided the US with an opportunity to contributie to end the Arab-Israeli conflict. The parties to the conflict were, themselves, no longer part of the antagonist rivalry between the superpowers. New challenges would arise and demand resources. As a unipole the US therefore had an incentive to devote resources to its post-Cold War aims rather than to previous zero-summing. Of course, the US still had vital interests in the area, and it was forced to deal with the region because of Iraq's invasion of Kuwait. In addition, the Iraqi experience had produced fear in Washington that another Arab-Israeli war could break out and might include weapons of mass destruction (Quandt 1993:398–9).

The US responded to the these changes and the invasion by initiating the Madrid process The invitation of the parties to the peace process came with a clear message: the US wanted them to make peace. None of the parties seemed to be ready to challenge the US. None of them were strong enough to solve the conflict on their own or to challenge the US, and each of them would oppose one or more of the others *and* the US if they did not join in.

Internally, both the PLO and Israel had problems with the Madrid process: the international changes came quickly after decades of campaigning against each other. The PLO was also facing strong anti-American internal opposition, while Israel was subject, in the middle of the process, to a change from a Likud to a Labour government.

It was the Likud government which had taken Israel into the Madrid talks and, on entering the talks, Prime Minister Shamir did not rule out or close any issues in advance (once in opposition, however, the whole Likud approach became much tougher). The break in Israel's basic bipolar positions which occurred during the Gulf Conflict, and which concerned self-reliance, the right of retaliation, and the refusal to allow foreign troops on Israeli soil, was carried out by Likud.

The outcome of contradictory developments and decisions within each camp, was that they both ended up with clear and distinctly changed positions; both agreed on US-proposed accords and adhered to the peace process in spite of the many challenges coming from their respective grassroots.

PALESTINIAN AUTONOMY

Clearly, the Declarations of Principles was an event that reflected something new and broke with bipolar patterns: the parties agreed to negotiate, recognized each other, changed their positions, and ended up by signing the DoP on Interim Self-Government Arrangements – 'the Gaza-Jericho accords'. A once bipolar issue and conflict about the rights of the Palestinians was changed into Palestinian autonomy.

The parties agreed to join an American initiative, in spite of serious internal opposition in both camps. They did it after they had both been affected by the systemic change and subject to changing positions but with different results. The Palestinians were weakened in terms of asymmetrical de-alignment as well as symmetrically: PLO had lost its Soviet superpower backing, and the Gulf Conflict had also damaged it. Israel was symmetrically strengthened but then weakened because of the asymmetrical US reassessment while important symmetrical adversaries were weakened because of Soviet dealignment and being on the losing side in the Gulf War.

These developments caused the PLO to realign: after the Iraqi defeat, which also ended the Organisation's dependence on Iraq, it opted for US support. The US support was not too difficult to achieve because the opportunies concerning the peace process appeared to be brighter in a situation where the US had no adversaries; the PLO had nowhere else to go and responded to the incentive to flock and to the single option.[3] The US provided a new offer as part of the reassessment it made of all the Middle Eastern actors prior to embarking on its new strategy for the area. A solution to the Palestinian problem would also help the other part of the Madrid process: the Arab-Israeli negotiations.

Israel was struggling harder to keep its privileges and its freedom of action, a struggle reflected in the efforts of the Shamir Government. The circumstances did not favour the choice of the 'Occupation is safer' strategy which the US opposed: although it faced its Arab neighbours from a slightly strengthened position within the subsystem, Israel was asymmetrically weakened and not joining the process would therefore one or more of them plus the US. The War against Iraq had made the potential power of the US obvious, as it had the pros and cons of being with or against the US. Israel's decision to join the talks and later to sign the accords reflected this structural change: it would be far better off accepting its new, albeit diminished position (compared with that in bipolarity) within the US camp and to continue to rely on superpower backing, than standing alone outside the US project, facing the Arab states and the US. Of course, after the Madrid conference, the Israeli-US relationship was not free of clashes. Indeed, it was not free of clashes in the past and will not be in the future. The single option, however, probably fuels the dilemma between backing and interference for Israel.

In addition, compliance with the US peace plan would pave the way for Israel to obtain a better position in the subsystem. If the DoP was followed by further steps in the peace process between Israel and its Arab neighbours, Israel might achieve a normalisation of its intra-regional relationships. This project depended on US involvement and goodwill. (It should be noted that the Israeli diplomatic relations were increased by 55 more countries after the Madrid Conference and the signing of Declaration of Principles.)

The signing of the Declaration of Principles had a high unipolar content: After redistribution of strenth, realigment took place, and the single option, flocking as well as hard work seem to explain the DoP and the Palestinian autonomy..

Additionally, the settlement may represent a fission outcome. Parts of the 1967 occupied territories were removed from Israel. Whatever the long term prospects for the Israeli-Palestinian settlement, the mutual relationship will never be as it was before: the enmity was interrupted. If the process proceeds and in the long term results in the creation of an independent Palestine, it will have been demonstrated that the systemic change has left another mark typical of such changes: the birth of a new state.

Chapter 13

The Arab-Israeli Peace Process

The Israeli-Palestinian negotiations were only one part of the bilateral Madrid track. The other parts concerned Israeli negotiations with Jordan, Lebanon and Syria, respectively. Since the formation of the Israeli state in 1948 and the following war, the surrounding Arab states had upheld declarations of war against Israel. Only Egypt agreed to the Camp David Accords with Israel in 1978. This technical state of war was moderated by the ceasefire agreements and interrupted by real wars, and was accompanied by an Arab boycott of Israel in all fields.

The declarations of war and the boycott isolated Israel in the subsystem and produced a three-fold Israeli strategy of pursuing strategic depth, self-reliance, and great power backing. Within the area there were no potential allies, and Israel considered itself to be in constant danger from a threatening environment.

After the Camp David accords, Syria, Jordan and Lebanon were Israel's neighbouring enemies. In spite of their common Arab position against Israel, individual Arab states had different relationships to Israel. After Israel's peace treaty with Egypt, Syria became Israel's main enemy because of its military capabilities, its radical positions and its Soviet backing. Jordan and Israel disputed the West Bank, but Jordan's weakness made the relationship less volatile, as did the Jordanian link to the US which dated back to the 1950's. Lebanon broke down into anarchy during its prolonged civil war, and it became a battlefield between Israel and Syria. From the Israeli point of view, Lebanon was a base for militant Palestinian struggle, for Syrian power and, potentially, for Syrian attacks on Israel, rather than a danger in itself. From the Lebanese point of view, Israel was one of the intervening external states contributing to the continuance of the civil war and threatening Lebanon's very survival. After the end of the civil war imposed by Syria, the Lebanese position vis-à-vis Israel was, during the 1990's, determined by Syria, although the Lebanese governments also promoted some specifically Lebanese positions.

During bipolarity, the front-line states to Israel pursued different and competing individual Arab aims as well as joint attempts to weaken Israel. Syria's performance was based on enmity; Lebanon was in civil war since 1975; and Jordan was torn between its Arab connections, Western affiliation, and the constraints of acting from a weak position, which favoured settlement, or at least an acceptable relationship.

Even though the Arab-Israeli wars had exhausted all parties, the declarations of war, the boycott, and the Israeli efforts to meet these threats were maintained. The parties never met officially and their mutual tension was not resolved. When they all agreed to meet and begin a process of settlement in Madrid on US' initiative, the bipolar deadlock was broken.

Since the process began, Jordan and Israel have signed a full peace treaty. Syria, Lebanon and Israel have been negotiating; although these negotiations seemed to have reached a stalemate after their early momentum. Steady progress was made during 1994: for example, there was direct talks between Syrian and Israeli military leaders.

The breakthrough in the Israeli-Palestinian negotiations came when the Declaration of Principles was signed in 1993. The Gaza-Jericho accords paved the way for further progress in Arab-Israeli negotiations because the Arabs had made the Palestine problem the centre of their rejection of cooperation with Israel. It was also a centre of their inter-Arab competition: who should take over the occupied territories? This question has so far been solved by common agreement on autonomy and throughout the Arab world the DoP was approved.[1] Syria and Lebanon, however, were critical but remained in the process, and Syria declared that the relationship was a matter for the Palestinians and that there was now the prospect of an independent Palestinian state. On the one hand, Palestinian autonomy, was beneficial to all the Arab states in that it prevented a full Israeli annexation and consequent geopolitical extension and strengthening. On the other hand, the Palestinian autonomy implied that none of the Arab states would directly benefit by taking over the area.

The peace process has made progress in a changed international context which included a superpower committed to Palestinian autonomy. Jordan exploited the opportunity to close a costly and potential front. Syria, and its vassal, Lebanon, chose to give the negotiations a try. Other Arab states have abolished part of the boycott of Israel and announced the establishment of normal relations. There has been an obvious break with the bipolar pattern of non-negotiation between Israel and the front-line states following the event of direct Arab-Israeli negotiations from the Madrid conference. It also brought about something new: the peace-process, the Israeli-Jordanian Peace Treaty, and the moderation of the parties' mutual positions in light of their changed situation. In the first place, the end of the Cold War had affected all the parties. In the second place, the unipolar world order and the peace process produced new games among the participating states.

END OF THE COLD WAR AND THE ARAB-ISRAELI RELATIONSHIPS

The end of the Cold War affected the subsystemic balance of power among the states of the Arab-Israeli conflict both in terms of a redistribution of capabilities, realignment, and a more complex security environment.

Initially, Syria was the most affected party. It had been a stable and well supported Soviet ally throughout bipolarity. When Mikhail Gorbachev began to give up Soviet positions in the Middle East, Syria was one of the victims. Military and economic support decreased, and Syria was told that it could no longer to opt to try and match Israel by achieving strategic parity. The Soviet Union was still there, however, and until the end of the Cold War no there were no dramatic changes in Syria's foreign policies. These were, however, being substantially reconsidered. President Assad was, at first, seriously concerned: he stated that the global changes had favoured Israel more than any other party (Drysdale, (1993:282). The risk of full war between Israel and Syria had already decreased substantially, even though no progress had been made towards a solution to their mutual animosity. Syria had also been subject to other adverse external developments during the 1980's. The Egypt-Israeli Camp David Accords had broken the monolithic Arab alignment against Israel, and in 1982 Israel's invasion of Lebanon had shown Syria that Israel was still the superior military force (Indyk 1992:89).

Syria was not able to aim for Arab leadership after Egypt's change of camps. The Syrian bargaining position was weakened vis-à-vis the other Arab states during and after the 1973 oil shock, because of its lack of oil. On the other hand, Syria benefited from the fact that Iraq, its adversary, was preoccupied from 1980–88 with the war against Iran. Because of that war, Iraq could not take over from Egypt either. Instead, Syria began to lower its ambitions. It continued its hostile but quiet relationship with Israel on the aspect of direct state-to-state relations, carefully watching Israeli moves and inteventions in Lebanon, which had become the Israeli-Syrian proxy theatre. It also pursued a policy of destabilisation towards Israel by supporting Palestinian terrorism from Lebanon and by fighting the moderate Palestinian factions there. When the Cold War was over, Syria was challenged with the new strategic environment. Syrian thinking was given fresh impetus by Iraq's invasion of Kuwait. Syria had to choose sides – as did others; it chose the US side because of the promising prospects for economic gains and an improved political position, including participation in a post-war regional settlement, and because of US pressure on Iraq, a primary Syrian rival in inter Arab competition.

Syria had been one of the most radical and pro-Soviet Middle Eastern states during bipolarity; it had adhered, internally, to a planned economy and an Arab version of socialism. As the Soviet Union withdrew, Syria was substantially weakened. The entire Syrian strategy was endangered : in its relationship with Israel it had given priority to the following elements: reliance on the Soviet Union, alliances with Israel's other adversaries (Egypt and the front-line States), and access to the resources of the oil rich states in the Gulf area (Drysdale 1993:276–77). Within the subsystem, the alignment factor made Syria – especially after Egypt's 'defection' in the late 1970's – put pressure on Lebanon, Jordan and the Palestinians to strengthen their positions against Israel. When the Gulf Conflict began in 1990, these four Arab parties were divided: Syria was in the US camp, while Jordan, because of the practical effect of its neutrality, and the Palestinians sided with Iraq; Lebanon was still in a state of civil war until the imposition of the Syrian solution.

When the Soviet Union began to retreat, Syria increased its efforts to align within the system; it also became open to a better relationship with the US. Without the Soviet Union, Syria could not aspire to face Israel from its former position of strength. Syria had been aiming at parity, but Mikhail Gorbachev had told Syria as early as 1987, that it could no longer rely on the Soviet Union in this aim. When the Soviet Union signalled its willingness to resolve regional disputes as part of the New Thinking, the Syrian position was further endangered. Syria had to reconsider its general position and the ways in which it could advance its demands of Israel, primarily with respect to the Golan Heights. The demands included total Israeli withdrawal, a reduction of Israeli forces in the border area (and a more general change in Israel's military posture) and economic benefits (Strategic Comments 1994:2). When the US asked Syria to join the Coalition, Syria agreed: an improved relationship with the US might help offset the Syria's decline vis-à-vis Israel.

During the 1980's Jordan had drawn closer to Iraq. In 1989 they had formed the Arab Cooperative Council (ACC) together. Jordan refused to go against Iraq (see Chapter 7) in the Gulf Conflict. After the end of the Conflict, however, Jordan became the most obliging Arab state when the US launched its peace plans. It was also the first to produce a result for the US: in July 1994 it signed a peace treaty with Israel. Before signature, the parties agreed the Washington Declaration in which the US confirmed its "devotion to the cause of peace" (Washington Declaration 1994:1). Jordan thus withdrew fully from the Arab commitment against Israel and chose the available option of superpower backing. Until this change, Jordan had attempted to pursue a policy of neutrality, trying to avoid real conflicts with any of its neighbours, while siding with the Arabs. Israel was the major adversary, but the majority of its adversaries were Arab. Jordan was one of the weakest Arab states and geopolitically extremely vulnerable with borders to five other states. At the beginning of the bipolar period, however, it had a minor advantage which gave it an edge over its adversaries: Jordan's close British connection had given it one of the best Middle Eastern armies at that time. But this edge was, however, due to external support and not matched by Jordan's own resources.

Jordan was even more in doubt about its affiliation to the states in the subsystem than were its neighbours. From the late 1950s, it had an understanding with the US and began to obtain support. It participated in the Arab-Israeli wars, albeit reluctantly in the later ones; but it had once had the offer of security backing from Israel (during the so-called Black September of 1970) where it accepted potential Israel support against a Syrian intervention (Walt 1990)). After 1989 Jordan first aligned with Iraq and the ACC, and during the 1990–1 Gulf Conflict it sided with Iraq against other Arab states and its US superpower connection.

Lebanon had few choices when it came to post-Cold War adaptation. It had effectively become a Syrian vassal, but the Gulf War provided an opportunity to end the fifteen year long civil war.

Lebanon's internal chaos ended, and it had a government, which, in spite of the country's vassal status, was able to rule internally in a way that had not been possible during the civil war. Because its foreign policy actually resided in Damascus, it should be treated as Syrian. Lebanon had not been able to resist foreign influence, but, on the other hand, it also gained the prospects of future revival as a state. The Arab-Israeli peace process provides the possibility for Syria to withdraw in the longer term as part of a guaranteed US package.

Israel was relatively strengthened by the weakening of the others after the Soviet retreat. The disappearance of the danger of superpower escalation, however, also provided Israel's adversaries with greater freedom of action (Inbar and Sandler 1995:48). The Gulf War improved Israel's position vis-à-vis Iraq, but it did the same for its Arab adversaries. On the other hand, the US reassessment of the subsystemic units made Israel relate differently to Syria, Lebanon and the Palestinians; Israel's value as a US ally had declined.

This was the immediate post-Cold War background to the Arab-Israeli negotiations within the framework of the Madrid process. The end of the Cold War and the Gulf War affected the parties. Figure 5 shows the impact in terms of strength ('+' indicates a strengthening, "indicates a neutral effect, and '–' indicates a weakening), and realignment at the time of the Madrid Conference ('+' indicates realignment, '–' indicates no realignment).[2]

The peace process itself, however, affected the subsystemic position of the participating states. It was in one way a compromise in the sense that it consisted of bilateral tracks as well as multilateral.

	After the Cold War: impact on strength		After the Gulf War: impact on strength		Realignment	
	A	S	A	S	A	S
Israel	(–)	+		+	–	–
Jordan		+	–	–	+	+
Lebanon	n.a.	n.a.		+	–	+
Syria	–	–	+	+	+	+
Palestinians	–	–	–	–	+	+

A = Asymmetrical
S = Symmetrical

Figure 5

A bilateral approach to negotiations had traditionally been favoured by Israel, being stronger than each of the other parties, while a multilateral approach had been favoured by the Arab side, prone to gain from joint efforts against Israel. The direct security issues, comprising the ending of previous conflicts and the conclusion of peace treaties, however, were part of the bilateral Madrid concept. Practically, the security negotiations were not only bilateral but part of a complex game in which the parties carefully watched each other. In addition to mere strength, the parties also came to the table with different assessments of the potential benefits of joining: Jordan was eager, Syria reluctant, Lebanon depending on Syria, the Palestinians with no alternative, and Israel under US pressure. Peace had become an option, and the next question was what kind of peace each of the participating actors would be able to achieve.

ISRAEL AND JORDAN

Israel and Jordan had a two-fold relationship throughout bipolarity. They were in conflict over the West Bank and the Palestinian problem, but they also had converging interests in an acceptable relationship and in preventing other Arab states becoming involved in or benefiting from a continuing conflict.

The traditional Jordanian approach to its environment has been deeply affected by its strategic position in the middle. It has been described as playing an external role "that corresponds to states with far more resources, a broader demographic base, and larger territorial size" (Hamarneh 1992:41). The stable elements of Jordan' external orientation have been decribed as conservatism, non-confrontation, and non-antagonistic approach to Western interests (Hamarneh 1992:43).

In 1957 the US began to support Jordan economically. Jordan repaid this by maintaining a pro-Western policy. When the 1967 War took place, Jordan was forced by its fellow Arab states to choose sides and join in the fighting. In spite of the war, ties between Jordan and the US grew stronger, and Jordan came to rely heavily on US military assistance.

Although Jordan, since the end of its British connection, had promoted policies against external presence in the area and for Arab cooperation, it was weak and faced many unpredictable adjacent relationships, which favoured relying on the US. Jordan is surrounded by as many as five stronger states, which have competed and conflicted with each other. Jordan therefore opted for a strong ally and while trying not to alienate itself from any local option – trying to be on good terms with as many Arab states as possible while limiting its disagreements with Israel.

Jordan was, therefore a moderate and pro-US state until Iraq's invasion of Kuwait, and in this respect it was surprising that it chose to side with Iraq. But what did Jordan choose to do after the Iraqi defeat?

King Hussein immediately accepted the US invitation to the peace process. Jordan entered with almost no demands, and caused no procedural or political obstructions during the process. Its overall approach was identical to that of the other Arabs: a comprehensive peace based on the UN Resolutions 242 and 338. When the Declaration of Principles was signed between Israel and the Palestinians, Jordan was the first to endorse it and did so without reservations officially, although the timing did cause concern. That Israel and the PLO were first to achieve an agreement might have decreased Jordanian influence on the Palestinian issue, and Jordan was therefore encouraged to speed up its efforts to sign a peace treaty with Israel in order to gain such influence (Garfinkle 1998).

Jordan had strong interests in the resolution of the Palestine problem: it hamstrung the relationship to Israel, the majority of the Jordanian population is Palestinian, and whatever the solution (autonomy, statehood, or confederation) Jordan would have a long border with the Palestinian entity.

Quick progress was made in the bilateral negotiations between Jordan and Israel. It seemed as though both parties were ready to make peace, and as if Jordan appreciated being released from the old squeezed between rival and stronger Arabs (some Soviet-supported) and the challenge from US-supported Israel: the Arab states had been divided by the Gulf War and the majority, including the important northern neighbour, Syria, joined the Madrid process.

Jordan was actually facing an easy choice: it was a state poor in resources, the Gulf Conflict had further weakened it, and the available prospects were miserable. If the Hashemite Kingdom chose to stay out of the peace process, it would have no regional backing, as Syria had signalled a willingness to come to terms with the US, Iraq was defeated, and the Southern Gulf States had all depended on the US during the Gulf War. Moreover, Jordan would have to face other neighbours linked to the US. In addition, Jordan was already under US pressure (the Aqaba blockade) because of its stance in the Gulf

Conflict, and a refusal to join the peace process would have meant a real delinking from the US. A willing and constructive Jordanian approach could, however, restore the US link and provide it with an ultimate security guarantee via the US commitment to the results of the process.

This was the background to Jordan's entry into the process, and to the Israeli-Jordanian peace treaty which the first tangible result of the process. The agreement was first formalised in the Washington Declaration of July 25, 1994 which included the following specific agreements: the state of belligerency was terminated; both parties would seek a 'just, lasting and comprehensive peace' in accordance with to UN Resolutions 242 and 338; Israel would respect the special Jordanian role in Muslim Holy shrines in Jerusalem; there would be a delimitation of the international boundary; and there would be a normalisation of the mutual relationship in all fields (The Washington Declaration 1994). The US committed itself to the declaration by signing it, and in the declaration it was stated that it "bears testimony to the President's vision and devotion to the cause of peace" (Ibid.).

The Declaration showed that the major conflict issues between the parties had been solved, and that a peace treaty could be worked out. The Declaration was followed in October by the Israeli-Jordanian Peace Treaty whose detail were based on the above agreements. (Israel-Jordan Peace Treaty 1994).

The Treaty included minor Jordanian gains – the return of two tiny parcels of territory, which had been occupied by Israel in the wars; whereas Israel achieved the important aim of normalisation of interstate relations. The moment the Treaty was reached, Arab states led by Saudi Arabia and Kuwait cancelled part of their boycott of Israel, and then Jordan and Israel began to implement the agreements.

By making peace with Israel, Jordan would be better off for the foreseeable future. A front was closed and the relationship may even turn into one of cooperation, and without estranging other neighbours. If Syria were to choose differently, Syria would then be the isolated party. Leaving the Palestinian problem to the Palestinians and settling with Israel provided Jordan with time and resources to focus on internal improvement and there is now the prospect of external assistance to do this. These potential benefits can be highlighted by the alternative. If Jordan had decided to stay out of the process, it would have lost any superpower backing, and would have risked being isolated within close surroundings in which it was weak. It had no other superpower to turn to.

Israel began the talks with Jordan against the background of a similar weighing of the pros and cons about its future subsystemic position. Israel would be able to close a front, it would make an opening in the total Arab boycott, and it would reduce potential external regional support to those Palestinians who rejected the Gaza-Jericho accords. A settlement with Jordan might also put pressure on the major threat, Syria, which would then face local isolation and a loss of leverage in the Israeli-Syrian talks.

Israel certainly had incentives to make peace with Jordan. Peace had become an option, because the Jordanian incentives to refuse had been undermined. Israel also had to face the new international condition, being subject to a declined strategic value to the US.

ISRAEL, SYRIA AND LEBANON

Syria has much to gain from negotiations with Israel. Firstly, Syria aims to retrieve the Golan Heights, which were lost to Israel during the 1967 War. The Golan Heights are only 40 kilometres from Damascus, and were a heavy loss for Syria both in terms of strategic value and prestige.[3] Secondly, strategic parity with Israel has become totally unattainable after the Soviet retreat. Although parity appeared to be a long term prospect in military terms even during the Cold War, it was dependent on balanced superpower backing. The loss of superpower backing created a strong incentive for Syria to work for a new relationship with Israel. In particular, Syria wanted to see a total Israeli withdrawal, a reduction of Israeli forces in the border area and a more general change towards a less offensive Israeli military posture. Thirdly, Syria aimed to secure its traditional interest in the status of Lebanon. Control of this border state has always been of great concern to Syria, and as long as the conflict with Israel remains unsettled, Syria regards its presence there as necessary (see the Ta'if Accords). Syria also gave vital priority to the following three aspects of Lebanese politics: the integrity of the territory, the unity of the country and internal order. In talks with Israel, Syria also linked the status of Lebanon to the Israeli presence in southern Lebanon.

Its participation in the Desert Shield and Storm Operations was a beneficial experience for Syria and it revealed the advantages of a redirection of its foreign policy. The US let Syria back into international diplomacy and let it take control of Lebanon. Both gains strengthened Syria and were only exceeded by an even larger one: Syria was able to join the club of states whose external relationships are guaranteed by the US. There are other indications that a redirection of Syria's foreign policy was taking place: the strategic concept of matching Israel was substituted by the aim of retrieving the Golan Heights through the negotiations, and maintaining control of Lebanon for as long as it is considered necessary (Hinnebusch 1998).

For Israel, the debate about the strategic importance to it of the Golan Heights has always been a classical one. In the new situation, however, the debate seemed to be superseded: the loss of specific military advantages will be more than compensated for by a peace treaty with Syria – including a withdrawal from Golan Heights – which will be guaranteed by the US.[4]

The Israeli incentive to withdraw was further emphasised by the change in the subsystemic security environment with respect to potential threats to Israel. Israel was now surrounded by relatively weak Arab states, while the two stronger states Iran and Iraq had made progress with regard to their qualitative military capabilities (weapons of mass destruction). Although Iran and Iraq were both weakened for the time being, there are long term concerns in Israel. As a result, Israel had an incentive to improve its relations with the former front-line states, as well as to maintain close relations with the US. The specific conditions of withdrawal were less easy, and during the late 1990's Israeli-Syrian cleavages arose concerning early warning measures and water resources in the case of withdrawal.

Another Israeli concern has been the normalisation of its relationship with the Arab world in general. The end of the Cold War challenged Israel's previous priviliged position in the US camp and increased the urgency of regional efforts and hard work. In the past, Israel was prevented from making such efforts by the Arab boycott. The Treaty with Jordan led to a cancellation (endorsed at the Casablanca Summit) of certain parts of the boycott, but the main part is still in operation and provides an incentive for Israel to settle with Syria as well.

Israeli national interests has been described as normalization internationally, Middle East peace, secure borders, free trade, and enhancing the Jewish dimension (Klieman 1994:109). At least the first three objectives depend on a successful outcome of the negotiations with Syria as the main challenge which strengthens the incentive to achieve a peace deal with Syria after a series of trials of strength with respect to achieving the best possible deal and testing out each other's will to comply afterwards.

Lebanon has an incentive to settle: to end the Syrian presence and not to be a battlefield for external powers in the future; and it would also provide Lebanon with the opportunity to benefit economically and to rebuild after the civil war. Since the end of the Lebanese civil war and throughout the 1990's, Lebanese and Syrian positions in the peace process were almost identical. Lebanon, however, had a specific problem with the peace process: it feared an unfavourable agreement about the Palestinian refugees in Lebanon.

A COMPLEX PROCESS

The systemic shift to unipolarity left the parties in the Arab-Israeli peace process in different situations and with different interest, while new necessities as well as new opportunities were present. The parties could no longer rely on alternative superpower backing (the single option), and they chose instead to join the US peace initiative (flocking); they all have to struggle for their future because the end of the Cold War has deprived them of the huge, bipolar superpower interest and support (hard work). The led to the Madrid peace process between previously non-negotiating parties, and in addition to the negotiations, presumably confidence building, a peace treaty between Israel and Jordan was signed in 1994.

The peace process itself altered the Middle Eastern balance of power. Reconciliation between the parties might strengthen them, and inside the peace process the Palestinian autonomy and the Israeli-Jordanian peace treate affected the puzzle. In addition, when the parties had committed themselves to the project, detail and minor issues gained importance as did the steps in the process.

To all the parties an issue related to the peace process came onto the agenda: to preserve internal cohesion during peace talks and normalization. Not only in the case of Israel but also Jordan, the Palestinian community and, to a lesser extent, Syria, the dramatic shift from standing together against an enemy to negotiating with the enemy created domestic division. To all the parties it was important to deal with the divisions in order not to suffer a decline in the capability of 'politicall stability' which would offset the gains from external agreements.

Chapter 14

Survey: The Middle East 1989–1998

This chapter deals with potential *non-events*. Non-events are understood as bipolar issues and patterns of conflict and cooperation which were not broken and/or unipolar impacts which did not appear. Actual events, as shown above, broke with bipolar patterns in a way which could be attributed to a unipolar impact. Non-events, however, are just as important when examining the unipolar impact on the Middle East: even though some events suggest a positive conclusion to the argument the conclusion might still be negative if the overwhelming picture was one of a continuation of the patterns which prevailed during bipolarity. Likewise, the conclusion might be exaggerated, if only the obvious events were considered. The way forward was to deal with major Middle Eastern powers which were not or only modestly involved in the events dealt with in the previous chapters.

Assessing the non-events, however, is not so simple. Some issues and patterns may have survived 1989: those issues still crucial to the US may have survived because the US remained in its position as a superpower, winner of the Cold War; and some patterns may have survived, possibly in a moderated form (as in the case of the US-Israeli relationship), because the US has new reasons for recycling former relationships, and because a pole assumingly prefers allies to non-allies. Finally, other issue and patterns may have persisted because they are as unimportant to the US unipole as they were to the bipolar powers: these will, instead, be mainly subject to the hard work condition.

The main focal points of the survey are: Turkey's new role, the positions of Iran and Libya, and the fate of Algeria. The three latter countries were not directly involved in any of the events. The survey also deals with the subsystemic alignments, particularly the Arab Cooperation Council (ACC), Gulf Cooperation Council (GCC) and the Maghreb Union (UMA).[1]

STATE STRATEGIES

Turkey

During bipolarity Turkey was a member of NATO – and still is. 1989, however, brought Turkey closer to the Middle East. Immediately after the end of the Cold War, Turkey seemed to have become redundant to the US and the Western alliance, because the Soviet threat had disappeared. During bipolarity, Turkey's geostrategic position, adjacent to the Soviet Union, was vital to the US and NATO as part of the strategy of Containment; Turkey in turn sought protection against the Soviet Union and protected its strategic straits joining the Black Sea to the Mediterranean.

As the most peripheral NATO country Turkey claimed a role as 'bridge' between Europe and Asia. However, it orientated primarily towards Europe, serving a specific Middle Eastern role only in countering Syria in the Arab-Israeli conflict.

Except for a an active period in the 1950's, when it joined the Baghdad Pact, Turkey kept a low profile in the Middle East during the Cold War, and it developed an almost isolationist approach to the area, often seen as deriving from its Kemalist heritage. The two main principles were non-interference in interstate disputes in the area and the distancing of Turkey's role in NATO from that in the Middle East (Robins 1991:66–67).

The systemic change of 1989 removed the Soviet threat from the agenda of Turkey, the US and the other NATO countries; Turkey began to drift away from its European affiliation. In 1987 Turkey applied for membership of the EC, but in 1989 the European Commission reply put forward such strict conditions for membership, that it was tantamount to a rejection (Op.cit.:12).

The Iraqi invasion of Kuwait, however, provided the opportunity for a new role for Turkey. It joined the Coalition, closed the two Iraqi pipelines, provided the bases for air operations against Iraq and participated in Operation Desert Storm.

For Turkey, joining the US would not only help to halt growing Iraqi ambitions but, most importantly, it would prove to the US that Turkey was still a worthwhile ally. The Turkish approach implied, however, a break with its bipolar principles of non-interference in terms of its participation on the Kuwaiti side against Iraq, and of distancing its Western affiliation from its Middle Eastern role in terms of its close cooperation with the US. Turkey did have some tactical considerations to make about the pipelines transporting Iraqi oil. It did not want to close them before the pipeline in Saudi Arabia was closed but this lasted only one day. Turkish efforts were successful: after Desert Storm, it was clear that the US Administration had an interest in preserving Turkey as an ally but for another purpose. Turkey would play an important role in the post-Cold War US Middle East policy; its regional strength and geographical position made it an instrument against the two socalled rogue states of Iran and Iraq. Turkey could also be used by the US to balance the new northeastern former Soviet republics. To prevent Turkey from aligning Iran and/or Iraq, and to reduce the rise of political islam, was also important to the West.

Turkey welcomed the new role. It would help Turkey pursue its own ambitions in the Middle East, where commercial opportunities were attractive compared with the difficult (highly-developed) European markets and economies; and it might halt Western pressure on Turkey over the Kurdish problem. The Turkish record in dealing with the Kurds had been subject to severe Western criticism; but the new role would probably mean that though the criticism would continue, it would not turn into stronger pressures.

In January 1998 Turkey with the US and Israel carried out naval mauoeuvres in the Mediterrean, reflecting the cooperation among the three parties. Turkey and Israel had entered en military cooperation, an entente, with the primary objective to deter a war against either party (Waxman 1999:27). The combination of Turkey's large military force and Israel's technology was powerful (Op.cit.:26). As both Turkey and Israel had been subject to declining strategic value to the US after 1989, the alignment indicated both their efforts to gain more value for the US, and hard work.

Contrary to this cooperative measure but similar to its more active Middle East policy, Turkey clashed with Syria in Autumn 1998. Turkey had strongly pressured Syria in order to halt the activities of the Turkish-Kurdish PKK in and from Syria. Eventually, Syria gave in, and closed down PKK camps. The two parties signed and agreement on October 20, 1998. Syria agreed, among other things, to cut off the support for the PKK.

Turkey flocked and was rewarded. It flocked in order to maintain its international position, which was endangered by the end of the Cold War, and it quickly redirected its ambitions and principles. During the 1990's Turkey adapted to unipolarity and became a major pro-US Middle Eastern power.

Iran

The end of the Cold War did not help Iran's search to maintain or improve its international position. Iran was not directly weakened because after the revolution, it had already disentangled itself from both camps. Since then, however, it pursued a policy directed first against both superpowers, and then a foreign policy of a more isolationist character when the Soviet Union left the US in an unbalanced great power position. This made renewed Iranian opposition even more difficult: zero-summing and the danger of escalation no longer restrained the US from pursuing its interests. Developments in the northeastern periphery of the subsystem also brought about difficulties for Iran: the secession of the former Soviet republics, from the Caucasus to Tadjikistan, was followed by internal unrest in these new states, and Iran became surrounded by potential conflicts. Iran's traditional rival, Iraq, was severely weakened by the Gulf War. This meant a relative subsystemic strengthening of Iran, though the Kurdish rebellion in the aftermath of the War posed another problem of unrest and potential conflict in the neighbourhood. Another and larger problem was that Operation Desert Storm had led to a US presence and a strong US foothold in the Gulf (for example, it received permission to establish military bases in Kuwait). These developments have been characterised as an effective encirclement of Iran (Chubin 1994).

When the US was gathering support and members for the international Coalition, it was feared that Iran might join the Iraqi challenge of the US World Order to weaken the US and US proxies in the area. This did not happen: although Iran did not welcome the US/ UN efforts, it remained passive and did not support Iraq in any way. During the Gulf Conflict Iraq flew a number of aeroplanes across the border to Iran to save them from destruction. Iran received them, but they were later seized as 'war indemnity'. In general, Iran preferred to take a neutral stance in the Gulf crisis. Its rival was, thereby, passively balanced when Iran did not obstruct the Coalition's weakening of Iraq.

Iran has also had a cooperative approach to the Caucasus and Central Asia where it has strong commercial and strategic interests. However, the area also containted the risk of clashes with other states with competing interests: Turkey, Russia and Pakistan. Iran was most careful and modest in its relations with Russia, and least towards Turkey, in spite of joint participation in the Economic Cooperation Council (ECO) with the latter.

In the course of the 1980's, Iran moderated its foreign policy compared with that of the first hectic years of fundamentalism. The war against Iraq had forced this moderation, which since the late 1980's was termed Realist Islam or Pragmatic Islamism (Mozaffari 1993:614). A major shift characterized the new Iranian notion of Islamism, which turned from 'Universal Islamism' to 'National Islamism' and had a far less expansionist connotation (Ibid.). In general, Iran gradually normalised its relationships to other states. Some remarkable exceptions remained because of the Rushdie *Fatwa*, Iran's support of Hizbollah groups and the rejectionist stance toward the Arab-Israeli peace procss. Iran's behaviour during 1990–91 showed further moderation: its reluctance to join Iraq, its withdrawal of the Iranian guards from the Lebanon when Syria took control, and its improvement in its relations with the Southern Gulf States.

In spite of this moderation Iran was at the top of the US list of potentially hostile powers; it was subject to pressure to stop its nuclear program; and the US pursued its strategy of 'Dual Containment' of Iran and Iraq. The US regarded Iran as the strongest of the potentially hostile powers (White House 1994). US criticism of Iran focused mainly on Iran's nuclear programme, its opposition to the peace process, its support for terrorism and its bad human rights record (Kemp 1994).

Iran was, like Iraq (see Chapter 6) also in deeply difficulties after the end of the 1980–88 war. In Iran's case, its economic and societal troubles were made even worse by the first years of fundamentalist experiments. Iran was therefore still in a state of reconstruction and was diverting most of its resources to internal purposes.

The reconstruction included the development of a nuclear capability. This partly represents a modernisation of its defence, which has been marked by severe technological deficiencies (Cordesman 1994); and is partly a result of its experiences in the 1980–88 war, which showed that self-reliance and qualitative improvements in capacity were decisive assets (Chubin 1994). A nuclear capability would definitely strengthen Iran's position, not least against the unbalanced unipole. On the other hand, the US is concerned that a nuclearized Iran would limit US freedom of action.

Why did Iran not turn against the New World Order in a stronger way? Given its 'encirclement' and its disagreements with the US, it seems as if Iran had good reasons to oppose that Order. The Iranian experiences of the Iraqi invasion in 1980 and of *Operation Earnest Will* (the US escort of tanker convoys through the Gulf) during the

Gulf War offensives called for caution, however. (Cordesman 1993). Secondly, and most importantly, there was Iran's temporary position of weakness. Apparently, Iran chose to benefit from US world leadership to continue its reconstruction and come to terms with the extension of the subsystem to the north. Given this, it is not surprising that Iran did not challenge the US World Order; nor is Iran's choice incompatible with unipolar expectations.

Libya

Since the Gulf Conflict Libya – a formerly prominent radical, Soviet proxy – tempered its foreign policy. Libya abstained when the vast majority of Arab states condemned the invasion of Kuwait, and in the Arab League Summit on 10 August 1990) it voted no (with Iraq and the PLO only) to sending troops against Iraq. It did, however, condemn the irresponsible actions of Saddam Hussein (Garnham 1991:77). All in all, Libya took a neutral stance, and after the Conflict it continued to keep a low profile, drawing closer to its moderate neighbour, Egypt (Heikal 1993); and it continued to cooperate in the UMA in spite of the different positions of UMA's members on the Conflict.

With respect to the US, Libya began to change its signals. During 1991 these even became rather positive (The Middle East, May and June 1991) – but the US preferred to await further developments. The only political clash between Libya and the US during the 1990's was the dispute over the extradition of those suspected of planting the terrorist bomb aboard the Panam passenger flight which exploded over Lockerbie in Scotland in 1988. Libya would not comply with US demands for extradition, preferring an Arab trial. The US was initially firm in its demands, relating them to its post-Cold War offensive against terrorism. Libya accepted the SC Resolution 731/92 to deny 'all sorts of terrorism regardless of its origin' (People's Committee 1992), a process went on, and in the beginning of 1999 Libya actually extradited the two suspects.

Libya still opposes the Arab-Israeli peace process, but its rhetoric has been moderated and reduced. Instead, the Libyan leader, Moammar Ghaddafi, was preoccupied with improving Libya's relations both with Egypt and with its fellow UMA states, even Morocco, in spite of the ceasefire in Western Sahara on Moroccan terms), because the North African states constitute Libya's core interest (M.-J. Deeb 1991:9). In addition, it did not seem as if Libya could align any formerly radical states: Algeria was in serious internal difficulties surviving as a state, Syria was engaged in the peace process, and Iraq was isolated and still struggling with the victors of Desert Storm victors about its future. The Libya's alternative to a cooperative approach was, therefore, isolation.

The tempering of Libya's foreign policy also has to be seen in light of the disappearance of Soviet Union – to which it originally turned for support because it feared Egypt. Although Libya did not flock, it did not oppose the US World Order; and the cooperative approach towards the other North African states is evidence of an adaptation to the unipolar hard work dynamic.

Algeria

In Algeria the post-Cold War period has been marked by internal unrest. The Soviet Union's scaling down of its support during the Gorbachev years caused severe economic difficulties. Algeria decreased its foreign commitments, for example to the Polisario Front, while internally a politically strong Islamist opposition grew up. The Islamic Salvation Front (FIS) gained a majority of the votes municipal elections held in Summer 1990 and at the following parliamentary elections the FIS won the first round, even though their victory was based on a turnout of only one third of the voters. The government stopped the election procedure before the second round, and within a year it was resorting to strong repression, suspending political rights and imprisoning FIS leaders. The popular reaction to this was strong, and the FIS gained even more support. During the first years after military rule was imposed, resistance became violent and the situation developed into a low-level civil war. An estimated 80,000 people were killed during the 1990's. The military regime was violent but also oppositional violence took place. Evidence of the atrocities was overwhelming while it was often difficult to demonstrate the specific responsibility (Spencer 1998).

Algeria had been a radical state belonging to the Soviet camp. After the collapse of the communist alternative to the free market and the liberal democracy, Algeria, given the weakening of the country, divided internally over which course to follow.

Algeria kept a low profile when Iraq invaded Kuwait. At the Arab Foreign Ministers meeting the day after the invasion, Algeria supported the condemnation of the invasion, and at the Arab League Summit on 10 August, Algeria abstained in the vote to send troops against Iraq, preferring an Arab to an international solution. Algeria (with Yemen, Libya and France) appealed to Iraq to withdraw before the 15 January deadline. But Algeria was ready to shelter Iraqi planes (Garnham 1991:77). Algeria was far away from the theatre, and mass demonstrations in favour of Iraq were taking place in Algeria – an already divided country; and the US did not regard Algerian participation in the Coalition as vital, not least because the Maghreb countries were already represented by Egypt (which sent as many as 40,000 troops) and Morocco. Algeria neither flocked nor opposed the US World Order; it just did not join the Coalition. It was comparatively free to take these positions because of US priorities about Arab backing.

SUBSYSTEMIC ALIGNMENTS

Though interstate cooperation in the post-Cold War Middle East is still evolving, it seems as if the dominant tendency from 1989 and throughout the 1990's was to form groups with a strong geographical element rather than ideological or related to any specific issue.

During the war between Iran and Iraq the states in the Arabian Peninsula[2] formed the Gulf Cooperation Council (GCC). The GCC had a military dimension, the Peninsular Shield Force, because it was created in the light of the threat from the Northern Gulf. After a short period at rest, the GCC revived after Iraq's invasion of Kuwait. Bahrain, Oman, Qatar and the UAE all contributed to the multilateral force with GCC forces. A fter the end of Desert Storm, GCC political cooperation intensified and it increased the links to the US, which intensified its relations with individual member states. Since the Gulf War the US concluded or strengthened bilateral defense cooperation agreements with almost all the Southern Gulf States (Cordesman 1997:68), Bahrain, Kuwait, Oman, Qatar, Saudi Arabia and the United Arab Emirates.

The dissolution of the Arab Cooperation Council (ACC), formed in 1989, was caused by the Gulf Conflict. Egypt fought against Iraq, while the Republic of Yemen and Jordan supported Iraq. The Yemeni support of Iraq was, however, more a question of balancing of Saudi Arabia than challenging the US World Order (Garnham 1991:76), and Jordan joined that Order and the Arab-Israeli peace process immediately after the end of the Conflict. During and after the Conflict the ACC was divided: two states were US affiliates (Egypt and Jordan), one state (Iraq) strongly opposed the US World Order, and one state (the Republic of Yemen) was preoccupied with the subsystemic balancing of Saudi Arabia. After the Gulf Conflict, the Republic of Yemen's policy was interrupted by civil war, but the end of internal fighting has so far revealed a cooperative approach. The ACC broke down, but the group of states in the peace process may evolve as a pro-US group with its centre in the Levant.

Members of the 1989 Maghreb Union (UMA) also took different positions during the Gulf Conflict: Morocco participated in Operation Desert Storm; Libya voted against the fighting; Algeria (and Mauritania) expressed reservations; and Tunisia kept a low profile, supporting the Arab condemnation of the Iraqi invasion on 3 August, but absenting itself from the voting on sending troops against Iraq (Garnham 1991:80). After 1991 UMA members were reconciled and increased their cooperation, which had, during bipolarity, been constrained by moderate-radical clashes of interest between Algeria and Libya, and Tunisia and Morocco, respectively. UMA like the GCC is now extending its political cooperation.

The UMA received strong encouragement from the US, which addressed UMA mainly through its ally, Morocco, but also through collective arrangements. The Casablanca Middle East/North Africa Economic Summit in Autumn 1994, which included the US, promoted four specific objectives: To dismantle trade restrictions, to counter terrorism, to promote better contacts between Israel and the Arab world, and to ensure the status of the Casablanca Conference as the beginning of a long term process (Pelletreau 1994:2). At the Summit the US supported its institutions and projects, which had been initially planned in UMA, and encouraged new initiatives under the heading 'free-market and democracy'. It also encouraged cooperation between the states: Secretary of State Warren Christopher said, in his address at the Summit, that Western Europe had been reconstructed and integrated after the Second World War by structures of cooperation, which began with economic ties, and that the US "purpose here in Casablanca is to apply that same lesson to this region, as we work to create a more peaceful and secure Middle East" (Christopher 1994). However, the European orientation of the UMA is strong, the EU being the closest daily cooperative partner. In 1995 the EU launched the socalled Barcelona process on Mediterranean Partnership which comprises economical, political and cultural cooperation between the EU countries and 12 partners from the southern shore.[3]

In the northeastern part of the Middle East another set of groups was formed at the beginning of the 1990's. In the northeast, ECO, mentioned above, was revived and changed. It included the three major regional powers, Turkey, Iran and Pakistan, as well as the former southern Soviet republics. ECO is almost a new organization if compared to its predecessor the almost inactive Regional Cooperation for Development formed in 1965; ECO had a new name, many new members and more tasks. Iran, Turkey and Pakistan were the founders of ECO, but Afghanistan, Azerbaijan, Kazakhstan, Kyrgyzstan, Tajikistan, Turkmenistan and Uzbekistan became members (Kemp 1994:117). The ECO has its headquarters in Teheran, and since 1992 it had a revival and a greater role in the area. Turkey and Iran cooperated in this forum, mainly in economic areas, but they had very different views about the ECO's future, and none of them had sufficient resources to fullfil the purposes of ECO.

Two other groups have also been formed by almost the same states: Turkey formed the Black Sea Economic Cooperation Zone (BSECZ) with Russia, Azerbaijan and the Central Asian states; Iran, with Russia, formed a similar group, the Caspian Sea Organisation (CSO) which includes Kazakhstan, Turkmenistan, and Azerbaijan (Kemp 1994:118).

The northeastern groupings represent both cooperation (ECO) among the major subsystemic powers as well as competition (BSECZ – CSO). It is too early to assess them, but they all represent the unipolar incentive of hard work.

GEOGRAPHICAL AND POLITICAL COOPERATION

This chapter addresses the policies of the states only modest or not directly involved in the events dealt with in the previous chapters, or apparently unaffected by the systemic change, and the Middle Eastern alignments.

Turkey flocked and remained to a US affiliate, but in a different context and with a new role. Iran did not flock, but tempered its opposition to the US World Order. This also goes for Libya, which developed a more cooperative approach in the subsystem. Algeria did not flock either, but like Libya its approach towards its neighbours became more cooperative. Algeria was, however, deeply troubled by the civil war which broke out in 1990–91.

Regarding subsystemic alignments in the area during the 1990's, the general tendencies thus, were:

• Geographically centred groups
• Symmetrical political and economical cooperation

- Evolving US cores in the 'middle' and south of the Middle East
- Strong US influence in security matters

It seems that the unipolar statement on hard work and increased regional activity is applicable to the alignments: ECO's revitalization; the UMA, whose members were reconciled and increased their cooperation, the GCC, and the formation of the BSECZ and the CSO. Also the Arab-Israeli peace process could develop into a cooperative group. The ACC lasted only shortly, but the former ACC members Jordan and the Republic of Yemen each opted for cooperation: Jordan for the peace process, the potential outcome of the peace process, and the Republic of Yemen in its approach to the GCC countries after its civil war. The regrouping also reflects flocking in security matters.

The development of both the state strategies and subsystemic alignments thus seem to have broken, or substantially moderated, bipolar patterns and to have been affected by unipolar dynamics.

Chapter 15

The Transformation of the Middle East – Conclusion

The initial argument was that Middle Eastern international politics were strongly affected by the end of the Cold War and the systemic change into unipolarity; the problem was to investigate how it was affected, and to demonstrate that the model for unipolarity was able to explain the 1989 to 1997 development. The investigation and the empirical analysis confirmed that the 1989 systemic change manifested itself in a series of significant events measured in number as well as in range. The events met the expectations of effects caused by the very systemic transformation resulting from the termination of the Cold War.

The first step was to describe each event, and to determine whether each event represented something new. When adding the findings, it is showed that all types of outcomes on the list of expected impacts of a systemic change were present: the outbreak of war, peace settlement, the end of/outbreak of civil war, state changes (fission, fusion, formation of new states and disappearance of others), symmetrical and asymmetrical realigment.

- *War*: the Iraqi invasion of Kuwait; Operation Desert Storm
- *Peace settlement*: the Gaza-Jericho accords; the West Saharan ceasefire; the commencement of the Arabi-Israeli peace process, including the peace treaty between Israel and Jordan
- *End of/outbreak of civil war*: the end of the Lebanese civil war (the Ta'if accords); the outbreak in the united Yemen (indirectly, as the outbreak followed the direct effect of the unification of the Yemens); and the Kurdish rebellion in Iraq(indirectly as well because the rebellion followed the direct effect of the Iraqi defeat)
- *State changes*: the formation of the Republic of Yemen (which include the disappearance of the two former Yemeni states and the formation of a new state; fusion); reduction of Israeli control over

202

parts of the territories occupied in 1967 (fission; the Palestinian Autonomous territories may be counted as the formation of a new state depending on the future development, so far it is only state-like); the creation of the UN safe haven for the Kurds in Iraq (fission)

- *The asymmetrical patterns of alignment* were changed by: the former pro-Soviet states' dealignment from the Soviet Union; the Arab participation in the international Coalition and Operation Desert Storm; the acceptance of US bases on the Arabian Peninsula; the new relationship between the US and the PLO
- *The symmetrical patterns of alignment* were changed by: the short life of the Arab Cooperation Council (formation and dissolution); Israel's total isolation came to an end; new groups of Arab states cooperated throughout the period in the Arab League (and also in the Coalition and in Operation Desert Storm[1])

The end of the Cold War (bipolarity) thus resulted in a series of events in the Middle East, which in total reflected the depth and the range of the 1989–impact.

The method demanded two additional steps to be taken in order to assess whether Middle Eastern politics were subject to a unipolar impact and not only to the impact resulting from the end of the Cold War. The questions were: did the event represent a break with bipolar issues and patterns of cooperation and conflict; and was the event compatible with the statements on (the US-specific) unipolarity, i.e., was a unipolar content traceable in the individual events when applying the explanation. The findings and the analysis resulted in the following conclusion regarding each of the events:

The unification of the Yemens. The end of Soviet support for the PDRY (asymmetrical dealignment) and the subsystemic weakening of both the Yemens following the disappearance of the bipolar zero-summing and the lack of superpower interests led to the unification of Yemen (a fusion outcome). The unification contained hard work with regards to the struggle for position in the light of the Yemens' weakening in the subsystem. The unification was explained by the statement on the single option' as well, as there were no alternative great power guarantees available for either of the two parties. The Republic of Yemen did not display flocking but neither did it actively challenge the US World Order. The Yemeni civil war took place in 1994 and resulted from the unification outcome: the war between the

Southern and the Northern factions was a struggle for the internal control of the Republic of Yemen, in which a robust monopoly of violence had still not been established.

Iraq's invasion of Kuwait. Iraq lost support from the Soviet Union (dealignment), and this led to a weakening of Iraq vis-à-vis the US-aligned states in the region. Iraq apparently – and correctly understood that the US had become the only superpower in existence in the post-Cold War situation. On the other hand, Iraq miscalculated the US commitment to the region in the absence of Soviet competition. Iraq's responded to the perceived threat of further weakening of its position (already suffering from the damages and subsystemic political isolation resulting from the war against Iran) by the invasion of Kuwait. The invasion represented a break with bipolar patterns and led to a trial of strength. The Iraqi invasion was closely connected to the 1989 transformation, and it was unique in the sense that it shortly afterwards led to a manifestation of the new: the US position became obvious during operation Desert Storm. With respect to unipolar content, the Iraqi invasion qualifies in terms of the single option', because Iraq could not have its problems solved by means of asymmetrical support vis-à-vis the US aligned states. The unipolar content is also reflected in terms of hard work', as Iraq calculated on a lesser degree of superpower support and was left to resolve its serious internal problems and strengthen its international position by own means. However, flocking' was absent, and the Iraqi response to the US reactions to the invasion almost neutralizes the unipolar content.

The formation of the international Coalition. The formation of the Coalition broke with the firm bipolar division of the Middle East into the two asymmetrical camps. The US and Arab states aligned in the Coalition. Syria is a clear example of asymmetrical realignment, and symmetrically of a radical state realigning with the moderates. The formation of the Coalition represents a substantial degree of the unipole's agenda, and of flocking: only Jordan, which until then had been in the US camp (and the PLO) should be treated as not flocking among those which were supposed to. Also a content of hard work' was traced, as it was very difficult for any of the relevant Arab states to free-ride regarding the Iraqi aggression, and they could not pass the ultimate responsibility for their security to the superpowers.

The end of the Lebanese civil war. The Ta'if accords and the disarmament of almost all the Lebanese militant factions followed the disappearance of the bipolar proxy struggle. The Lebanese factions had lost external support, and Syria had achieved a position from which it could impose a true vassal governance. The Syrian vassal governance resulted from the end of the Cold War and Syria's participation in the Coalition. To the US an end to the civil war was beneficial as it was part of creating peace, and regarded a prerequisite concerning a future peace process. The unipolar content was traced, though only to a limited degree. Ending the Arab-Israeli conflict in the was part of the (US specific)unipole's agenda', andthe single option' provided the opportunities for the Syrian solution.

Operation Desert Storm. In many ways operation Desert Storm was similiar in content to the formation of the MLF. The similarities occur with respect to break of bipolar patterns, realignment, and the content of the unipolar agenda, flocking and hard work. The war, however, emphazised the importance of the content. When the Coalition was gathered it was not clear whether the conflict would lead to war, or if Arab members would leave in the event of war. The Arab members did not, and this confirms the assessment of their adaptation to the US world order as well as emphasizes the unipolar character of the operation Desert Storm.

The ceasefire in West Sahara. The conflict about the status of West Sahara was tempered by the ceasefire. The ability of Algeria and Libya to prevent total Moroccan control by supporting the Polisario Front was weakened by the loss of Soviet backing (dealignment). The UN initiated ceasefire was primarily on Moroccan terms, but it also holds the promise of a referendum. The dispute was dealt with in the context of Moroccan strength (the single option) and decreased fear of an independent West Sahara turning into a battlefield for Soviet influence.

The Gaza-Jericho accords. The agreements on Palestinian auton-omy reflect the breaking of bipolar patterns and high degrees of unipolar content. During bipolarity, the Palestinian problem was an issue between the superpowers, and the zero-summing made a solution impossible. 1989 de-linked the Israeli-Palestinian conflict from the zero-summing, and it also changed their mutual relations of strength. In addition, the emergence of unipolarity led to de-/ realignment of Syria and the PLO, and to US reassessment of all parties and the international agenda. The US changed its strategy for the conflict, took on the role of mediator and demanded a start to the peace process. The accord resulted in Israeli abandonment of some control over parts of the previously occupied territories (fission), and it may lead to the rise of a new state eventually: a Palestinian state may be within the reach. The unipolar content of the Gaza-Jericho accords was traced in all dimensions: the unipolar agenda, flocking, the single option, and hard work.

The Arab-Israeli peace process. The peace process between Israel, Jordan, Syria, and the Lebanon was initiated in the same way as the Israeli-Palistinian track. The Israeli-Arab parties met publicly in Madrid and negotiated for the first time directly and publicly, under US auspices. So far the negotiations have produced an Israeli-Jordanian peace treaty. The commencement of the negotiations, in itself, represented a break with the bipolar agenda and the patterns of cooperation and conflict, and the Israeli-Jordanian peace treaty confirmed the break. Symmetrical as well as asymmetrical realignment was present, and the degree of unipolar content was high: the connections to the statements onthe unipole's agenda',flocking',the single option', andhard work' were all demonstrated. Whether or not the process will lead to additional peace treaties, the unipolar impact was there: the parties, remarkably, began to negotiate.

In addition to the analysis of the major international political events, which have taken place, a survey of apparently stable Middle Eastern politics between 1989 and 1998 was provided in order not to overlook bipolar patterns still in operation. The survey did not challenge the above results, rather the general tendencies were confirmed. There were no bipolar patterns and issues which were not affected, and actions of the subsystemic units not involved in the events did not deviate substantially from expectations. The model for unipolarity is about outcomes; cf. the emphasis on the events. Yet it is possible to interpret state behaviour to some extent by means of the model, because a unipolar content would not be traceable if the states did not change their behaviour.

Turkey (involved only in the Gulf Conflict operations) adapted and flocked. Turkey has also been involved in increased regional activity concerning the ECO and the Black Sea Cooperation (hard work), and it has changed its foreign policy and become a more active Middle East power. Libya and Algeria did not flock, but Libya has become more integrated i UMA, and Algeria is still haunted by the civil war.[2]

The analysis revealed only a few deviations concerning the individual units: Jordan's choice of neutrality in 1990–91 (and PLO's support of Iraq), continuing Iraqi non-compliance, and the Iranian resistance to adapting. As for Jordan's choice it took place before the manifestation of unipolarity by the victorious operation Desert Storm, and Jordan immediately flocked afterwards. As for the PLO, it was analysed as an organisation which was severely weakened by the end of bipolarity (asymmetrical dealignment) and mainly influenced by Iraq being the only former Soviet proxy with relative, subsystemic strength on its own. PLO's choice took, like Jordan's, place before the Iraqi defeat, only on even harder terms. Like Jordan, PLO also flocked afterwards.

The puzzling aspects according to the analytical framework, therefore, are Iraq's continuing non-compliance with the US world order despite the military defeat in operation Desert Storm, and Iran's troubled relationship with the West. Given Iraq's defeat, it is interesting that adaptation has not taken place yet. The answer probably lies in the fact that the US stopped short of making Iraq areal' loser, as was seen in the US lack of will to go to Baghdad or to encourage the formation of a Kurdish state. These options were ruled out in favour of what is interpreted to be a quest for stability: imposing a real partition of Iraq would change the subsystemic relations of strength, create a new power vacuum to be filled, and the Middle Eastern development would be very difficult to manage. The US policy has given Iraq the possibility to breathe and test the limits for restoring its position. However, Iraq has also been labelled arogue' state and has been subject to a very strong international pressure in order to deprive Iraq of its weapons of mass destruction since the end of the fighting in February 1991. Nuclear and other WMD non-proliferation in general is a part of the US unipolar agenda, and non-proliferation in particular is a part when it comes to what the US perceive a hostile threshold states.

During the 1990's Iran had the threshold dimension in common with Iraq (and to a lesser degree with Libya but which had kept a low profile and not challenged the US world order as have Iraq and Iran). Although Iran had left most of its early fundamentalist positions, and although Iran remained neutral during operation Desert Storm, the US still had it at the top of the list of the so-called rogue states. As mentioned in Chapter 3, the so-called rogue states have in common that they deny the US world order and are nuclear threshold states. The US expressed concern about the Iranian opposition to the Madrid peace process and international terrorism. Iran withdrew its revolutionary guards from Lebanon, but it still supported the Hezbollah. Iran was against the increased US presence in the Persian Gulf, while the US accused Iran of supporting international terrorism.[3] Finally, but not least, Iran refused to close its nuclear program. Iran and Iraq fell out with the US with respect to a very important part of the US unipolar agenda: the non-proliferation of nuclear weapons. For various reasons Iran and Iraq did not comply with important parts the world order, and their special cases during the period in question are thus explained with a reference tothe unipolés agenda'.

Another question still needs an answer: were the initial theoretical connections between changes of strength and realignment reflected in the analysis? The subsystemic relations of strength were definitely changed by the end of the Cold War in 1989: firstly, states and organisations supported and influenced by the Soviet Union were weakened. These states were Algeria, Libya, the PDRY, Syria, and Iraq; and the organisations were the PLO and the Polisario Front. Secondly, the subsystemic positions of states supported by the US, in the context of the US aim to contain the Soviet Union and to reduce Soviet influence, were endangered. After the end of the Cold War the positions of the US aligned states depended on the US reassessment of its allies. This group included Morocco, Tunisia, Jordan, North Yemen, and, to a lesser extent, the Southern Gulf States, which (especially Saudi Arabia) had been central in the US aim of securing the oil supply. Similarly, US support for Israel was at stake, but again to a lesser extent because of the general US commitment to the security of a Jewish state.

It was inevitable that the Middle Eastern states, once supported by and aligned to the Soviet Union, were weakened. Their future position, however, depended – and depends – on their relationship with the US, which was bound to reassess its foreign connections after 1989, including its support for states in the Middle East. So far the US has reassessed its connections in accordance with its post-1989 objectives for the Middle East. These objectives were broadly announced immediately after 1989, and progressively developed during the first following years, most notably in the aftermath of operation Desert Storm. A unipole is expected to pursue the aims of keeping challengers down, of trying to avoid exhaustion and other states' free-riding, andof managing world affairs which may affect a major part of world affairs or the unipole's direct interests. Specifically for the Middle East in the 1990's, the US declared its commitment to halting the proliferation of nuclear weapons, to securing the oil supply on reasonable terms, and to working for an Arab-Israeli peace.

The US reassessment created an opening for states which could, potentially, take advantage of the US world order. Thus, the oil rich states in the Arabian Peninsula have been subject to renewed US commitment (and the US has increased its presence),[4] and the states which joined the US Madrid peace initiatives had the opportunity of US commitment (the group includes the former Soviet allies of Syria and the Palestinians). On the other hand, opposing states are ruled out and regarded as adversaries (to an extent which would depend on what part of the US world order that is opposed – especially nuclear proliferation, how much they oppose, and, of course, if it make any difference to the US) until they comply with the US world order.

The connections between the states in the Middle East and the US are by no means fixed, and they may change during unipolarity. The fact, however, that there is only one superpower in existence and that there are no alternatives for the subsystemic units to use in bargaining or to realign, makes the post-1989 Middle East comparatively stable with respect to strength resulting from asymmetrical alignment. This needs three qualifications: firstly, in case of a peaceful development, the connections between the US and its Middle Eastern allies may loosen. States tend to flock only when it is necessary, and the presence of an un-checked superpower may become troublesome and turn into dominance. Secondly, with regard to subsystemic interaction, states continuously respond to the minor, quantitative changes of strength, which is part of the international daily life and this may lead to different and shifting subsystemic (symmetrical) constellations. Thirdly, if unipolarity is transformed by the rise of successful challengers, the subsystemic units will have new options – and the unipolar dynamics will disappear.

Within the Middle Eastern subsystem, the units responded to the systemic change and to their new conditions, including their different relative positions, which became clearer during the years between 1989 and 1998. The overwhelmingly prevalent way, however, was adaptation. The process of adaptation was definitely assisted by the clarification of the US unipolarity by the US reaction to the Iraqi invasion of Kuwait, and the process has not been smooth. Jordan and the PLO initially opted against adaptation by remaining neutral, in effect supporting Iraq, during the formation of the Coalition and operation Desert Storm. However, both Jordan and the PLO changed their strategies, when the price of their support of Iraq had to be paid, and, when new options were available, they immediately joined the peace process – and later signed accords with Israel. Syria has been flocking in three cases: the formation of the Coalition, operation Desert Storm, and the participation in the Arab-Israeli peace process. Only a peace treaty with Israel is still lacking to complete Syria's inclusion in the US unipolar network, but Syria's choice is still not finally made.

Israel has gone through different phases of adaptation. When the Shamir Government was only reluctantly joining the Madrid process and maintaining a series of procedural demands (which in effect obstructed any progress in the process), the US reacted strongly and showed its will to reassess all parties (examples of the US reaction are the adverce UN vote after the Temple Mount incident, and the loan guarantee delay). The Rabin Government restored the US-Israeli relationship and signed treaties with the PLO and Jordan. The international progress in the peace process, however, resulted in very high internal Israeli costs, primarily brought about by the more than thirty terrorist attacks in Israel and thus challenged the Israeli gains from the process. The Netanyahu government tried to address the challenges. The efforts, however, had a negative impact on the process, but they also reflected the changed relationship between Israel and the Palestinians: when the process began, Israel was in a superior position and gave concessions to a much weaker part. The concessions strengthened the Palestinians, now in possesion of soil, government and organsition. Therefore, it is obvious that the new situation demanded response. For Israel the challenge to its position as a privileged US ally was expressed in the US declaration of its commitment to all sides in the peace process, as against its once exclusive commitment to Israel's security.

The unipolar incentive to hard work was not only reflected in the individual events. During the period from 1989 to 1996 the formalised regional – subsystemic – activity increased in the Middle East, not only in case of the peace processes. Several Middle Eastern organisations were expanded or revitalised: UMA, ECO and the GCC. Only the ACC dissolved (after only one year in operation), and the Arab League is in a process of what appears to be redifinition and adaptation to the changing positions and relations of its member states. The activity reflects another dimension of the current power arangement. The activity in the subsystem appears to increase geographically rather than along the previous patterns.

In sum, the expected impact of the 1989 systemic change into unipolarity according to the analytical framework was present in the Middle East as demonstrated in the analysis. Individually and in total the events have met the criteria for both the disappearance, or significant moderation, of the bipolar patterns, and led to something new and compatible with the statements on the US unipolarity. The only exception was the Iraqi response to the US and international pressure subsequent to the invasion of Kuwait, where the unipolar content was traced only to a low degree. The connection between the Iraqi invasion and the transitional perspective was, however, fully demonstrated; and it is important that the invasion took place before the full manifestation of US unipolarity. Regarding bipolar patterns still operative, the findings suggested that extremely few important bipolar patterns have survived 1989 (this, of course, does not mean that the parties making up the patterns have reconciled or changed their aims; only that the conditions and dynamics are different and lead to different patterns). The US-Israeli relationship may be the only example, but it was shown that the relationship is now less privileged to Israel and that it has changed in more ways.

When the post-1989 events are aggregated, they make up a picture of post-1989 Middle Eastern politics which clearly differs from the pre-1989 picture: the unipolar US camp so far comprises the Southern Gulf States, Israel, Jordan, Egypt, Morocco, Tunisia, Turkey, the Palestinians, and, though not fully or definitely, Syria and Lebanon. The states outside the camp are Algeria (in civil war), the Republic of Yemen, Libya, Iraq, and Iran. Among these states only Iraq and Iran in various degrees opposed the US World Order seriously.

As for the subsystemic patterns of cooperation and conflict, the bipolar division between radical and moderate states was changing into a pattern of geographical groupings: the Maghreb states in UMA, the states in the peace process, and the GCC states. Iran and Turkey is involved in cooperation with the former Soviet republics in Trans Caucasus, and Turkey entered into military cooperation with Israel.

Unipolar issues also differ from the bipolar issues. The US has put the following issues on the agenda, which it now alone defines: to contain Iraq and Iran; to limit proliferation of weapons of mass destruction, especially of nuclear weapons; to achieve comprehensive Arab-Israeli peace accords (during bipolarity the aim was the process itself and less comprehensive); and, which is not new, to secure the supply of oil, primarily from the Arabian Peninsula.

Even the concept of the Middle East has undergone some changes. The former Soviet republics from Azerbaijan in the West to Tajikistan in the East have enlarged the subsystem; and Turkey in the northeast is becoming a much more active Middle Eastern power rather than in the bipolar period. On the other hand, the Maghreb states are strengthening their mutual relations as a group which disentangles itself from the Middle East in favour of Europe, especially the Mediterranean EU countries; and the Soviet attempt to include the

Asymmetrical patterns	Symmetrical patterns	Issues
• US camp vs. 'rogue' states	• Geographical and political/economical groupings (GCC, UMA, ECO, BSECZ)	• The Peace Process • World Order compliance • Kurdish nationalism • Democratization • (US dominance)

Figure 6 Unipolar patterns of conflict and cooperation in the Middle East

Bipolarity	Unipolarity
• Maghreb	• (Magreb + Mauritania)
• Mashrek	• Mashrek
• Northern Gulf states (incl. Afghanistan)	• Northern Gulf states (excl. Afghanistan)
• Horn of Africa	• Arabian Peninsula
• Arabian Peninsula	• Turkey
	• Caucasus (ex-Soviet republics)

Figure 7 The political Middle East across the systemic change

Horn of Africa into Middle Eastern politics is history. The size and stretch of the political Middle East have changed.

Unipolarity is not a static state of affairs, and the continuously changing subsystemic relations of strength as well as the changes in the US agenda and priorities may have effects on patterns of conflict and cooperation, and issues in the Middle East. From 1989 to 1998, however, Middle Eastern international politics were deeply affected by the systemic change into unipolarity, and the demonstrated connection between the theoretical statements and the events provides the explanation.

THE MODEL FOR UNIPOLARITY

When a theory is used, the usage reveals both the shortcomings and advantages of the theory itself. In this case the advantages of both the classic neorealist theory and the specific model for unipolarity was on trial.

One element of the framework may appear to be disputable. This is the distinction which has been made between flocking (unipolarisation) and the concept of bandwagoning.[5] It is an essential neorealist notion that states tend to balance each other.[6] More specifically, states tend to balance the stronger rather than to follow, as the states want to enhance security and avoid being dominated. The balancing thesis thereby contradicts the bandwagoning thesis (see Walt 1990), which says that states will follow the stronger in order to enhance power. The debate is relevant in the case of unipolarity, and not least in the case of the model for unipolarity emphazising the tendency to flock. Unipolarity may in some respects resemble a hierarchic system, where bandwagoning tends to prevail unlike in cases of anarchically organised systems. However, as argued in chapter 3, polarisation and bandwagoning are still different phenomena in the case of unipolarity, and even though the effects may appear to be similar, the causes differ: Bandwagoning is understood to conceptualize lack of balancing within symmetrical relations, whereas flocking and polarisation conceptualises asymmetrical relations. Minor states will tend to flock around the poles in order to obtain effective security guarantees or not to be worse off than their symmetrical adversaries.

Asymmetrical alignment (for example the Saudi Arabian-US defence cooperation during the Gulf conflict 1990–91) should, therefore, be dealt with in terms of flocking rather than bandwagoning. In general, the analysis has proven the value of relying on the neorealist notion of balancing, even across the systemic change. In the aftermath of 1989, the Middle Eastern states, with the exception of Jordan of those expected to do so, have pursued balancing strategies *and* flocked, rather than bandwagoning strategies.

However, as a framework for the analysis, the model for unipolarity apparently worked, and the statements on unipolar dynamics apparently have explained the immediate post-Cold War development of Middle Eastern politics and the very different events. So far there has been a lack of *general* explanations of the transformation of Middle Eastern politics. In addition, the model makes it possible to analyse the connections between the different events because of the model's emphasis on the continuous development of the relations of strength. Consequently the model possesses a dynamic potential together with its capacity for pointing to deep trends during unipolarity.

The study of the effects of the 1989 systemic transformation in one particular area is also of more general interest because the analysis and results encourage generalisations based on the theoretical statements. The affirmative answer to the initial argument strengthens the basis for dealing with other areas in the same way in order to search for similar effects (but not for identical outcomes or an identical breaking of patterns, because other subsystems and areas were subject to the bipolar impact in different ways depending on specific superpower interests).

The next steps will be to further elaborate the concepts of the model for unipolarity, to infer and test hypotheses thoroughly, and to apply it to other geographical areas as well as to other chronological phases of unipolarity. Only such research processes will improve the model and point to its advantages and limitations.

One specific dimension of neorealist theory which appears particularly useful and worth elaborating could be labelled capability analysis. Capabilitiy analysis was carried out in the basic analyses of all events though not much explictly applied (Hansen 1998). That is, to focus on developments in aggregate capalities of each state, not forgetting the capability of 'political stability' (Waltz 1979), often overlooked as a part of the neorealist conceptual framework. Capability analysis is crucial when putting emphasis on redistribution of strength and power balancing.

The conclusions have lead to an understanding of the security dynamics of the Middle East as having being transformed, and the conclusions also suggest considerations about future developments in the Middle East.

FUTURE RESEARCH

It seems it will be valuable to place a stronger emphasis on systemic change when dealing with international politics. In spite of the Middle East's apparent potential for resistance to systemic change, the 1989 transformation deeply affected the region. This points to a broader use of the analytical framework elaborated here: other areas could be analysed in the same way; and the Middle East itself could be analysed in terms of earlier systemic change. For example, the emergence of the post-1918 and post-1945 systems might be dealt with by means of a general framework rather than the specific contexts often used. Theoretically, however, the statement on systemic change needs elaboration (cf. Chapter 3). The extensive amount of empirical material in existence will facilitate the task.

For the Middle East, a reinterpretation of the bipolar conflicts appears to be beneficial according to the above analysis, which showed that simple relations of strength were the crucial barrier to peace – as well as preventing some conflicts.

The model for unipolarity may prove to be of use for more general research in international politics after 1989: firstly, it provides a consistent way to analyse the many events which have occurred all over the world since 1989. Secondly, it also provides a way to deal with future international developments. So far no other general – or unipolar – models have been proposed.

In light of the results of this study, it seems reasonable to propose the following suggestions for future research strategies:

- There is a need to put a strong emphasis in analysis on strength – in the neorealist way where relative international strength matters.
- The model for unipolarity (or an improved version of the model) may contribute to analyses of the post-1989 world affairs. Even though other analyses credit the existence of only one superpower, there is a need to draw the full consequences. An extreme illustration of this, which goes outside the academic world, is the thinking of Saddam Hussein, who acknowledged the singe superpower arrangement but failed to draw the full consequences.
- Kenneth Waltz' phrase that states are states and act accordingly' is also applicable to the Middle East. The Middle Eastern states acted according to the general expectations regarding state behaviour and outcomes after 1989, and consequently the Middle Eastern states should not be treated as exceptional cases in International Politics.
- It is important to make a distinction between the effects of the end of the Cold War (bipolarity), those of the systemic change itself, and the effects of the emergence of unipolarity. However, it is important to investigate the longer term effects of unipolarity in phases less close to the systemic change.

Whatever the final result of the ongoing processes in the Middle East, all parties have fundamentally changed their positions, and the Middle East has been transformed. The states have different patterns of conflict and cooperation, new policies, and the risk of (bipolar) proxy wars has gone. There is only one superpower to call on if conflicts arise. There is still a risk of conflict, and many problems remain and new ones have emerged. But the context of the problems is different, and the unipolar transformation of the Middle East may well have brought about an improvement in security.

Chapter 16

Security Challenges in the Middle East

Ten years after the end of the Cold War the Middle East had clearly undergone a series of changes. Unipolarity had not eradicated conflicts or completely changed what lies behind earlier patterns of conflict and cooperation. The unipolar dynamics, however, have had their impact, and so did the specific US unipolar state of affairs. When looking to the future it is important to incorporate the unipolar dynamics of politics as well as the US policy in analyses of Middle Eastern. The dynamics are expected to remain in operation until a different international arrangement of power emerges, and they will affect the outcomes of the variety of unit level interactions which will undoubtedly take place. In the future the US policy may be subject to greater variations as the US reacts and responds to Middle Eastern politics from a position as a global power and arguably attempts to remain so. In addition, the subsystemic relations of strength will gain importance according to the statement on hard work. These dimensions are crucial to further analysis when applying the suggested theoretical framework. It is also important to address the range of unit level activity which was excluded from the bipolar agenda: the management of problems like poverty, inequality, growth of population, and scarcity of resources (anything fluid) were to a great extent subordinated to superpower rivalry during the Cold War.[1] Now these problems are growing and are less likely to escape attention, and they may given higher priority in the Middle Eastern subsystem. Furthermore, the US unipolarity has added democratization and the spread of the free market to the agenda. On the other hand, democratization will advance only with difficulty in an area characterized by serious problems concerning leadership succession. While the Middle Eastern states will be *working hard* within the context of unipolarity, their current problems and challenges thus indicate that their mutual interaction will include a multitude of

216

dimensions, and the states are challenged on several internal dimensions.

When the urgency presented by international threats (like the Iraqi invasion of Kuwait) is absent, states have a greater room for maneouvre, they are less inclined to subordinate daily national interests, and they are able to manage a greater range of foreign political issues simultanously, which leads them into less clear mutual relations. When a state does not have to choose between allies, to choose side in a conflict, or give concessions, it often tends not to make that choice. Moments of truths are revealing (and useful when analysing), but fortunately they are rare phenomena in international politics. Furthermore, with respect to any analysis of coming Middle Eastern events it will be necessary to pay attention to the current – and ever changing – relations of strengths and balances of power within the subsystem. While changing relations of strength do not change the global (systemic) power arrangement, the changes may bring about major impact within the subsystem.

In the light of these considerations on the model for unipolarity, and the development between 1989 and 1998, it appears that the following issues will be important parts of Middle Eastern politics in the foreseeable future as they particularly relate to the power balancing: the development of the Israeli-Arab-Palestinian peace process, the problem of succession, the future international role of the major powers in the subsystem, the problem of nationalism and potential Middle Eastern failure states, and potential US dominance. All this in a region itself being transformed in size and orientation.

THE ARAB-ISRAELI-PALESTINIAN PEACE PROCESS

In the Spring of 1996 the peace process deteriorated and became subject to severe problems. The triggering factors were the series of militant Palestinian terror attacks against Israeli civilians within Israel and the decision of the then Israeli Prime Minister, Benyamin Netanyahu, to begin the construction of new Jewish settlements (Har Homa/Abu Gnaym) in East Jerusalem. Until then, breaks and problems had also been part of the process but not to the same extent.

Both the triggering factors reflected the changing relations of strength between the Israeli and the Palestinian parties, which were the result of the previous development and the accords between the parties. When the Madrid process began, the parties joined the process from their post-Gulf War positions. The PLO, behind the

Palestinians, was weaker than it had been since all positions won during the 1970's and 1980's were lost as was its superpower ally of the Soviet Union. Israel, on the other hand, was strenghtened in the first place as the superpower ally of most of its opponents had gone, and because Iraq being a major regional threat had been defeated. The Palestinians appeared to have no alternatives to joining the process, and Israel appeared to be in a position to achieve substantial concessions by joining the peace process, which Israel was also under a strong pressure to do from the United States.

The process resulted, rather quickly, in a redistribution of gains and strenght between Israel and the Palestinians. The Palestinians gained their first real autonomy ever, and by obtaining the autonomy they gained the prospects of achieving a state in the long term, and they gained a series of instruments to make the prospect of a state come real. They were now able to organise themselves, recognized as a negotiator, and had become a state-like political actor. In addition, but not least, their autonomy provided them with a relative gain vis-à-vis Israel, which had given up some control over Gaza and parts of the West Bank, since 1967 under total Israeli control; and the Palestinians, relatively speaking, gained the position of becoming a negotiator formally equal to Israel (though not, in spite of the gains, an equally strong one).

Israel gained little in this first phase relative to the Palestinians. only Israeli gain has been the improved prospects for the Israeli aim of acomprehensive' peace with its neighbours. In return Israel gave up control over territory formerly providingstrategic depth' and suffered severe civilian casualties as a consequence of the process. In terms of relative strength Israel was in the superior position to the Palestinians when peace became an option. The gap between Israel and the Palestinians has narrowed in the sense that they are now facing each other as two negotiating actors rather than being in quite different classes.

The narrowing of the gap in strength should not blur the evident fact, however, that Israel is still the stronger part. If the process totally fails, Israel would be in a position to regain control if facing only the Palestinians. Israel is thus in a position of being the better suited part for ignoring American brokerage. The problem for Israel is that a failure of the peace process would imply serious difficulties regarding the potential long term gains for Israel: to reduce regional threats and increase regional cooperation while maintaining a close relationship to the US and the Western democracies.

The phase of the peace process in the late 1990's was consequently difficult for especially Israel, which was giving concessions while still awaiting the gains. And because the concessions created internal political instability, that was a further decrease in capability. To the Palestinians the first years of the process was been beneficial though creating new problems: those of forming a society, preparing for a state and establishing the range of necessary social structures. In addition to the redistribution of bargaining power between the parties, the process came closer to the most difficult issues as the status of Jerusalem. This apparently triggered another trial of strength running between 1996 and 1999. The trial of strength was further affected by the 'deepening' of the process into the parties' societies. The first agreements were negotiated by Yassir Arafat and Yitzhak Rabin. However, both parties needed to 'swear in' also parts of their societies with less acceptance of the terms.

However, in the current context three factors, in particular, favour the development of the peace process between Israel and Palestinians. Firstly, both parties share a common threat. If Iraq rebuild its strength or if Iran perceives itself to be cornered, and if these two states aquire the adequate capability of weapons of mass destruction, Israel and the Palestinians will share the danger – and the incentive to counter it rather than to concentrate on mutual strife. That is, they both face long term challenges more serious than those of each other. Secondly, both parties cannot ignore the residual subsystemic context. Israel has other opponents than Iran and Iraq as well as a need to obtain normal regional relations, while the Palestinians cannot count on assistance from the neighbourhood. They get political and moral (and some financial) support, but they cannot count on getting any military support against Israel. Thirdly, and most important, both parties need some kind of superpower support, and they can ill afford a fall out with the United States. Neither of the parties have strength to do that, and they both have an incentive to commit the US – which might re-prioritate its resources

If the peace process comes to a complete stop, the Palestinians would risk a complete loss of what has been achieved recently, and Israel would expose itself to regional threats or at least see the vanishing of any potential improvement of its regional position.

Owing to the US position, both parties have a strong incentive to stay in the peace process. They may choose not to stay in the process, but the consequences will be serious. Probably the long term result will be a small Palestinian state (demilitarized and without

Jerusalem). An alternative but less likely proposal may, in the longer term, reappear: a Palestinian confederation with Jordan.

With respect to the Israeli-Arab peace process the prospects are similar. During the stale-mate in the mid-1990's Syria improved its (bad) relations to Iraq, it has not given up its connections to Iran, but Syria still remains a part of the peace process. Syria risks becoming completely isolated, and the alternatives appear to be a Syrian-Iraqi-Iranian axis or a continuation of the peace process. If the US maintains its commitment, the favourable option for Syria appears to be the peace process. If an agreement is reached, an inner core with longer term prospects of close cooperation, guaranteed by the unipole, will have materialised among the formerly conflicting parties. Then the Middle East would be partitioned into two centres with US commitments (the inner cores' consisting of the states in the peace process, respectively the GCC states), and this would affect the whole subsystem. A central question would arise concerning the Egyptian role in such a case. One option for Egypt would be to join the peace process core. The relatively weaker states in the core, however, might fear Egyptian dominance and thus try to keep Egypt at a distance. This points to another option, which is a further Egyption orientation towards the African continent, most notably the Maghreb. In sum, the results of the peace process will influence the whole region and its alignments.

It has been argued that the distribution of water will create new dangers. The area in general is rich in oil but poor in water supplies.[2] If the general organisation of security is in place, the problems with water should be solvable, too. The water problems are also serious among the countries involved in the peace process, but because they are in that process, they have the best prospects of general security.

SUCCESSION AND DEMOCRATISATION

In many Arab states tendencies towards democratisation have evolved recently. The economic-ideological alternative to liberal democracy and free market capitalism disappeared with the Soviet Union. It is too early to assess whether this dimension of the US World Order will prevail, but there are already indications that it might. The pressure which the market-democracy dimension exerts is strong: it is the only successful model left, and is probably the only way to enter the new, united organisation of the world – which embraces economic competition. It is most likely, therefore, that the spread of the market-democracy dimension will trigger internal tensions in many states and among many groups poorly suited for adapting to it. The rise of radical political islam is evidence of that. To integrate in the US world order and to adapt to democratization therefore pose a major challenge to the Middle East.

The spread of democracy accentuates problems of succession. Problems of succession are unit level phenomena, but they have so far proved to possess a potential for creating international tensions. The reasons for that is probably to be found by drawing an analogy to the results and explanations worked out by Stephen Walt in case of revolutions (Walt 1988): when internal change takes place, channels of information are disturbed and insecurity arises about how to manage the problems of the state in which the changes take place (although this should be considered to be a much lower risk than compared in the case of revolution). If, however, the change takes place in a formerly authoritarian state, civil urest or even civil war may break out (Anderson 1991). In such cases the international effects may be similar to those of revolutionary changes, and at least power vacuums may emerge.

In the Middle East the ruling generation is ageing, and most of the leaderships are authoritarian though in different ways and to different degrees. By 1999 a series of Arab leaders face the challenge of succession (Hansen 1998):[3] Colonel Muammar al Qaddafi (born 1942/achieved power 1969) in Libya, King Hassan II (1929/1961) in Morocco, Palestinian Yasser Arafat (1929/1969), President Saddam Hussein (1937/1979) in Iraq, President Hosni Mubarak (1928/1981) in Egypt, President Hafez al Assad (1930/1971) in Syria, King Fahd (1923/1982) in Saudi Arabia, Emir al-Sabah (1926/1977) in Kuwait, and Sultan Quaboos Ibn Saud (1940/1970) in Oman. In Jordan, King Hussein (1935/1953–99) died in February 1999, and his son Abdallah (II) became the new king of Jordan. The change of power took place peacefully and, at least in the short term, without major difficulties.

During bipolarity successions could shake the region because a new leadership might change its superpower affiliation. This option no longer exists. Of course, new leaderships may opt for a strategy of distancing themselves from the US, but this demands strength (as in the Iranian case), and, to carry out real opposition to the US, considerable strength. The single option will probably prevent new leaderships from making substantial changes in their foreign policies. But the changes in leadership themselves may increase the degree of international insecurity.

Unipolarity, however, contains probable counter-agents regarding the creation of international tension: unipolarity provides a buffer, as unipolarity leaves no risk that the new leadership will fall into the wrong hands'. That is, the new leadership cannot align itself with the other superpower because there isno other superpower. In the case of the Middle East it may tilt towards political islamism, which is currently the main political anti-American tendency. But political islamism is not led by any competing superpower;[4] and it is a very diverse phenomenon. On the other hand the lack of an alternative option also leaves a major internal room for unrest and civil war, in the worst case for a failed state. The spread of the democratic dimension of the US World Order, however, provides the Middle Eastern states with a direction, when the whole generation of ageing Arab leaders have to be replaced not later than during the first decade of the new millenium. The democratic direction, however, is in competition with political islam and international conflicts.

THE MAJOR POWERS IN THE SUBSYSTEM

Throughout the 1990's, the balancing of power in the Middle East was affected by previous and post-Gulf War puzzles of bringing the major regional powers in: Iraq and Iran were both preoccupied by their mutual war in 1980's, after that Iraq was subject to sanctions and air-strikes in the 1990's while Iran still had a post-revolutionary troubled international relationship. In the Western part of the Arab world, Algeria was suffering from serious internal problems during 1990's, and therefore three of the potentially most powerful Middle Eastern states (measured in terms of capabilities) were playing a lesser role than they might otherwise have played. On the contrary, Turkey began to become a more active Middle Eastern power in the same period. An important challenge for the first ten years of the new millennium will therefore be the incorporation and integration of these major powers into 'daily' Middle Eastern politics. The power balancing, in general, will be affected when three of the major powers, Iraq and Iran in particular, recover and reenter the political stage and another, Turkey becomes more active. They will also have to adjust their interests and ambitions according to their mutual relationship.

The gap between Iraqi policy and the US World Order may seem hard to bridge. Since the Gulf War and throughout the 1990's, the troubled relationship between Iraq and the US persisted. Iraq is in a very dificult situation. It has so far pursued an offensive strategy in order to restore its position and given priority to maintaining af WMD-capacity on cost of societal decay. Iraq will probably be forced to give up its offensive strategy – or face a breakdown. The US chose to make an example of Iraq, and it seems as a change of the US approach depends either on a US assessment of the Iraqi WMD-capacity being eliminated[5] or of the rise of more serious international problems which demands full US attention. It is, however, beyond any doubt that a change of leadership in Iraq would facilitate an improvement of the Iraqi-US relationship, also a change by a competing faction of the Iraqi regime. This would allow an alternative strategy for Iraqi reconstruction to be promoted, and it would provide the US with a reason for change.

Some slow progress and improvement in the US-Iranian relationship took place in the late 1990's. While dramatic change are probable agents for change between the US and Iraq, slow but steady development appears to be the agent in the case of Iran. Iran's foreign policy has been continuously 'normalized' over the years since the revolution. Still, some serious issues remains but their resolution appears to depend mostly on further incremental change of the Iranian policy.

NATIONALISM AND FAILED STATES

The Palestinians have hope to get their own state, the Kurds also have. Whereas the Palestinians have made substantial progress towards achiving a state, the Kurds have only got thesafe haven' in northeast Iraq. It is estimated that the Kurdish peoples total about twenty million spread over mainly fourstates with a geographic centre in the northeastern part of the Middle East. In contrast to the Palestinians, the Kurdish peoples are numerous and their centre is rich, including first class oil ressources. On the other hand, the Kurds are more divided than were the Palestinians, as many of the Kurds are integrated in or linked to the states where they live – the Palestinians outside the West Bank and Gaza are much less integrated. Also the cultural differences between the various Kurdish groups are greater; the Kurds are not confined to the Arab world but disseminated in such different societies as Persian Iran, Arab Iraq, and secular Turkey.

Kurdish aspirations are also undermined by the fact that a Kurdish state would endanger the Middle Eastern balances and give rise to instability. This would be contrary to the US aims, and the fear of instability might well have influenced President Bush in 1991, when he decided not to let troops continue into the Iraqi heartland, and when the US later refused to commit itself to the establishment of a Kurdish state in Iraq. Later, in the Spring of 1995 the US did not prevent Turkey from what may be interpreted as a launching of a preventive operation against an evolving Kurdish state in th UN safe haven in Iraq.

The Kurds in Iraq have rebelled several times, most energetically after the Iraqi defeat in 1991. Since then, however, they have also fought civil war, and the KDP-faction realigned with the Iraqi regime in 1996. In Turkey the efforts have been different and less coherent though even more continuous. The Kurdish struggle in Turkey have been met with repression, too. In both places the repression has fuelled Kurdish aspirations for a state, and the aspirations has also been encouraged by the apparent Palestinian success.

While the unipolar world order may provide a rare opportunity for new states to be formed, and while the international norms have been changing in favour of self determination, the Kurdish case apparently faces difficult prospects because of the problems such a state would create with regard to the subsystemic balance of power and to the existing states, and because of the so far lack of Kurdish cohesion. Iraq may break up, and it seems as if nobody wants failed states in the Middle East. The would create vacuums of power in an unstable context.

US DOMINANCE

To several states and many groups in the Middle East the greatest challenge of unipolarity is probably the risk of US dominance. If the US pursues a maximalist strategy or if it just slowly spread its world order, this may harm the interests and daily life of states and groups. Per definition, a unipole cannot help offending other states' interests. A unipole only qualifies in terms of superior capabilities, and in a globalized world as this, such a position equalizes global interests and activity. In addition, the specific American model of liberal democracy and free market capitalism endanger the life of many people and the political system of several states, poorly suited for taking up this challenge. They have to give up their own way and make (at least in the short term) painful adjustments. As Kenneth Waltz (1979) stated, socialization and imitation of the successful states by others are recurrent phenomena. Therefore, the challenges are not only to be found in the Middle East but also in the US unipolarity itself although it apparently also provides a series of important security opportunities.

FUTURE PATTERNS

The model for unipolarity cannot predict specific future patterns, only point to the expectation that during unipolarity the Middle East will be strongly influenced by the following security dynamics: the unipole's agenda, flocking, the single option, and hard work including increased regional activity. It is evident that the Middle East will still have to struggle with a series of serious problems such as growth of population and many kinds of conflicts. Above, challenges related to the power balancing were outlined

The general pattern of conflict and cooperation in the Middle East will most likely be characterized by two tendencies: a general flocking around the US together in the case of security problems alongside with opposing efforts to avoid US dominance, and the emergence of symmetrical security arrangements linked to the subsystemic development. The dangers of escalation and zero-summing have gone, and the Middle Eastern states have to work harder in order to enhance security.

Both the bipolar superpowers helped to end the period of mandates and protectorates. They then fought a cold war and deadlocked a series of conflicts among the then new states in the subsystem. This era has come to an end, and a new world order has emerged. The first chapter in the modern history of the Middle East is over, and a new one has begun.

Notes

Chapter 1 Introduction

1 The terms 'great power', 'superpower' and 'pole' are used interchangeably.

Chapter 2 Neorealist Analysis

1 Aggregate capabilities comprise size of territory and population, economic and military capacity, resource endowment, political stability and competence (Waltz 1979).
2 Alignment is understood simply and broadly as security cooperation between two or more states (Walt 1990:1).

Chapter 3 Bipolarity and the Middle East

1 The major exception was the case of Iran where the US sought influence and the Soviet Union initially refused to withdraw its troops from their positions.

Chapter 4 A Model for Unipolarity

1 Neorealism has been tested as well as elaborated since its emergence in the late seventies, particularly concerning interstate alliances, see Walt (1990), Walt (1988), David (1991), Morrow (1991); for alliance theory see also e.g. G. Snyder (1984), Christensen and J. Snyder (1990), and Garnham (1991).
2 The case is not uncontroversial, however, because it could be claimed that the Roman Empire did not exist in an international system, or that it did not exist in a state system.
3 Waltz has stated that multipolarity did last longer than bipolarity. However, if a distinction is made between the different multipolar systems which succeeded each other, multipolarity appears to be a more unstable arrangement.
4 The potential costs of allying are described by, for example, Glenn Snyder (1984), and Christensen and Jack Snyder (1990). Allying with other states

226

may cause a state to be drawn into the warfare of others, to lose autonomy, and/or to exclude other options.

5 The rise of new states and reorganization of others have been considered as essential parts of the post-Cold War world order. It is, however, a recurring phenomena in international politics that new states are formed after a systemic transformation, unipolarity probably holds the potential for the formation of states comparatively weak in capabilities, or even with no ability to defend themselves let alone to sustain economic growth by own means. The emergence of such small and vulnerable states may be a distinct unipolar feature: the neighbouring states may struggle for influence, but the state in question does not become part of a great power rivalry or game.

6 For a survey of the Cold War's final phase, see Garthoff 1994.

Chapter 5 The US World Order

1 The emphasis of the address was clearly on domestic reforms, and President Bush pointed to a series of planned military cuts and a reduction in defence expenditures.

Chapter 6 The Unification of Yemen

1 Reliable statistics concerning economy and migration are hardly available in the Yemeni case. However, specific divergence in numbers does not affect the general picture.

2 The analysis of the Yemeni civil was to some extent breaks with the chronology. However, one could argue that it completes the unification.

Chapter 7 Iraq's Invasion of Kuwait

1 Iraq's claims on Kuwait had no legal substance (Boxhall 1991; Mendelson and Hulton 1994; Schofield 1994).

2 Initially North Yemen was the member, but after the 1990 declaration of unification, the new Republic of Yemen joined the ACC.

3 The speech also indicated an Iraqi attempt to demonstrate the role as the leading Arab nation (Poulsen-Hansen 1997:3).

4 The Iraqi demands were also put forward at the preparatory meeting between foreign ministers; Iraq referred again to its war efforts against Iran (Heikal 1993:212).

5 This might have been an additional explanation to the Kuwaiti position: As Freedman and Karsh argues (1993:62), the Kuwaitis were fearing that a favourable approach to the Iraqi demands might just have lead to repetition, and was therefore a likewise dangerous strategy.

6 Mylroie refers to and quotes from statement by President Mubarak about Saddam Hussein's belief 'that the invasion of Kuwait would only cause verbal protest'. (Mylroie 1993:125).

7 When Kuwait gained full independence from Great Britain in 1961 Iraq forwarded a claim on Kuwait. However, the Arab League recognized the

independence of Kuwait and Great Britain, which was then representing'
the West, sent troops and deterred Iraq from proceeding. Iraq then
renounced.

Chapter 8 The Formation of the International Coalition

1 Bush's declaration is quoted from the chronology of events in Nye and
Smith (1992).
2 For a survey of the participants, see Cooper *et al.* (1991:392 and 392(n8)).
3 It was only during late in the Iraq-Iran war that Kuwait had sought US
protection by the reflagging of its tankers.
4 A state can choose to pass the buck, i.e. to let other states perform the
balancing, and the advantage is free riding while the risk is abandonment);
or to chain-gang, i.e. to link closely together with others against the threat ,
and the advantage is the addition of strength, while the risk is the high costs
incurred in being drawn into an ally's war (Christensen and Snyder 1990).
The concepts refineme neorealism with a particular focus on unit-level
strategies
5 The PLO supported Iraq. The support, however, can be seen as a
consequence of Iraq' s then dominant position over the Organisation.

Chapter 9 End of the Lebanese Civil War

1 The National Dialogue Committee, September-November 1975; The
Constitutional Document, February 1976; the Riyadh-Cairo Arab Summit
Conferences, October 1976; the Geneva-Lausanne Conferences, 1983–84,
and the Damascus Tripartite Agreement, December 1985. For a survey of
the major attempts to settle the conflict, see Faris 1995.
2 The incentive for Syria to do so and the US approach to Arab participation
in the Coalition was discussed in Chapter 8.

Chapter 10 Operation Desert Storm

1 The SC Resolution 678 passed with twelve votes in favour; only Yemen and
Cuba voted against, and China abstained.
2 Also the previous relationship between Iraqi governments and the Iraqi
kurds had been bloody. The 1987 Anfal Operations illustrates this: In
March 1987 the PUK and Iranian forces had captured the town of Halbja.
Iraqi forces retaliated with gas attacks, shelling their own town (McDowall
1996:357–58).
3 KDP (the Kurdish Democrati Party) was created in 1946 and during the
late 1990'es led by Masoud Barzani. It is the biggest and the pragmatic
faction which opts for a solution with Baghdad in opposition to PUK (the
Patriotic Union of Kurdistan) which opts for independence. During the late
1990'es, PUK, formed in 1976, was led by Jalal Talabani (based on
Cordesman and Hashim 1997).

4 Turkey was able to carry out what was in fact a preventive strike against an evolving Kurdish state structure in the safe haven area because of US acceptance, which was consistent with US care for its general objectives in the Middle East; but Turkey had to withdraw for the same reasons after the mission was completed (Hansen 1995b).

5 The assessment also credits Cordesman and Hashim (1997), Hollis (1993) and Rathmell (1996).

6 'Intransigence' according to Marr (1998:215). Also Hansen (1997).

7 Total elimination of a state's WMD-capacity is hardly possible today as biological and chemical capacity can be developed in a hospital laboratory.

8 The military option, however, is also limited in the case of unipolarity, when the superpower faces an adversary with nuclear (or other WMD-) capacity, see Chapter 3.

Chapter 11 The Western Saharan Cease-fire

1 This historical review of the Western Saharan problem is based on Cordesman 1993.

2 IBRU Boundary and Security Bulletin.

Chapter 12 The Gaza-Jericho Accords

1 The PLF action might have been backed by Saddam Hussein in order to force the PLO back to its radical positions and the need to rely on Iraq.

2 The US searched for and targeted Iraqi Scud missiles, partly in order to protect Israel and preventing it from acting unilaterally under increased pressure, and partly to weaken Iraq.

3 This, of course, is to treat the PLO, theoretically, as a state. The alternative would be still to treat like an organization, now being mostly influenced by the US.

Chapter 13 The Arab-Israeli Peace Process

1 Saudi Arabia immediately assured the US, that it supported the Declaration, and that it was ready to contribute financially to the development of the Palestinian entity – in spite of the PLO position during the Gulf Conflict (International Herald Tribune, September 13, 1993).

2 Until the end of the comprensive civil war in 1990, Lebanon is not assessed.

3 Important and lasting territorial losses have been a rarity in the modern Middle East, in spite of the high frequency of conflicts.

4 The US declared that it was open to the idea of deploying forces in the Golan Heights as part of an agreement between Israel and Syria: this "might well mean some kind of US forces in the Golan", said Secretary of State Warren Christopher in 1993 (International Herald Tribune, 13 September 1993). Later, contradictory statements were put forward.

Chapter 14 Survey: The Middle East 1989–1998

1 Next to the Middle East, Afghanistan has throughout the period in question been burdened by a full scale civil war, which broke out after the withdrawal of the Soviet Union which followed Gorbachev's 'New Thinking'. Afghanistan broke down into virtual anarchy and could hardly be considered a state during the 1990's. The contiguous states of Iran and Pakistan were carefully watching developments in Afghanistan and each others actions there; both had troops on Afghan territory and were supporting different opposing clans, but they did not engage directly in the civil war. The US did not interfere.

2 The Yemens were not members.

3 Morocco, Algeria, Tunesia, Egypt, Jordan, Lebanon, Israel, Syria, the Palestinian Autonomy, Tyrkey, Malta and Cyprus.

Chapter 15 The Transformation of the Middle East – Conclusion

1 The case of the Arab Maghreb Union illustrates that asymmetrical alignment subordinates symmetrical alignment: during the Gulf Conflict 1990–91 UMA was split. After the conflict the UMA states resumed their mutual cooperation.

2 The civil war in Algeria was not part of the analysis because of its internal character. The civil war, however, is probably another effect of the 1989 transformation.

3 After the trial in Nurnberg in May 1997 (where Iran was held responsible for the murderer of four Kurdish leaders in Germany in 1992) also the relationship between the EU and Iran deteriorated.

4 The Southern Gulf States, however, may be challenged with the quest for democratization.

5 The concept of bandwagoning was introduced by Kenneth Waltz with credit to Stephen van Evera (Waltz 1979:26).

6 The notion of balancing is referred to Waltz 1979; it is tested by Walt 1990 (who elaborated the notion into the concept of balancing of threats); and elaborated by Morrow 1991. A specific study on Middle Eastern alignments during the Gulf conflict 1990–91 is provided by Garnham 1991.

Chapter 16 Security Challenges in the Middle East

1 These problems may well become extremely important and the intention is not to underestimate their importance. They are, however, beyond the scope of the work which is about specific dynamics rather than specific issues, and that is why the are not analysed.

2 For a comprehensive study of the water problems in the Middle East, see Beschorner 1993.

3 About the challenges of succession, see Hansen (1997; 1998), and Brooks (1998).

4 The Soviet alternative to the American way has to some extent been replaced by a revival of polical Islam, which, however, lacks a pole at its centre. Unless Iran makes decisive progress, political Islam may be reduced to a movement of internal oppostion or to weak experiments. It will be a reaction to US progress and the emergence of pro-US cores in the Middle East, but it will be to weak become a real challenge.

5 Or at least reduced to an acceptable and minimalist level as it is hardly possible completely to eliminate a state's WMD-capacity (in particular its chemical or biological capacity).

References

Acharya, Amitav (1992): Regional Military-Security Cooperation in the Third World: A Conceptual Analysis of the Relevance and Limitations of ASEAN. *Journal of Peace Research*, Vol. 29:1.

Ajami, Fouad (1992): *The Arab Predicament*. Canto, Cambridge University Press, Cambridge.

Amirahmadi, Hooshang (1990): 'Economic Reconstruction of Iran: Costing the war Damage'. *Third World Quarterly*, Vol. 12:1.

Andersen, Lars Erslev (ed.) (1994): *Yemen. Mellem stamme og modernitet.* Systime, Herning.

Anderson, Lisa (1991): 'Absolutism and the Resilience of Monarchy in the Middle East'. *Political Science Quarterly*, Vol. 106:1

Baram, Amatzia: 'Baathi Iraq and Hashimite Jordan: From Hostility to Alignment'. The *Middle East Journal*, Vol. 45:1, 1991 (pp. 51–70).

Barnett, Michael N. and Jack S. Levy (1991): 'Domestic Resources of Alignment: The Case of Egypt, 1962–73'. *International Organization*, Vol. 45:3.

Beschorner, Natasha (1993): *Water and Instability in the Middle East.* Adelphi Paper 273, IISS, Brassey's, London.

Boxhall, Peter (1991): 'The Iraq claim to Kuwait'. *Army Quarterly and Defence Journal*, Vol. 121:1.

Breslauer, George W. (ed.) (1990): *Soviet Strategy in the Middle East.* Unwin Hyman Ltd., London.

Brooks, Risa (1998): *Political-Military Relations and the Stability of Arab Regimes.* Adelphi Paper 324, IISS, Oxford University Press, Oxford.

Brynen, Rex (1994): 'Palestinian-Lebanese Relations: A Political Analysis'. *Collings, 1994.*

Bulloch, John and Harvey Morris (1991): *Saddam's War.* Faber and Faber, London.

Bush, George (1989): 'Change in the Soviet Union'-speech. Department of State Bulletin, Washington DC, July 1989.

Cairo Agreement (1994) – Agreement on the Gaza Strip and the Jericho Area. *Ministry of Foreign Affairs*, Jerusalem.

Calvocoressi, Peter (1992): *World Politics Since 1945.* (6th ed.) Longman, London.

Christensen, Thomas J., and Jack Snyder (1990): 'Chain gangs and passed bucks: Predicting alliance patterns in multipolarity'. *International Organization*, Vol. 44:2.

Chubin, Shamran (1994): *Iran's National Security Policy: Intentions, Capablities & Impact*. The Carnegie Endowment, Washington DC.

Clinton, William (1993): Speech at the South Lawn, 19.09.93. *USIS*.

Collings, Deirdre (ed.) (1994): *Peace for Lebanon?* Lynne Rienner Publishers, Boulder.

Cooley, John K. (1991): 'Pre-war Gulf Diplomacy'. *Survival*, Vol. XXXIII:2.

Cooper, Andrew Fenton, Richard A. Higgot and Kim Richard Nossal (1991): 'Bound to Follow? Leadership and Followership in the Gulf Conflict'. *Political Science Quarterly*, Vol. 106:3.

Cordesman, Anthony H. (1997): *U.S. Forces in the Middle East*. CSIS, WestviewPress, Boulder.

Cordesman, Anthony H. (1994): *Iran & Iraq. The Threat from the Northern Gulf*. Westview Press, Boulder.

Cordesman, Anthony H. (1993): *After the Storm. The Changing Military Balance in the Middle East*. Westview Press, Boulder.

Cordesman, Anthony H., and Ahmed S. Hashim (1997): Iraq. Sanctions and Beyond. CSIS, WestviewPress, Boulder.

Dannreuther, Roland (1992): *The Gulf Conflict: A Political and Strategic Analysis*. Adelphi Papers 264.

David, Steven (1991): 'Explaining Third World Alignment'. *World Politics 43*, an.

Declaration of Principles on Interim Self-Government Arrangements – DoP (1993). *Ministry of Foreign Affairs*, Jerusalem.

Deeb, Marius (1991): 'Lebanon in the Aftermath of the Abrogation of the Israeli-Lebanese Accord'. *R. Freedman, 1991*.

Deeb, Mary-Jane (1991): *Libya's Foreign Policy in North Africa*. Westview Press, Boulder.

Encyclopædia Britannica, Vol. 8, 1993

Drysdale, Alasdair (1993): 'Syria since 1988: From Crisis to Opportunity'. *R. Freedman, 1993*.

Faris, Hani A. (1994): 'The Failure of Peacemaking in Lebanon, 1975–1989'. *Collings, 1994*.

Freedman, Lawrence and Efraim Karsh (1993): *The Gulf Conflict 1990–1991*. Faber and Faber, London.

Freedman, Robert O. (ed.) (1998): The Middle East and the Peace Process. The Impact of tyhe Oslo Accords. University Press of Florida, Gainesville.

Freedman, Robert O. (ed.) (1993): *The Middle East After Iraq's Invasion of Kuwait*. University Press of Florida, Gainesville.

Freedman, Robert O. (ed.) (1991): *The Middle East from the Iran-Contra Affair to the Intifadha*. Syracuse University Press, Syracuse.

Garfinkle, Adam (1998): 'The Transformation of Jordan 1991–95'. Freedman 1998.

Garfinkle, Adam (1993): 'Jordanian Policy from the Intifada to the Madrid Peace Conference'. Robert O. Freedman: *The Middle East after Iraq's Invasion of Kuwait*. University Press of Florida, Gainesville 1993.

Garfinkle, Adam (1991): 'The Importance of being Hussein: Jordanian Foreign Policy and Peace in the Middle East'. Robert O. Freedman: *The*

Middle East from the Iran-Contra Affair to the Intifada. Syracuse University Press, Syracuse 1991.

Garnham, David (1991): 'Explaining Middle Eastern Alignments During the Gulf War'. *The Jerusalem Journal of International Relations*, Vol. 13:3.

Gause III, F. Gregory (1993): 'Saudi Arabia: Desert Storm and After'. *R. Freedman, 1993.*

Garthoff, Raymond L. (1985): *Détente and Confrontation.* Brookings Institution, Washington DC.

Garthoff, Raymond L. (1994): *The Great Transition. American-Soviet Relations and the End of the Cold War.* The Brookings Institution, Washington DC.

Gold, Dore (1988): 'Toward the Carter Doctrine: The Evolution of American Power Projection Policies in the Middle East, 1947–1980'. *Spiegel et al., 1988.*

Golan, Galia (1990): *Soviet Policies in the Middle East – From World War II to Gorbachev.* Cambridge University Press, Cambridge.

Hansen, Birthe (1998): *Politik i Mellemøsten.* DUPI, København.

Hansen, Birthe (1995a): 'Staten i det internationale system'. *Jensen and Torfing, 1995.*

Hansen, Birthe (ed). (1995): *European Security 2000.* Political Studies Press, Copenhagen.

Hansen, Birthe (1991): Magt og forhandling – Kernevåbenpolitikken 1986–89. *MA-thesis*, January 1991. Institute of Political Science, University of Copenhagen.

Hansen, Birthe (1994): *Fredsprocessen i Mellemøsten.* Danish Commission on Security and Disarmament, Copenhagen.

Heikal, Mohamed (1993): *Illusions of Triumph.* Harper Collins Publishers, Hammersmith.

Heller, Mark A. (1988): 'Soviet and American Attitudes toward the Iran-Iraq War'. *Spiegel et al. 1988.*

Heurlin, Bertel (1986): *Kontrol med Kernevåben.* SNU, København.

Hinnebusch, Raymond A. (1998): 'Syria and the Transition to Peace'. Freedman 1998.

Hubel, Helmut (1995): Das Ende des Kalten Kriegs im Orient. R. Oldenburg Verlag, München.

Hunter, Robert E. (1993): 'U.S. Policy toward the Middle East after Iraq's Invasion of Kuwait'. *R. Freedman, 1993.*

Hunter, Shireen T. (1991): 'The Gulf Cooperation Council: Security in the Era Following the Iran-Contra Affair.' *R. Freedman, 1991.*

Inbar, Efraim, an Shmuel Sandler (1995): 'The Changing Israeli Strategic Equation: Toward a Security Regime. *Review of International Studies,* 1995:21.

Indyk, Martin (1992): 'The Postwar Balance of Power in the Middle East'. *Nye and Smith, 1992.*

Jensen, Carsten: 'Hegemony, Internationalization and the New World Order'. Conference *Paper,* DUPI Conference on the New International Order, Copenhagen 1997 (22 p.).

Jensen, Carsten, and Jacob Torfing (eds.) (1995): Nyere statsteorier. Ålborg Universitetsforlag, Ålborg.

Joffé, George (1994): 'Low-level Violence and Terrorism'. *NATO Conference Paper*, Conference on Security Challenges in the Mediterranean Region, Rome.

Karsh, Efraim (ed.): Peace in the Middle East. The Challenge for Israel. Frank Cass, Essex 1994.

Karsh, Efraim and Inari Rautsi (1991): *Saddam Hussein – A Political Biography*. Futura, Aylesbury.

Karsh, Efraim and Inari Rautsi (1991):

Kemp, Geoffrey (1994): *Forever Enemies? American Policy & the Islamic Republic of Iran*. The Carnegie Endowment, Washington DC.

Kemp, Geoffrey (1994): 'Cooperative Security in the Middle East'. *Nolan,*

Klieman, Aharon (1994): 'New Directions in Israel's Foreign Policy'. *Karsh 1994*

Kostiner, Joseph (1996): Yemen. *The Tortuous Quest for Unity, 1990–94*. The Royal Institute of International Affairs, Pinter, London.

Laqueur, Walter, and Barry Rubin (eds.) (1984): *The Israeli-Arab Reader. A Documentary History of the Middle East Conflict*. Penguin Books, USA.

Karsh, Efraim, and Inari Rautsi: 'Why Saddam Hussein invaded Kuwait'. *Survival*, Vol. XXXIII:1, 1991, IISS, Brassey's, London 1991 (pp. 18–30).

Lesch, Ann Mosely: 'Contrasting Reactions to the Persian Gulf Crisis: Egypt, Syra, Jordan and the Palestinians'. *The Middle East Journal*, Vol. 45:1, 1991 (pp. 30–50).

Maila, Joseph (1994): 'The Ta'if Accord: An Evaluation'. *Collings, 1994.*.

McDowall, David (1996): *A Modern History of the Kurds*. I.B.Tauris, London.

Mearsheimer, John J. (1990): 'Back to the Future'. *International Security*, Vol. 15:1.

Mendelson, Maurice and Susan Hulton (1994): 'Iraq's claim to sovereignty over Kuwait'. *Schofield, R. (ed.) (1994)*.

Moltz, James Clay, and Dennis B. Ross (1990): 'The Soviet Union and the Iran-Iraq War, 1980–88'. *Breslauer 1990*.

Morrow, James D. (1991): 'Alliances and Asymmetry: An Alternative to the Capability Aggregation Model'. *American Journal of Political Science*, Vol. 35:4.

Mozaffari, Mehdi (1993): 'Changes in the Iranian Political System after Khomeini's Death'. *Political Studies*, XLI/1993.

Mylroie, Laurie (1993): 'Why Saddam Hussein Invaded Kuwait'. *Orbis*, Vol. 37:1.

Nolan, Janne E. (ed.) (1994): *Global Engagement*. The Brookings Institution, Washington DC.

Nonneman, Gerd (ed.) (1992): *The Middle East an Europe. An Integrated Communities Approach*. Federal Trust for Education and Research (Report to the EC Commission), London.

Nye, Joseph S. Jr. and Roger K. Smith (1992): *After the Storm*. Madison Books, Lanham.

Oudraat, Chantal de Jonge (ed.) (1994): *Conference of Research Institutes in the Middle East*. UNIDIR 94/16, UN, New York.

Page, Stephen (1985): *The Soviet Union and the Yemens*. Praeger, New York.

Peace Treaty Israel-Jordan (1994): *Ministry of Foreign Affairs*, Jerusalem.

People's Committee of Foreign Liaison and International Co-operation (1992): 'Statement 13.5.1994'. *The People's Bureau of The Great Socialist People's Libyan Aran Jamhiriya.*

Pelletreau, Robert H. (1994): 'Casablanca and the New Middle East'. Remarks, US GCC Corporate Cooperation Committee, Arlington. *Department of State*, Washington DC.

Perry, William J. (1992): 'Desert Storm and Deterrence in the Future'. *Nye and Smith (1992).*

Pimlott, John, and Stephen Badsey (eds.) (1992): *The Gulf War Assessed.* Arms and Armour, London.

Pimlott, John: 'The International Ramifications'. *Pimlott and Badsey 1992* (pp. 193–218).

Poulsen-Hansen, Morten (1997): 'The Gulf War'. Unpublished Paper, Copenhagen.

Quandt, Willian B. (1993): *Peace Process. American Diplomacy and the Arab-Israeli Conflict since 1967.* The Brookings Institution/University of California Press, Washington DC.

Ramazani, R. K. (1991): 'Iran and the United States: "Islamic Realism"?'. *R. Freedman (ed.) (1991).*

Reagan, Ronald (1986): 'President's Statement on Interim Restraint'. Special Report 147, Washington DC.

Robertson, B.A. (1998): *The Middle East and Europe.* Routledge, London.

Robins, Philip (1991): *Turkey and the Middle East.* RUSI, Pinter Publishers, London.

Salamé, Ghassan (1994): 'Security Impossible to Achieve, a Region Impossible to Define'. *Oudraat (ed.).*

Salem, Paul (1994): 'Reflections on Lebanon's Foreign Policy'. *Collings, 1994.*

Schofield, Richard (1994): 'The Kuwaiti islands of Warbah and Bubiyan, and Iraqi access to the Gulf'. *Schofield, R. (ed.) (1994).*

Schofield, Richard (ed.) (1994): *Territorial Foundations of the Gulf States.* UCL Press, London.

Singer, J. David (ed.) (1968): *Quantitative International Politics: Insights and Evidence.* Free Press, New York.

Singer, J. David and Melvin Small (1968): 'Alliance Aggregation and the Onset of War, 1815–1945'. *Singer (ed.) (1968).*

Snyder, Glenn H. (1984): 'The Security Dilemma in Alliance Politics'. *World Politics* vol. XXXVI nr. 4.

Spencer, Claire (1998): 'Algeria. France's dissarray and Europe's conondrum'. *Robertson 1998.*

Spiegel, Steven L., Mark A. Heller, and Jacob Goldberg (eds.) (1988): *The Soviet-American Competition in the Middle East.* Institute on Global Conflict and Cooperation, University of California.

Stockton, Paul N., and James J. Tritten (eds.) (1992): *Reconstituting America's Defense – The New U.S. National Security Strategy.* Praeger, New York.

Taylor, Alan R.: *The Superpowers and the Middle East.* Syracuse University Press, Syracuse 1991.

Taylor, Alan R. (1982): *The Arab Balance of Power.* Syracuse University Press.The Middle East Peace Process: An overview (1994). *Ministry of Foreign Affairs*, Jerusalem.

The Military Balance. Covering 1990–95. IISS, Brassey's, London.

Trainor, Bernard E. (1992): 'War by Miscalculation'. *Nye, Joseph S. Jr. and Roger K. Smith (1992)*.

Tritten, James J. (1992): 'The New National Security and the Base Force'. *Stockton and Tritten, 1992*.

Wagner, Harrison R. (1993): 'What was Bipolarity?' *International Organization*, Vol. 47:1.

Walt, Stephen M. (1992). 'Revolution and War'. *World Politics*, Vol. 44:3.

Walt, Stephen M. (1990): *The Origins of Alliances*. Cornell University Press, Ithaca.

Walt, Stephen M. (1988): 'Testing theories of alliance formation: the case of Southwest Asia. *International Organization*, Vol. 42:2.

Waltz, Kenneth N. (1995): Hansen 1995.

Waltz, Kenneth N. (1988): 'The Origins of War'. *Journal of Interdisciplinary History*. Vol. XVIII:4.

Waltz, Kenneth N. (1981): 'The Spread of Nuclear Weapons: More May Be Better'. *Adelphi Papers* nr. 171, London.

Waltz, Kenneth N. (1979): *Theory of international Politics*. Random House, New York.

Washington Declaration (1994). Israel, Jordan, the United States. *Ministry of Foreign Affairs*, Jerusalem.

Waxman, Dov (1999): 'Turkey and Israel: A New Balance of Power in the Middle East'. *The Washington Quarterly* 22:1, Winter 1999 (pp. 25–32).

White House (1990): *National Security Strategy of the United States*. Washington DC.

White House (1992): The President's State of the Union Address. *White House Fact Sheet*. Washington DC.

White House (1994): *A National Security Strategy of Engagement and Enlargement*. Washington DC.

Zakaria, Fareed (1990): 'The Reagan Strategy of Containment'. *Political Science Quarterly*, Vol. 105:3.

* * *

Christopher, Warren (1993): Speech at the South Lawn, 13.09.93. *USIS*.

Christopher, Warren (1994): 'Building the Structures of Peace and Prosperity in the New Middle East'. Speech in Casablance, Morocco, October 30, 1994. *US Department of State*.

Husayn, Saddam. Speech delivered on the 22d anniversary of the 17 July Revolution. FBIS-NES-90–137, 17 July 1990.

Husayn, Saddam. Speech at a ceremony honoring ministers and commanders. FBIS-NES-90–064, 3 April 1990.

Aziz, Tariq. Letter sent to Arab League Secretary General Chedli Klibi on 16 July. FBIS-NES-90–138.

Keesing's Record of World Events. News Digest for April 1990. Middle East – Arab World. 37390–91.

The Middle East. The International Business and Current Affairs Monthly. IC Publications, London. (Issues 1989–1995.)

The Middle East Journal. Middle East Institute, Washington DC.

Strategic Comments (1994). *IISS*:0.
Strategic Survey. IISS, Brassey's, London. Covering 1989–1995.
United Nations and the Referendum in Western Sahara (1992). *Department of* Public Information, United Nations PS/DPI/17, March, 1992.
United Nations: Security Resolutions.
IBRU Boundary and Security Bulletin.
FBIS-NES
International Herald Tribune
The Middle East
Le Monde Diplomatique

Index

Abdallah II, King 221
Aden 95, 99, 102, 104
Afghanistan 36–7, 40–1, 42, 46–7, 89, 200
Ajami, Fouad 128
al Beidh 100
al Bid 102
Al-Hamdi 94
al-Sabah, Emir 221
Algeria 24, 25, 39, 47, 89, 130, 135, 162, 164, 197–8
Algiers Accord (1975) 111
Amirahmadhi, Hooshang 118
Amman meeting (1990) 115
anarchy 52; and balance of power 53–5
Andersen, Lars Erslev 95
Anti-Ballistic Missile (ABM) Treaty 75, 76
Aoun, General 144
Arab Cooperation Council (ACC) 47, 90, 99, 100–1, 112–13, 114, 115, 117, 121, 122, 127, 129, 132, 135, 183, 191, 198, 201, 210
Arab League 101, 106, 112, 133, 197–8
Arab Maghreb Union (UMA) see Union of Arab Maghreb
Arab Republic of Yemen (YAR) 24, 38, 47, 93, 94–6, 97, 99, 100–1, 104–5, 127, 133, 135; see also People's Democratic Republic of Yemen (PDRY); Yemen
Arab-Israeli conflict 2, 41, 46, 48, 89, 90, 91, 147, 165; see also Gaza-Jericho Accords

Arab-Israeli peace process 195, 206, 209, 217–20; background 179–81; complexity of 190; and end of Cold War 181–5; and Israel, Syria, Lebanon relationship 188–90; and Israel/Jordan relationship 185–8
Arafat, Yasser 169, 219, 221
Assad, Hafez al 128, 141, 142, 221
Aziz, Tariq 106

Baghdad Pact (1950s) 35, 36, 37, 108
Baghdad summit (1990) 113, 115
Bahrain 124, 130
Baker, James 90, 151, 172
Balkan conflicts 86, 88
Baram, Amatzia 132
Barcelona process 199
Barnett, Michael N. and Levy, Jack S. 37
bipolarity: characteristics of 52–3; and loosening/end of rivalry 46–8; move from 22–5; in practice 32–42, 211; and subsystemic alignments 42–6
Black Sea Economic Cooperation Zone (BSECZ) 200, 201, 206
Black September (1970) 183
Bosnia and Hercegovina 58, 72
Brynen, Rex 145
Bulloch, John and Morris, Harvey 113
Bush, George 82, 83–4, 87, 89, 135, 136, 151, 152, 153, 165, 175, 223

Cairo Treaty (1994) 166, 169
Calvocoressi, Peter 36
Camp David Accords 24, 44, 45, 129, 165, 170, 179, 181
Carter Doctrine 41, 109
Casablanca Conference (1994) 199
Casablanca summit (1989) 112, 113
Caspian Sea Organisation (CSO) 200
Central Treaty Organisation (CENTO) 36
Cheney, Dick 86
China 79, 137
Christensen, Thomas J. and Snyder, Jack 28, 126
Christopher, Warren 175, 199
Chubin, Shamran 194
Clinton, William (Bill) 84, 87–8, 175
Cold War: effect on Middle East 22–3, 24; end of 1–2, 11–12, 16–17, 45–6, 73–9, 181–5; neorealist analysis of 8, 16–17; timetable of events 43
Cooley, John K. 115, 120
Cooper, Andrew Fenton et al 126, 136
Cordesman, Anthony H. 142, 146, 155, 162, 196, 198; and Hashim, Ahmed S. 156
Crefeld, van 45

Dannreuther, Roland 115
David, Steven 28
Dayton Peace Agreement 58
Deeb, Marius 141
Deeb, Mary-Jane 196
Drysdale, Alasdair 144, 181, 182

Eastern Bloc 84
Economic Cooperation Council (ECO) 194, 200, 201, 206, 210
Egypt 23, 24, 25, 32, 35, 37, 38, 44, 90, 101, 112, 113, 114, 117, 124, 140, 179; and Gulf War 127, 129–30
Eisenhower Doctrine (1957) 36, 140
Europe: interest in Middle East 33, 34–5; and intervention in Bosnia/Hercegovina 58; Soviet interest in 35
European Union (EU) 79, 199

Fahd, King 100, 128
Faris, Hani A. 140
France 35, 69
Frangieyh, President 141
Freedman, Lawrence and Karsh, Efraim 29, 107, 120, 128, 131, 138
Freedman, Robert O. 29

Garfinkle, Adam 132
Garnham, David 28, 127, 132, 133, 196, 198
Garthoff, Raymond L. 39, 42, 91
Gaza-Jericho Accords (1993) 180, 205–6; background 165–8; Declaration of Principles 168–71; Israel, PLO and US 171–6; and Palestine autonomy 176–8
Gemayel, Bachir 143
Geneva talks 74, 75
Germany 79; reunification of 84
Glaspie, US Ambassador 120
Golan, Galia 34, 108
Gold, Dore 33, 34
Gorbachev Doctrine 97
Gorbachev, Mikhail 40, 89, 90, 111, 182
Great Britain 35, 69, 95
great powers, specific change of 15–16
Gulf Cooperation Council (GCC) 43, 111, 113, 119, 125, 131–2, 191, 198, 201, 210
Gulf States 44, 91, 99, 104, 106, 110–11, 113, 114, 116, 117–18, 120, 132, 137
Gulf War (1990–91) 2, 82, 83, 85, 89, 91, 100, 101–2, 105, 106–7, 111, 117, 118–19, 121–3, 145, 172, 174, 182, 183, 186, 202, 204; analysis of 160–1; effect on regional redistribution of strength 126–35; flocking in 125–6, 127, 132, 135, 137, 158–9; followers/leader in 126; and formation of international coalition 124–6; Great Scud Hunt 152; massive support for 137–8; Multilateral Force (MLF) in 124, 128, 135,

151, 204; Operation Desert Shield
(1990) 124, 131–2, 147, 151–2,
153, 188; Operation Desert Storm
(1991) 84, 85, 91, 92, 101, 125,
138, 149–61, 175, 188, 192, 194;
Operation Earnest Will 195;
participation in 126–35; unipolar
management in 135–7; US
reaction to 124

Hamarneh, 133, 185
Hansen, Birthie 17, 52, 74, 75, 78,
158, 169, 214, 221
Hassan II, King 163, 221
Heikal, Mohamed 101, 113, 129
Heller, Mark A. 39, 109
Helsinki summit (1990) 154
Heurlin, Bertel 74
Hinnebusch, Raymond A. 189
Hubel, Helmut 110
Hunter, Robert E. 91, 119
Hussein, King 117, 186, 221
Hussein, Saddam 106, 107, 111,
114–16, 117, 118, 120, 121, 122,
133, 147, 155, 158, 196, 215,
221

Ibn Saud, Quaboos 221
Indyk, Martin 181
Intercontinental Ballistic Missiles
(ICBMs) 76, 78
Intermediate-Range Nuclear Forces
(INF) 77, 86
international political structure:
anarchy 52, 53–5; functional
similarity 52; polarity 52
international system: asymmetrical
relations 66–7; and
bandwagoning 66, 213; free-
riding option 58–9; management
issues 58–60; minimalist strategy
58; and nuclearity 62–3; peace
and war 61; and realignment
69–73; specific interests 58; and
stability 60–1; transformation
of 68–73; and unipolarity
57–68
Iran 24, 34, 36, 37, 44–5, 113, 144,
200, 207–8; and Gulf War 134;

internal affairs 118; invasion of
109, 110–11; relationship with
Soviet Union 109; relationship
with US 109–10; state strategies
194–6
Iraq 2, 23, 24, 25, 33, 35, 37, 38,
44, 45, 47, 88; calculations of
invasions 120–1; and emergence
of unipolarity 121–3; invasion of
Kuwait 82, 83, 85, 89, 91,
101–2, 106–7, 124, 204;
relationship with Soviet Union
108; relationship with US 90–1,
116; response to balance of
power 112–19; and subsystemic
balance of power 108–12;
threat from 90; see also Gulf
War
Iraq-Iran War 89, 90, 109, 110–11,
121, 127
Israel 22, 24, 33, 37, 43, 44, 47,
107, 113, 116, 140, 144, 146,
165, 210; alliance with US 40;
and Gulf War 132, 134–5;
Operation Peace for Galilee 174;
Operation Wisdom of Stones
(1978) 142; Peace for Galilee 142;
wars with 141–2, 143; see also
Arab-Israeli conflict; Gaza-Jericho
Accords
Israeli-Jordanian Peace Treaty 181,
187, 206

Japan 79
Joffe, George 128
Jordan 23, 24, 36, 37, 38, 47, 101,
112, 114, 117, 165, 201, 206–7,
210; and Gulf War 132–3;
relationship with Israel 179, 180,
181, 183, 185–8
June War (1967) 38, 41, 188

Karsh, Efraim 106; and Rautsi, Inari
37, 111, 117
Kelly, John 120
Kemp, Geoffrey 195, 200
Klibi, Chadli 106
Klieman, Aharon 189
Kosovo 88, 159

Kostiner, Joseph 102
Kurds 193, 207, 223–4; safe haven
155–9; uprising 152, 155–9; and
US Operation Provide Comfort
155
Kuwait 24, 47; invasion of 2, 82, 83,
85, 89, 91, 101–2, 106–7, 117,
118–19, 121–3, 124, 204;
relationship with Soviet Union
131; see also Gulf War

Lebanon 23–4, 33, 36, 37, 165, 173;
challenge of 147–8; Civil War in
41–2, 46, 113, 139, 139–45, 202,
204–5; end of Civil War in 145–7;
foreign policy 140; from National
Pact to Ta'if Accords 139–45;
outside pressures on 140–2;
relationship with Israel 179–80,
183–4, 188–90
Lesch, An Mosely 128, 132
Levy, David 146
Libya 24, 25, 44, 47, 86, 130, 133,
135, 162, 164; state strategies
196–7
Lloyd George, David 71
Lockerbie disaster 196

Madrid Conference (1991) 91,
165–8, 177, 184, 209, 217
Maila, Joseph 144
Mauritania 47, 133, 162
Middle East 1; analytical procedure
29–31; asymmetrical patterns of
alignment 203; attributes of 2;
bipolar division of 24–5; and
Cold War 11–12, 38–42;
conflicts in 37, 38–40; European
interest in 33, 34–5; explanation
of analysis 25–9; historical
overview 32–3; internal conflict
in 11; as international subsystem
9; neorealist structural analysis of
2–6; non-events 191; and oil
interests 34, 37; symmetrical
patterns of alignment 203;
timetable of events 202–6; US
policy towards 89–92; US/Soviet
interest in 33–4, 35–42

Middle East Defence Organisation
35, 140
Mission for the Referendum in
Western Sahara (MINURSO) 163
Morocco 24, 25, 41, 44, 47, 124,
130, 162–4, 196
Morrow, James D. 9, 19, 28, 66
Mossadeq, Muhammad 36
Mozaffari, Mehdi 195
Mubarak, Hosni 90, 117, 129, 221
Muhammad Ali 95
multipolarity 44; characteristics of
52–3
Muslim Brotherhood 129
Mylroie, Laurie 121

Nasser, Gamal Abdel 140
NATO 58, 66, 67, 83, 84, 192
neorealist analysis 2–6; and Cold
War 8, 16–17; core concepts/
statements 7–10, 21; emphasis on
strength/power 10; and lack of
concrete predictions 10; problem/
argument 11–16; and security
7–8; and unipolarity 9, 10, 17–21,
51–7
Netanyahu, Benyamin 210, 217
New Pacific Community 87
New Thinking 77, 111–12
New World Order 82–3, 84–5, 86,
123, 195, 200, 222
Nixon Doctrine (1969) 40
Non-Proliferation-Treaty 87
Nonneman, Gerd 47
North American Free Trade Area
(NAFTA) 87
North Atlantic Council of
Cooperation (NACC) 87
North Atlantic Treaty Organisation
(NATO) 87, 88
North Korea 86

October War (1973) 38, 40, 44, 62
Oman 24, 124, 130
Operation Desert Storm (Jan 1991)
84, 85, 91, 92, 101, 125, 138,
149–50, 175, 192, 194, 205;
analysis of 160–1; and Kurdish
safe haven 155–9; leadership and

the coalition 153–5; US objectives/
agenda 151–2; US-Iraqi stand-off
157–9
Organisation of African Unity
(OAU) 163
Oslo Agreements 166, 170
Ottoman Empire 32, 69, 95, 139

Pact of Defence and Security (1991)
146
Page, Stephen 96
Pakistan 35
Palestine 23, 39, 41, 46, 107, 113,
140–1, 182
Palestine Liberation Organisation
(PLO) 23, 24, 25, 44, 46, 89, 115,
117, 135, 141, 143, 145, 165,
186, 206, 217–20; and Gaza-
Jericho Accords 167–78
Pelletreau, Robert H. 199
People's Democratic Republic of
Yemen (PDRY) 24, 37-8, 39, 44,
93, 94, 95, 96, 97, 98, 99, 104–5;
see also Arab Republic of Yemen
(YAR); Yemen
People's Republic of South Yemen
(PRSY) 25, 95; see also Arab
Republic of Yemen (YAR); Yemen
Perry, William J. 150
Pimlott, John 134
polarity, change of 15
pole, defined 52
Polisario Front 24
Primakov, Yevgeny 154

Qaddafi, Colonel Muammar al 221
Qassem, General Abd al-Karim 36
Qatar 124, 130
Quandt, William B. 40, 89, 176

Rabin, Yitzhak 169, 173, 210, 219
Reagan, Ronald 39, 40, 41, 42, 76,
82, 97, 142
Reykjavik summit (1987) 77
Robins, Philip 192
Rubayyi Ali 94
Russia see Soviet Union

Sadat, Anwar 142

Salem, Paul 141
Sarkis, President 141
Saudi Arabia 24, 36, 37, 44, 117,
124, 130, 144, 145; and Gulf War
136; involvement in Yemen 97,
98, 99, 100, 101–2, 103, 104–5
Saudi-Iraqi Treaty 113
Second World War 33–4
security 55–6; and Arab-Israeli-
Palestinian peace process 217–20;
challenges 216–25; future patterns
225; major powers in subsystem
222–3; nationalism and failed
states 223–4; succession/
democratisation 220–2; and US
dominance 224
Shamir, Yitzhak 89
Singer, J. David and Small, Melvin 5,
69
Snyder, Glenn H. 28, 56
South Yemen see People's Republic
of South Yemen (PRSY)
Soviet Union 1, 79, 91; and arms
limitation 74–8; in decline 73;
deténte-relationship with 83–4;
and Gulf War 137; hedging
strategy 109; and Iran 109; and
Iraq 108, 121; and Kuwait 131;
Middle East interests 22–5, 33–4,
35–42; nuclear strength of 73–4;
and policy of recognition 74;
retreat from Middle East 111–12;
retreat from Yemen 98–100;
surrender of 79; withdrawal from
Afghanistan 46–7; and Yemen
95–8
Soviet-Iraqi Treaty of Friendship and
Cooperation (1972) 108
Spencer, Claire 197
Strategic Arms Limitations Talks
(SALT) 74–8
Strategic Arms Reduction Talks
(START) 77, 78, 86
Strategic Defense Initiative (SDI) 76,
78, 86
subsystemic alignments 42–6,
198–200, 209; geographical/
political cooperation 200–1
Sudan 133

Suez Canal 32, 35, 37
Syria 23, 24, 25, 33, 37, 38, 41, 44, 47, 108, 112, 113, 165; and Gulf War 124, 125, 127–8, 135, 188; and Lebanese Civil War 141–2, 143, 144, 145–7; relationship with Israel 179, 181–3, 188–90
systemic change 3–6, 11, 12–14; leading to realignment 69–73

Ta'if Accords (1994) 103, 139, 144
Taylor, Alan R. 17, 24, 29, 47
Third World 91
Trainor, Bernard E. 90, 121
transformation 14–15, 68–73, 213–14
Treaty on Brotherhood, Cooperation and Coordination (1991) 146
Tritten, James J. 86
Truman Doctrine (1947) 35
Truman, Harry S. 35
Tunisia 24, 47
Turkey 34, 35, 37, 192–3, 200, 206
Two Camp Strategy 35

Union of Arab Maghreb (UMA) 47, 111, 135, 191, 196, 199, 201, 206, 210
unipolarity 9, 10, 211–12, 222; agenda 19–20; balancing strategies 213; and change 80–1; dynamics of 17–21; and end of Cold War 73–9; flocking 18–19; and flocking 65–7, 212–13; future research on 214–15; hard work 19; and hard work 67–8; importance of 49–50; and international system 57–68; model for 1–6, 49–51, 212–14; move towards US 22–5; and neorealism 51–7; and number of poles 79–80; and other states 63–8; single option 19; and single option 64–5; strength/strategies 56–7; and systemic transformation 68–73
United Arab Emirates (UAE) 24, 107, 124
United Nations (UN) 33, 101, 103, 138, 186

United States 1, 20; actions immediately post-Cold War 82–3; approach to international politics 82, 83–9; and arms limitation 74–8; Bottom-Up Review 86–7, 88; Central Command 90; deténte-relationship with Soviet Union 83–4; dominance of 224; 'Don't bully your neighbour' 82; dual containment policy 92; and the Gulf States 120–1; and Gulf War 124, 135–7, 151–61; 'Integrated Regional Approaches' 86, 92; and Iraq 116, 121; and Islamic legitimacy 131; issue of Defense Condition III Alert 39; 'It is time to go beyond Containment' 82, 83; Middle East interests 22–5, 33–4, 35–42, 89–92, 208–9; military position 86–7; 'National Security Strategy of Engagement and Enlargement' 85–8, 91, 92; nuclear strength of 73–4; Partnership For Peace Programme 86; position of 82; Quadrennial Defense Review 88; Rapid Deployment Force 90; 'Realism, Strength and Dialogue' 82; relationship with Iraq 109–10; relationship with Yemen 95–8

Walt, Stephen M. 28, 29, 35, 36, 66, 70, 183, 221
Waltz, Kenneth N. 1, 2, 4, 10, 13, 20, 28, 49, 50, 51–2, 54, 55, 59, 62, 66, 70, 73, 74, 214, 224
Warsaw Treaty countries 66
Washington Declaration (1994) 183, 187
Waxman, Dov 193
weapons of mass destruction (WMD) 18, 62–3, 86, 157, 158, 159, 173, 223
Western Sahara 23, 24, 41, 48, 130, 196, 205; disputes in 162–4
Wye River memorandum (1998) 166

Yahya, Imam 95
Yemen 2, 23, 41, 46, 48, 84, 112,
121, 202; choice of Yemens
98–100; Civil War (1994) in
100–4; foreign interest in 95;
Soviet retreat 98–100; unification

of 93–5, 104–5, 203–4; and
US-Soviet rivalry 95–8; *see also*
Arab Republic of Yemen (YAR);
People's Democratic Republic of
Yemen (PDRY)
Yugoslavia 72, 88